MAKING SENSE OF SOCIAL WORK

Also by Michael Preston-Shoot

CONTRACTS IN SOCIAL WORK (*with John Corden*)
EFFECTIVE GROUPWORK

Making Sense of Social Work

Psychodynamics, Systems and Practice

Michael Preston-Shoot

and

Dick Agass

MACMILLAN

First published 1990

Published by
MACMILLAN EDUCATION LTD
Houndmills, Basingstoke, Hampshire RG21 2XS
and London
Companies and representatives
throughout the world

Printed in Singapore

British Library Cataloguing in Publication Data
Preston-Shoot, Michael, *1951–*
Making sense of social work : psychodynamics, systems and practice.
1. Welfare work. Theories
I. Title   II. Agass, Dick
361.301
ISBN 0–333–49302–8 (hardcover)
ISBN 0–333–49303–6 (paperback)

Contents

List of figures

Preface

Our initial attempts to achieve a working synthesis in practice between psychodynamic and systems theories were shared with other members of Leeds Family Therapy and Research Centre (Leeds University): Peter Stratton, Gill Tagg, Helga Hanks and Dorothy Heard. From the team we learned a great deal and many of our ideas were worked out in common with them.

Dr Ronald Markillie has been a consistently encouraging teacher and supervisor. Vic Sedlak and Mary Twyman from the Society of Psychoanalytical Psychotherapists have led thought-provoking seminars in Leeds for the past three years. Brian Sidey, Iain Dallas (Bradford Social Services) and Don Wright (Leeds Social Services) have been challenging and helpful colleagues and friends. Suzy Braye (School of Social Work, University of Manchester) read the manuscript and provided welcome support, critical comments and illumination. Alison Cummings and David Hughes, Fiona, Sean and Rachel Agass, and Kay Barella all provided personal support whilst we completed our project.

Jean Ashton, Ruth Carter and Ursula Miley helped to type the manuscript.

We are grateful to them all.

MICHAEL PRESTON-SHOOT
DICK AGASS

Introduction: concerns, curiosity and visions

Although a much abused word, crisis currently typifies much of social work. It is no exaggeration; social work is approaching turmoil. Increasing workloads, multiplying responsibilities contrasting with static or contracting resources, the emotional and physical impact of the work, the deletion of posts in some fields to meet financial targets or the demands of child protection work, apparently contradictory public expectations and vitriol from the media which often sees little other than tragedies: these are all reflected in low morale, vacancy levels and burn-out. Practitioners face a plethora of pressing problems and yet do not feel highly regarded. Some conceal their occupation or derive little pride from their work. Few believe it commands public respect (Davies and Brandon, 1988). Given the work's complexity and difficulty, this absence of public commitment to social work – and the concomitant low morale, confusion and frustration among practitioners – must be of major concern. Moreover, major changes are imminent: the privatisation of parts of the National Health Service and the possible reorganisation of social services whereby departments co-ordinate packages of care rather than provide directly many of the services currently within their remit. Other, arguably more beneficial, changes have been dismissed. Qualifying training will not be extended into a third year and, apart from courses in child protection, social work education at post-qualifying and short course levels is underfunded. Thus, although the number of potential recruits to social work courses remains buoyant and the commitment of many social workers impressive, there is no margin for complacency. As one practitioner graphically described it, social work is like mining coal with teaspoons.

This book has evolved from our concern both about the crisis and the permanency towards which this state of affairs is drifting, together with curiosity about the reasons for it and a belief in the urgency of finding constructive ways forward. The ideas presented in this book result from our practice experience.

What is social work? The battle of definitions

One battle rages over social work's soul. Some advocate a narrow, restrictive definition. Social work is defined simply in terms of its statutory responsibilities. All activities are relegated behind social control. The work is defined by the law and the function of employing agencies. This framework provides social work's mandate (Blom-Cooper, 1988). Stevenson (1988) opposes this view. She argues that an ethical duty of care to the user, not the law, should define social work. In practice, the picture is not as simple as these polarities would suggest. Practice places social workers uncomfortably between the two positions and daily confronts them with dilemmas (Braye and Preston-Shoot, 1990): for instance, the legal grounds for action may exist but that response may not be in the user's best interests. It may or may not be appropriate. On the other hand, social workers may wish to empower users and protect their rights, as part of their ethical duty of care, yet operate from a context of services which are resource- and provider-led, not need- and user-led.

Another battle centres on the elevation of economy and value for money above the development of effective care packages. Users have to fit the services available rather than provision being tailored to individual needs and wishes. In both child care and social work with older people, this can lead to inappropriate placements or admissions to institutional care, or to increased risk in the community because of the non-availability of resources. Paradoxically, therefore, emphasising economy over effectiveness may, ultimately, not be economical in the longer term.

Each of these struggles may be subsumed within the controversy: what is social work? There has been a long search for the definitive answer. Some propose a radical activity, to change social and economic structures which oppress and alienate whole groups of people. Their focus is on public ills. Others suggest a residual activity, to control the 'deviant' and the 'useless'. They may focus on private ills. The choice is often presented as being between the intra- and interpersonal, the internal and external. A third position focuses neither on the individual nor the environment but on the interaction between them. Thus Pincus and Minahan (1973) describe social work as aiming to enhance people's problem-solving and coping capacities, to link them with systems which provide resources and services, to promote the effective operation of these systems and to contribute to social policy development. There is, therefore, no agreed purpose for social work. Where its vision should be concentrated remains confused. Wootton (1959) criticises social workers for their uncritical focus on the individual and individual pathology as opposed to the social situation and the individual's interactions with it. Parsloe (1986) criticises practitioners for failing to hold both the individual and social aspects in a balance, the third position. She laments social work's tendency towards polarisation, and its failure to connect in a dynamic interaction individual problems and the public context of social and political systems.

Despite this criticism that social work has falsely divided the person and the situation, concentrated on individual adjustment at the expense of social change and promoted consensus rather than conflict strategies, the 'person-in-situation' focus (the third position) seems little clearer as a result. In part this is due to a clear clash of ideologies. Community care, and by implication the frontiers of the state, are defined differently by the radical left and radical right. The values promulgated from these positions differ substantially: for example, attitudes regarding the role of women, family roles and adult responsibilities, or the value attributed to unemployed, older or disabled people. More disturbingly, the differential value attributed to some groups of people, together with the dominant political values in society, are reflected in the marginalisation of older and disabled people and the relative neglect of carers within social work provision.

A further reason for the difficulty in retaining hold of the person-in-situation focus, and for maintaining a critical edge to practice, is that the task of synthesising knowledge regarding the individual, family, social and political contexts is complex. In theory, as in practice, a false divide has been perpetuated, a closed system characterised either by the advocacy of exclusive panaceas (such as casework) without any crossover to other methods and theories, or by an uncritical, chaotic eclecticism.

The time is right for synthesis, to move towards integration of practice methods and theories. There is, after all, no such thing as an individual; there is always a context. Neither is there such a thing as a society or situation without its component parts. The complexity is such that no one theoretical or methodological approach will suffice (Evans, 1976). Interventions at different levels are required. This requires understanding of those levels. The major challenges of racism, sexism, unemployment, HIV/AIDS, ageism and poverty, the need to develop anti-discriminatory practice and the need to challenge policies which stigmatise disadvantaged groups does not invalidate psychodynamic and psychological theories or work, but merely recognises that work is required at different levels. The need, therefore, is for an integrated approach, based on a perspective which sees individuals, families, groups and communities in dynamic interaction with economic, social, cultural and political systems characterised by mutual influence and feedback. As structural inequalities and problems of relationships persist (reflected in continuing poverty, the development of an underclass, in the increasing incidence of child abuse and divorce and the uneven geographical and social class distribution of health), theories to understand this complexity and methods to structure the work are required which recognise that effective social functioning requires social and individual resources, social and individual work (Specht and Vickery, 1977).

We hope to make a contribution here, believing that social workers have an obligation to develop practice, and theories for practice, to locate points for intervention and to explore new ways of intervening to effect change. We further believe that the integration or synthesis of psychodynamic and systems theories can provide a helpful way forwards for practitioners attempting to work with the person-in-situation.

Practice concerns: 1. Is theory relevant?

In a child care review, an adolescent boy was attempting to sabotage proceedings by throwing furniture, running out of the room and attacking both his father and teacher physically and verbally. The reviewing officer suggested to him that children often convey their powerful feelings by actions, finding behaviour easier than words to describe what they want to communicate. The reviewing officer asked what he was trying to convey. The adolescent boy said that he was 'bloody mad' about what his family were doing to him. He then sat down and the review proceeded more calmly and was able to address his needs and feelings.

Many would no doubt consider this an example of 'intuitive' social work, and would see themselves doing much the same thing in the same situation, with no thought of any 'theory'. However, there *is* a theory at work here, to do with behaviour as communication, even if it is one which many of us have absorbed into our intuitive repertoire. In this particular case, there might be other theories, perhaps relating to the effects of early emotional deprivation, which we would formulate more consciously.

As this example illustrates, theories suggest actions which promote and achieve change. They enable workers to continue to function, even under extreme pressure, rather than be sucked into problem sequences. This holding function comprises both an understanding of people's behaviour and outcomes. Theories can provide, therefore, both understanding and meanings and, from this, a focus for change and techniques for bringing it about. They provide frameworks which give coherence to techniques, to understanding how problems may develop and be maintained (Jenkins, 1985). The use of theory is, therefore, crucial to outcomes.

However, social workers have an ambivalent relationship with theory. Uncertain of its relevance, social workers lack an adequate theoretical and conceptual base for purposeful practice. They are often unable to articulate the skills and knowledge which guide their practice, or the specific forms of intervention or practice theory they are applying to their work. Where theory is used, social workers appear to rely on preferred ways of understanding and intervening, irrespective of user need, and devote considerable time to particular cases, often with little positive outcome. Theorising is abandoned to academics (Carew, 1979; Corby, 1982). Smale (1983) has rightly pointed to the urgency of improving on practice which he asserts can be of poor quality, characterised by long-term support and occasional hectic activity which rarely results in change or growth. Otherwise, with theory abandoned or seen as unhelpful, practitioners will be caught in a downward spiral: the more they ignore theory, the more social work will be experienced as ineffective and stressful, and the more ambivalent practitioners will be about theory since they will not see that it offers a way forward. Theory-less practice can easily become a mindless activity, lacking purposeful, clear and consistent approaches to practice situations.

One explanation for this position is the structure of the social services, the organisational context of social work. Largely ignored in the literature on theory development and application, this context severely restricts opportunities for post-qualifying training, provides caseloads which preclude opportunity for critical reflection and therapeutic work in depth, and prioritises the performance of statutory responsibilities, such as six-monthly child care reviews, but does not provide the resources to implement the plans agreed at these meetings (M. Allen, 1988). Rather than positive planning, crisis prevention and an emphasis on change, there is crisis intervention, reactive social work and the processing of users through procedures, policy guidelines and instructions. The specific use of therapeutic methods of intervention with users whose difficulties frequently include profound psychological, social and/or economic disadvantage and deprivation has largely been replaced by a bureaucratic approach, social control, resource rationing and soft policing (R. Allen, 1989).

Moreover, this is despite the key ingredients for successful work being well-known:

1. problem-cornering, where problems are well defined and translated into specific objectives and further into tasks precise enough to be managed quickly;
2. agreed, clearly focused tasks;
3. active support from significant people in the worker–user environment;
4. agreed goals, expressed within a working agreement which acknowledges differences between worker and user, which takes seriously the user's problem definitions, in which both user and worker actively contribute to the decision-making and the work, and in which targets for change may include systems with which the user interacts (Stein and Gambrill, 1977; Mullender and Ward, 1985; Preston-Shoot, 1985; Sheldon, 1986; Corden and Preston-Shoot, 1987).

These key ingredients are difficult to operationalise for several reasons: the organisation of welfare services and the underlying political and economic philosophies and social structures; clashes in perspective between workers and users; concentration in theory building on assessment rather than on-going intervention.

Not surprisingly, therefore, there is a theory–practice divide (Sheldon, 1978b) in which the practice sub-culture is forced to develop in unpropitious circumstances. Research regularly encounters a depressing picture (Stevenson and Parsloe, 1978; Clare, 1988). Social workers are overburdened and depleted physically and emotionally by the feelings and disadvantages experienced by service-users, and by the distance they feel from managers. Managers are not felt to have, and perhaps because of their position in the hierarchy relinquish the struggle to retain, any idea of what social workers do or encounter. Supervision is regularly criticised for being unconcerned with the practitioner's development, professional or personal needs, or with theory, concentrating instead on procedures and statutory obligations. Predictably, coping defence mechanisms emerge. Administrative procedures and bureaucracy may be emphasised, with organisational arrangements and ideologies of need devised to reduce pressures through the use of routinised, stereotyped solutions and a textbook approach (G. Smith and Harris, 1972; Dunham, 1978; Prodgers, 1979; Addison, 1982). Service provision then becomes characterised by authoritarianism, an emphasis on expertise, and withdrawal.

Another result is that social workers become suspicious of theory and research, largely ignore or remain unaware of it, and even deny its relevance and applicability to their work (Carew, 1979). The real world is felt to be different from that envisaged by the theoretical sub-culture: it concerns not problem-solving but problem containment, control and maintenance of stability, and is often a restricted practice not linked to or requiring any particular method of intervention (Corby, 1982). Commonly, students on qualifying report feeling unprepared for practice (Davies, 1984) and, indeed, have perhaps been trained to practise in one world, where notions of change and empowerment reign, only to find another, very different, planet.

We believe theory, and especially psychodynamic and systems theories, to be essential to informed, open, self-aware and purposeful practice, and to creative ways of effecting change. We regard practice as essentially informing and evaluating theory. The process is circular, involving feedback. Four convictions lead us to this position. First, if social workers devalue their own theorising, others will fill the vacuum. Medical and psychiatric models did once manoeuvre social work away from focusing on social reform and towards individual diagnosis and treatment. Presently the advocates of social work as social control seek to impose their theoretical prescriptions. Second, social workers must 'know what' and 'know how' (Howe, 1980). Social workers face highly charged, complex situations and work with people seriously disadvantaged economically, politically, socially and emotionally. To survive the stress and emotional demands made upon them, to make sense of what they encounter and to intervene effectively and with direction, social workers require more than common sense. They must understand what influences client–worker relationships in order to work through conflict and misunderstanding. They must be able to sort out their own reactions to the behaviour or situations they encounter if they are not to be plunged into tangled re-enactments of the very problems and conflicts they are struggling to deal with (Temperley and Himmel, 1986). They need frameworks to guide assessments, determine methods of intervention and provide a professional justification for decisions taken. Ineffective work results from a lack of in-depth theoretical and practice understanding, from uncertainty about what is going on and how then to intervene. Third, social workers require the skills and critical edge to survive, to make sense of their occupation, and to rescue it and themselves from the turmoil and context in which it currently resides. Finally, everyone carries around theories and belief systems (ways of looking at the world). As these frameworks determine what is seen and looked for, and the sense made of phenomena, social workers must be clear about the theories they have and their influence. Actions are determined by how we interpret what we encounter. No one can be atheoretical. Values, culture, gender, socialisation and professional training all shape our theories and belief systems which we take into life and work and which must, therefore, be owned and critically appraised. Otherwise, social workers may leave some areas unexplored and become boxed in by their own bias. In place of dialogue and curiosity, we then find emphasis on technical purity, with a reliance on one view and that work with users is characterised by a formalised approach and distance from – rather than openness to – their experience.

Practice concerns: 2. Dilemmas in working for change

Counselling remains an appropriate role (Barclay, 1982), popular with practitioners (Davies and Brandon, 1988). However, social work also displays a willingness to abandon therapeutic expertise. Social workers have been withdrawn from some locations where counselling is especially appropriate (for example, child guidance clinics and hospitals), the vacuum being filled by nurse counsellors, community psychiatric nurses and psychotherapists. Furthermore, some practitioners regard therapeutic work suspiciously. Methods which might have a valuable contribution to make to change are dismissed, especially if they appear to challenge the notion of user self-determination, with nothing put forward in their place. It is difficult to draw the line between risks and rights: to decide when a user's right to take risks should give way to an equal right to be protected, or to accept the authority and responsibility to work for change. Denying expertise can then serve as a defence against the anxiety created by such practice dilemmas.

In our view social workers have to use therapeutic skills, not just because of the insufficient numbers of other professionals available to be therapists but also because of what they encounter in practice. Emotional carnage surrounds social workers, as does non-rational behaviour and serious emotional and practical problems. They must understand and work with the dynamics of family relationships (for instance, in child abuse). They require psychological strength and personal resources to perform and survive the job. They must understand organisational dynamics and relationships to make sense of and creatively intervene in, for instance, the abuse of residents in institutional care and the state's apparent lack of concern for older people once the private sector has obliged by 'taking over' the problem.

Social work practice comprises many dilemmas. Some are infamous, such as care as opposed to control. Others are more insidious, amounting at times to double-binds: social work is damned if it does and damned if it does not. Results are required without agreed definitions of what is expected. Social work is caught in the midst of society's own confusions and ambivalence: between the conflicting rights of those involved in child sexual abuse, say; or between conflicting definitions (for instance, of who may be seen as victims of structural and economic inequalities or as scroungers). Social workers often find themselves at odds with definitions and values promulgated elsewhere.

Consequently, not only must social workers formulate and articulate the political and practice questions which arise for them from their work (Timms and Timms, 1977) but they must also confront practice dilemmas such as rights versus risks; needs versus resources; agents of the user versus agents of the department (Braye and Preston-Shoot, 1990). Failure to do so will result in defensive practice and attitudes. Assessments will centre not on needs but on resources. Tasks and goals will become procedural and by-pass the user's experience. When rationing, prioritising and economics rather than effectiveness shape social work practice, retaining and articulating an ethical duty of care to the user and a professional justification for practice decisions is difficult. In the fight not to collude with the pressures of the context and system, theoretical knowledge is crucial. To illustrate these remarks: dominant images of people's worth are acted out in service provision. Work with older people is seen as straightforward. It can wait. Child care is seen as complex and immediate. However, both require the same social work skills, present the familiar social work dilemmas and require sensitive handling of separations, placements and culture. In addition to physical resources, psychological knowledge is required, especially concerning loss and change, human growth and development. Theoretical knowledge will help practitioners articulate the professional justification for the aims of their work. Theoretical knowledge will help practitioners resist the automatic 'solution'.

Practice concerns: 3. Social work: a difference or more of the same?

A major question for social work is how practitioners can work effectively for change rather than become part of the problem and perpetuate more of the same in a game without end (Watzlawick *et al.*, 1967). The question is how can social workers make a difference? This curiosity led us to seek a conceptualisation which integrated individual, family, organisational and social perspectives and which provided both a framework for understanding and techniques for intervention. In this book we hope to demonstrate that a synthesis of psychodynamic and systems theories offers some promise for social work to make a difference at both micro and macro levels.

Psychodynamic theory: a case for rehabilitation?

By psychodynamic we refer to the entire theory and practice which derives from Freud and which has been expanded and modified subsequently by the work of Melanie Klein and object-relations theorists, as well as by such other influences as Bowlby's attachment theory.

At first glance, our choice of psychodynamic theory may appear odd given the shift in focus from the intrapsychic to the interpersonal in social work (from what goes on inside people to what goes on between them). However, object-relations theory is itself interactional, although concerned primarily with intrapsychic phenomena. Moreover, psychodynamic concepts have been helpfully applied to clarify group and organisational phenomena. Indeed, psychodynamic theory has found some apparently surprising partners. Hinshelwood (1983) and Kovel (1976b) have compared, and found connections between, psychodynamic and Marxist theory. Marx may have begun with social phenomena and Freud with individual behaviour but each approach extends into the domain of the other. Seagraves and Smith (1976) reported on a similar surprising alliance between behaviour therapy and psychodynamic psychotherapy, finding that the only problem was the competition between therapists.

Nonetheless, the relevance of psychodynamic concepts must be demonstrated since to many workers the approach still smacks of an ivory-tower activity, largely discredited and far removed from the harsh realities of life in an area team. It is commonly seen as a self-indulgent pastime which encourages its participants to be even more neurotically self-preoccupied than they already are. Davies (1985), whilst heartily endorsing the injunction to 'know thyself', nevertheless decries the supposition that social workers need to be in tune with their own inner selves in order to cope with the complex problems found in other people's lives and dismissively adds that 'a narcissistic concern with self-knowledge is not a pre-requisite for effective social work practice'.

We reject this all-too-familiar parody of the psychodynamic approach. We recognise that it has had a bad press and has not always given a good account of itself. Certainly the practice of psychotherapy has never been directly transferable to social work and much misunderstanding and confusion has arisen from the belief that such a transfer of skills could be made. This has produced practice which was a bad parody of half-understood, watered-down psychoanalysis, bringing the psychodynamic approach into disrepute (Temperley and Himmel, 1986). Wootton (1959) rightly criticised the penetration of psychiatric terminology, models and language into social work but the response, of reasserting the social in social work, has regrettably included the reaction of dismissing almost wholesale the relevance of psychodynamic theories. We would caution against such blanket rejection since, while therapeutic activity is only one of many social work roles, psychodynamic concepts illuminate not only that one role but also many other daily social work tasks. The concepts have a major contribution to make.

We agree with Yelloly (1980) and Casement(1985) that practitioners would be able to use psychodynamic thinking and approaches if they had a clearer sense of what was involved and if the language and terminology were more easily accessible. The relevance of psychodynamics lies mainly in its knowledge-base and framework, and in the understanding it offers of processes and dynamics. For instance, in direct work with children, concepts such as transference, countertransference and defence mechanisms, an understanding of attachment theory and the use of symbols are useful not only in unravelling the dynamics which arise, the emotional impact on and possible repercussions for the worker involved, but also in suggesting particular approaches to the work. The utility of the concepts are further highlighted when considering practice around bereavement, loss and change, human growth and development, and marital conflict. Furthermore, psychodynamic theory has an immediacy now in terms of its relevance for practitioners understanding the impact of the work on them since social work is increasingly becoming a stressful occupation. It is often unloved by recipients and regarded ambivalently by society. Public hostility towards, and yet expectations of, social work escalate and spiral. Burn-out and low morale are common. If ever there was a need to understand and counteract these processes, it is now.

The case for reassessment and rehabilitation also originates in the tendency within social work literature to present psychodynamic theory as nothing more than Freudian instinct theory and neo-Freudian ego-dynamics. Thus, Howe (1987) confines his treatment of psychodynamics for social workers almost entirely to Freud, failing to detail the influence of attachment theory and object-relations theory on social work practice. This is a misrepresentation for, like Marxist theory also, psychodynamic theory is not one unified body of knowledge (Rojek, 1986). There have been many developments alongside Freud, largely ignored by social workers. For instance, psychoanalysis is not concerned just with unconscious and intrapsychic processes but also with how individuals define their own existence and find meaning in life. Whilst Freud saw adulthood defined and determined in the early years of life, existential psychotherapists affirm the individual's freedom of choice and responsibility for their own actions. Thus, not all analysts are pessimistic about overcoming blocks which originate in early experience, or accept that understanding the origins of difficulties in the past is essential for change in the present. Equally, British object-relations theorists marked a major change in focus and conceptualisation, as yet barely impinging on social work consciousness (Yelloly, 1980). Social work knowledge largely seems to begin and end with Freud. This has led to a rejection of psychodynamics as narrow and outmoded. One aim of this book is to present a more up-to-date object-relations approach in the hope that this may contribute to the process of rehabilitating psychodynamics within social work practice.

Psychodynamic theory is evolving. Freud's own work showed this evolution. It is concerned as much with interpersonal conflicts as with intrapsychic processes, although accepting that the latter are often played out in the former. It does not necessarily mean that a person's current interactions are less important than a consideration of intrapsychic processes. Some analysts would differ from Freud in their therapeutic approach to patients, preferring a more open, honest stance rather than a blank screen model (Lomas, 1987). Others have quarrelled with Freud's and Klein's reliance on hypothetical instincts and constructs to explain personality development, preferring instead to centre ideas on experiences, the meaning people derive from relationships and the presence or absence of secure attachments (Fairbairn, 1952; Winnicott, 1965; Bowlby, 1979). Malan (1979) questions concepts such as primary narcissism, libido theory and the death instinct. He and Bowlby (1979) find the view that everything can be reduced to sexuality and feeding simplistic and a distortion. Both believe that attachments develop instead from survival and protection instincts. Viewed in this way, a fear of the dark is not neurotic but a fear-arousing situation indicating a risk of danger. Fear in this context has survival value. Bowlby also departs from Freud by seeing anger, as a response to loss, as part of a grief reaction and not indicative of pathological mourning. He criticises analysts for their concentration on the early months and years of an individual's life at the expense of childhood and adolescence generally, and for failing to realise the importance of affectional bonds in the lives and problems of clients. Bowlby's contribution has been to develop a framework for understanding their formation, maintenance and disruption. Psychodynamic theories have also been applied to child abuse and organisational dynamics, reflecting an increasing acknowledgement of the importance of the context in which an individual lives alongside intrapsychic development (Dowling and Osborne, 1985). In summary, some of Freud's ideas have been confirmed, others disproved and others modified. This has yet to be reflected in social work's vision of psychodynamic theory.

Vision

Our aim in writing this book is to provide a perspective on social work practice, which we believe to be relevant to the contemporary practice problems faced by social workers, derived from a combined psychodynamic and systemic approach to human motivation and behaviour. We are not seeking to produce a primer on how to practise psychodynamic psychotherapy or systemic family therapy, or to provide an introduction to psychotherapy or to family therapy. Good literature exists on this already, either in the form of general introductions to the whole field of therapy (Kovel, 1976a; D. Brown and Pedder, 1979; Bloch, 1982), or more specialised guides to specific approaches (Malan, 1979; Hoffman, 1981). Neither are we trying to argue that all social workers should become psychotherapists or that social work should be viewed primarily as a psychotherapeutic activity. As Yelloly (1980) has rightly observed, there is a borderline between psychotherapy and social work. They have different objectives, social work being characterised by its social focus and perspective and its concern with outer reality as well as inner experience, even when the social worker is engaged in counselling or is using a psychological understanding of dynamics.

Instead, we are concerned to show how the insights and techniques embodied in these two theories can be applied not just to direct work with service-users but across a wide range of social work practice; not just when social workers adopt a counselling/therapeutic role but also in other roles, too. Apart from books for social workers which focus on the use of particular techniques in particular settings (Burnham, 1986), there is a dearth of material dealing with this wider applicability of therapeutic theory and practice within social work. There is little detailed guidance on ways in which psychodynamic and systems concepts together can be used to survive, make sense of and be creative in practice.

This is not, therefore, a book for social workers who wish to be therapists, though it may encourage them to work therapeutically and provide frameworks and techniques for such work. Rather, it is designed to explore the theoretical background of two therapeutic approaches, the psychodynamic and the systemic, to spell out their ingredients simply, and to demonstrate how they can be applied in synthesis by social workers, both for understanding and for change, in their work and interactions with individuals, families and organisations.

The theoretical groundwork for a combined systemic–psychodynamic approach will be presented first. Initial chapters will provide definitions and illustrations of the major concepts, argue for their relevance to social work and explore criticisms made of the two theories. Later chapters will apply these ideas not simply to an individual social worker's exposure to particular service-users or situations and the effect worker and user may have on each other, but beyond that to the whole series of concentric and overlapping systems in which even the smallest social work transactions take place: the dynamics of the team or agency; the influence or pressure exerted by management or by other parts of the organisation; the effect of different systems coming into contact and dealing with each other. At any one time, and especially in contentious or highly-charged areas of work, such as the physical and sexual abuse of children, pressures will be exerted on social workers from many directions, including from within. We feel that it is vitally important to make sense of this complex interaction of personal and organisational pressures. By encouraging social workers to look with understanding at themselves, at service-users and at the wider context in which worker and user meet, we hope that they will be more able to work effectively.

No book is ever finished, or indeed any theory. Knowledge is always partial and incomplete. We can only sing our song. Readers will understand, appraise and shape it in their own way, from their own experience. We invite curiosity, not uncritical adoption or rejection of our ideas. We seek to discover but yet also to retain uncertainty since this encourages exploration. Social work is in the process of becoming. To believe otherwise, from the pressure on social workers to be competent, to know, is to seek premature closure, to take flight for the illusion of certainty, often 'found' in off-the-peg social work, dogma and rules. We are truly in danger if we think that we have arrived (Casement, 1985). No universal answers exist to social work's everyday dilemmas.

1

Defining the theory: psychodynamics

Our purpose in the next three chapters is to explore as clearly as possible the main features of a combined psychodynamic and systemic approach to social work practice. For the sake of clarity we have decided in the first place to treat 'psychodynamics' and 'systems' as separate bodies of theory, and then to attempt to bring them together by showing how they provide different perspectives on the same basic phenomena. In subsequent chapters this bringing together of the two approaches, this working synthesis, will be applied directly to practice.

This chapter offers a detailed investigation of psychodynamics, particularly in its more recent guise of object relations. It will be argued that the so-called 'British school' of object-relations theorists – relatively neglected in social work literature – achieved a fundamental reworking of Freudian instinct theory, and that in effect they constructed a 'dynamic bridge' (Slipp, 1984) from the intrapsychic domain to the field of interpersonal relations. We will be touching here on the work of Klein, Fairbairn, Balint, Winnicott and Guntrip. The contribution of Bowlby's attachment theory will also be considered, as this constitutes one of the most significant variants of British object-relations theory (Bowlby, 1988), and is probably familiar, in outline at least, to many social work practitioners. The remainder of the chapter will be devoted to a discussion of key psychodynamic concepts, with particular attention to the ways in which they might deepen our understanding of social work practice.

The Freudian base

All psychodynamic theory and practice derives from the work of Freud. Although we will not attempt a comprehensive survey of

Freudian theory, it is at least necessary to set down some of the basic concepts. This will serve the purpose not only of laying out the groundwork of psychodynamic theory but also of providing a yardstick by which some of the more recent developments in psychodynamic theory and practice can be assessed. Direct access to the *Standard Edition* (*SE*) of Freud's complete works has now been made even easier by the advent of the *Penguin Freud Library* (*PFL*). In addition there is a convenient one-volume collection of Freud's writings entitled *Sigmund Freud: The Essentials of Psychoanalysis* (1986), edited by Anna Freud, which gives the key sources for Freud's most important ideas. 'Introductions' and 'commentaries' abound, and most social workers will be familiar with at least some of them (J. Brown, 1964; D. Brown and Pedder, 1979; Bloch, 1982). Stevens (1983) provides a more detailed introduction, tracing the development of post-Freudian ideas. Storr (1989) provides an excellent brief guide to Freud's life and work, together with a balanced assessment of the value of psychodynamic therapy. Of particular interest to social workers is the well-written introduction to Freudian and post-Freudian theory from a 'political' perspective by Frosh (1987). Finally we recommend Malan's (1979) compelling and highly readable therapeutic account of what we might call basic psychodynamics in action.

We offer a deliberately brief account of some of the main themes of Freudian theory. The term 'psychoanalysis' has a two-fold application, referring to a body of theoretical knowledge as well as to a treatment technique. Here we are not primarily concerned with psychoanalysis as a treatment method, though some of the key issues relating to Freudian technique will be referred to in our discussion of transference and countertransference below. Our general aim is to show how Freud's original theories have been modified by the object-relations school. Our discussion of Freud is divided for convenience into four sections.

The dynamic unconscious

Although he was not (and never claimed to be) the first person to discover or investigate unconscious mental processes, Freud brought a mixture of courage, imagination and rigour to the task which took him into new territory. From his starting point of trying to explain the origin of certain neurotic symptoms he gradually evolved a general theory of human motivation and behaviour. Central to this theory is his belief that nothing is trivial or arbitrary in the way an individual's life is determined. Through a process of self-analysis, and by investigating the manifestations of unconscious processes in symptom-formation and in dreams, Freud uncovered a whole realm of which most individuals are still only dimly aware.

The Interpretation of Dreams (S. Freud, 1900) contains the clearest expression of Freud's discoveries about the unconscious mind. For Freud, dream-interpretation offered 'the royal road' to understanding unconscious mental processes. His central thesis is that dreams are disguised, hallucinatory fulfilments of repressed wishes (Storr, 1989). He explores the processes involved in what he calls the 'dream-work': that is, the ways in which unconscious impulses and desires are 'condensed' or 'displaced' in dreams, or the various forms in which they come to be disguised or 'represented' (for example in symbols). He distinguishes between primary and secondary mental processes, the primary process referring to the condensing, displacing and representing which characterise the inchoate world of the unconscious, and the secondary process referring to the more ordered and 'rational' thought processes of waking life (cf. Rycroft, 1975). The primary process, according to Freud, ignores the normal categories of time and space and treats opposites as if they were interchangeable. These features are characteristic of the primitive, pleasure-seeking part of the psychic apparatus which he later referred to as the 'id'.

In *The Psychopathology of Everyday Life* (1901) Freud explores the various ways in which everyday lapses of memory and slips of the tongue betray underlying unconscious forces. The term 'Freudian slip' has now become part and parcel of everyday vocabulary, and it is applied to almost any slip of the tongue which appears to reveal someone's 'true' feelings or motives. Although usually treated as something of a joke, it is worth reflecting that a great deal of unconscious communication occurs in such inadvertent ways.

Freud's concept of the unconscious is *dynamic*. It is pictured as an arena in which quantities of energy are constantly on the move, a seething cauldron of raw emotion and irrationality. In keeping with the scientific orthodoxy of its day, it is also a biological concept, in that the psychic energy is fuelled by bodily drives.

Instinct theory and psycho-sexual development

Central to Freudian theory is the belief that 'there is a basic driving urge to satisfy instinctual need which provides the source of all psychic energy' (Stevens, 1983). For many years Freud emphasised the sexual drive above all others, only later (after the First World War) stressing the paramount importance of human aggression. These two powerful instinctual drives, the sexual and the aggressive, are variously referred to by Freud (1949) as 'Eros' or the 'love instinct' and the 'destructive' or 'death instinct'. It is important to remember that for Freud these instincts have a physiological basis: they represent the somatic demands upon mental life (S. Freud, 1949). 'Libido', or sexual energy, is pictured as streaming into the ego from various organs and parts of the body. In keeping with this organic view Freud framed his understanding of infantile sexual development in terms of parts of the body: mouth, anus and genitals.

In 1905 Freud published *Three Essays on the Theory of Sexuality*, a work which shocked and offended his contemporaries and 'contributed considerably to Freud's social and scientific isolation from his environment' (A. Freud, 1986). The second essay deals with the subject of infantile sexuality. Freud understands 'sexual' in a broader sense than simply 'genital'. It includes activities designed to obtain pleasure from different zones of the body. Hence, 'sexual life does not begin only at puberty, but starts with clear manifestations soon after birth' (S. Freud, 1949). According to Freud the evolution of the sexual drive passes through successive developmental phases, each associated with a particular 'erotogenic zone'. Hence the well-known stages of human development, the *oral* (first year), the *anal* (1–3), the *phallic* (3–5) and the *genital* (post-puberty). Human sexual development is pictured as occurring in two major 'spurts': from birth to five, and then again around puberty. Between these two phases is the period referred to as 'latency'. Undoubtedly the best-known and most contentious element in this whole scheme is the so-called 'Oedipus complex' which is said to occur in the phallic phase. This was only really worked out in relation to boys, and in any case may well be a peculiarity of the Western nuclear family (Storr, 1989). At this stage the boy is said to turn away from auto-erotic preoccupation and to take a sexual interest in his mother, thus coming into rivalry with his father. Whatever we think about the

Oedipus complex as such, many would see evidence of a sort of Oedipal dynamic which is frequently reactivated in adult life, particularly in competitive situations (cf. Malan, 1979).

As we have seen, 'libido' is pictured as investing itself in (or 'cathecting') particular bodily zones at particular stages of human development. In keeping with the science of the day, this is the picture of 'a closed energy system regulated by the physical law of conservation of energy, so that libido withdrawn from one area must inevitably produce effects elsewhere' (J. Brown, 1964). Conflicts or difficulties experienced at one or other developmental stage may lead to a fixation of libido at that point, or may cause it to 'flow back' to an earlier developmental stage. Hence the common usage of terms such as 'oral' or 'anal' to describe specific personality types deemed to be 'fixated' at a particular point in their development.

If these vicissitudes are successfully negotiated, the Freudian developmental pathway leads on to 'full genitality': mature heterosexual relations. Freud believed that the origins of adult neurosis were to be found in early childhood, and that they were invariably related to disturbances of sexual development. It is well known (and of particular topical interest to social workers) that Freud felt obliged to abandon his early ideas about hysterical disorders being the result of actual childhood seduction in favour of a view which highlighted the powerful role of sexual fantasy. Although Freud remained aware of trauma as a cause of disturbance, he pictured the infant's development as an internal process only tenuously connected with interaction with care-takers (Storr, 1989). For Freud, the ideal state of the human organism is one where there is an absence of tension, need having been met and feelings having been discharged. It is considered almost in isolation. This 'closed system' aspect of Freudian psychoanalysis will be taken up and developed in our discussion of object-relations theory.

Psychic structure

Freud's ideas about the structure of the psyche passed through their own developmental phases, from the early formulations about conscious and unconscious levels, through the so-called 'topo-graphical model' (unconscious/preconscious/conscious) and on to the fully-fledged 'structural model' of *id*, *ego*, and *superego*. Indeed,

Freud's theories were never static: from around 1920 onwards, he developed a new theoretical framework for psychoanalysis which encompassed the life and death instincts, the idea of repetition compulsion and a new theory of the nature of anxiety, as well as the 'structural model' of the psyche (J. Brown, 1964).

Ego and id correspond to what was earlier called 'conscious' and 'unconscious', whilst superego approximates to 'conscience'. The id represents 'the basic biological aspect of the psyche, the inherited instinctual and constitutional aspects which we share to a large extent with the higher primates' (D. Brown and Pedder, 1979). As such it is primarily pleasure seeking and governed by primary process thinking. The ego is the executive part of the personality concerned with rational, self-conscious functioning. It is reality-oriented, and governed by secondary process thinking. It keeps watch over the id, and monitors the id-impulses which pass through its 'territory' on their way to gratification (A. Freud, 1968). It is the ego which deals with the outside world. The superego consists of what has been internalised from parental figures from infancy onwards. This naturally includes the moral precepts and day-to-day code of practice of the functioning personality, the 'do's' and 'don'ts' which all of us carry around inside us. To this picture should be added the 'ego ideal', a more benign version of the superego which provides a positive example to follow rather than a list of prohibitions.

One of the main interests of this model in the light of our discussion in the rest of the chapter is that Freud's concept of the superego begins to point away from the purely intrapsychic sphere towards the family and society as a whole. It enters the territory of 'others in the external world who become internalised and set up as internal representations or images' (D. Brown and Pedder, 1979). 'The formation of a superego thus implies a process by which the functions of the external object are installed within the psyche' (Ogden, 1983). Subsequent theorists, such as Fairbairn, acknowledge that this was an important point of departure on the way to a fully developed theory of object relations.

Neurosis: Conflict, Anxiety and Defence

Basic to Freud's formulations about human nature is the idea that past emotions are the cause of present problems, and that such emotions are invariably shameful, painful or frightening, so that they need to be repudiated and *repressed*, or pushed down into unconsciousness (Storr, 1989). As we have seen, *sexual* feelings are regarded as the key to the process; not necessarily memories of actual traumatic events which occurred in childhood, but instinctual impulses manifesting themselves as fantasies (Storr, 1989). At the root of *neurosis* there is a *conflict* between some powerful feeling which seeks to become conscious and to be discharged, and another part of the psyche which finds that feeling repugnant or frightening, and which therefore seeks to keep it away from conscious awareness. Repressed affects do not simply 'go away': they continue to exert a powerful pressure on the ego to allow them out. The result may well be the emergence of neurotic symptoms which, according to Freud, represent a sort of compromise solution to the struggle being waged between different parts of the psyche.

This basic picture of *repressed feelings* or impulses, struggling to find expression but being held in check by *defences* deployed by the ego to protect itself from the *anxiety* aroused by those repressed feelings, could be said to sum up the essence of psychodynamics. The whole concept of defence mechanisms has been developed by Anna Freud (1968). She points out that Freud used the term 'defence' in the 1890s to describe the ego's struggle against painful or unendurable ideas or affects, and that this was subsequently refined into the concept of repression, the core concept of psychoanalysis. The notion of defence is therefore basic to our understanding of psychodynamic process.

Defences are not only normal but essential. We all have them, we all need them, and none of us could function properly without them. The term 'defensive' is often used pejoratively, but defences are not necessarily negative. Occasionally one comes across the attitude that defences 'stand in the way' and are there to be 'broken down'. It cannot be stressed too strongly that people's defences have to be respected, and that the way to approach them is not with a battering ram but with patience and sensitivity.

Repression is the primary form of defence: 'the witholding or expulsion of an idea or affect from the conscious ego' (A. Freud, 1968). Amongst the other defence mechanisms elaborated by Anna Freud, the following are noteworthy.

1. *Regression*: returning to an earlier maturational stage in order to avoid a damaging or disappointing present.

2. *Denial*: this is a more 'conscious' form of repression, and involves simply denying that something is a problem or causing distress, and banishing it from awareness. This is perhaps one of the crudest forms of defence and one of the most difficult with which to deal.

3. *Projection*: 'In repression the objectionable idea is thrust back into the id, while in projection it is displaced into the outside world' (A. Freud, 1968). In other words, the unacceptable feeling (for instance jealousy or anger) is disowned and attributed to someone else who may then be attacked as a result. This sometimes takes the form of surrendering one's own impulses or wishes to another person and then encouraging that person to fulfil them, thus gaining a vicarious gratification. Examples here might be people who get extremely aggressive for *someone else's* good cause, or people with anorexia who are notoriously successful at catering for other people's culinary desires.

4. *Reaction formation*: this form of defence manifests itself as a complete reversal of the feeling or impulse being defended against, a sort of massive overcompensation in which the subject ends up at the opposite end of the emotional spectrum (for example, being extremely kind and considerate when defending against intense anger and hostility).

5. *Identification with the aggressor*: this takes the form of the subject identifying with the person who is treating them badly and then dishing out the same treatment to someone (or something) else. The child who gets a telling off and then attacks their teddy-bear would be a simple example. Adults who defend themselves against the persistent effects of their own hurtful treatment as children by doing the same to their own children, provide another example.

6. *Reversal:* occurs when the real situation is reversed in fantasy, so that (perhaps most commonly) something dreadful is converted to something much nicer. Again social workers will be familiar with children who persist in believing, against all the evidence, that their parents love them.

7. *Turning against self*: this describes a situation in which a powerful emotion – for example, anger – is turned against oneself rather than directed at its rightful target. Hence, a husband who is intensely angry with his wife, but who cannot

acknowledge or express this anger, is quite likely to turn the anger upon himself and become depressed.

Object relations

Immediately there is a problem. The term 'object relations' conveys something impersonal, something to do with discrete physical entities or 'things'. This is very confusing for those unfamiliar with psychodynamic discourse, and may simply confirm their belief that it occupies a remote world which has nothing to do with everyday life. 'Object' is in fact an analytic code-word for 'person', although it means 'person' in a rather specialised sense, referring as much to an internal representation of another person as to the actual person in the outer world. Confusingly, 'object' may also be used to signify part of a person (otherwise called 'part-object') – for example, a breast – and thus may actually come closer to being a 'thing'. This usage derives from Freud, who conceived of drives as having sources, aims and objects, and of 'objects' as denoting the person or thing which is the target of an individual's libidinal urges and the means of instinctual gratification. As in simple English grammar, an 'object' here is not a person being considered in his or her own right, but solely in terms of the activity of a particular 'subject'.

Freud did develop an object-relations theory within his work, but one which was firmly based on the primacy of the drives and which viewed the object as being an intrapsychic mental representation 'invested' with sexual and aggressive energy (Buckley, 1986). Two aspects of Freudian theory are crucial here. First, there is the supposition that individuals have instinctual drives, and that the primary aim of an individual is to seek instinctual gratification. Second, there is an overriding concern with intrapsychic phenomena. Although the Freudian scheme undoubtedly evolved through several major revisions, it retained its focus on the individual as a 'closed energy system' in which libidinal urges seek satisfaction through particular objects (Greenberg and Mitchell, 1983). In other words, the 'drive' is primary and the 'object' is required as a means of satisfying it.

Fairbairn (1943, 1952) completely recast the classic libido theory, constructing 'a fundamentally different conceptual framework in which relations with others constitute the fundamental building blocks of mental life' (Greenberg and Mitchell, 1983). He traced the development of Freudian theory from its initial concentration on 'impulse' to its later concern with the 'ego', and advanced this development a stage further. For Fairbairn, the vital concern is not the ego's struggle with its impulses, but 'the object towards which impulse is directed'. Acknowledging his debt to Melanie Klein's concept of 'internalised objects', he sees object relationships and not libidinal aims as the determining factors in human development, so that 'a relationship with the object, not of gratification of impulse, is the ultimate aim of libidinal striving' (Fairbairn, 1952, ch. 2).

Effectively, Fairbairn turns the Freudian model on its head. In place of Freud's theory of the various 'erotogenic zones' (oral, anal and genital), through which libido 'flows' to seek discharge, Fairbairn proposes that these libidinal phases are no more than 'techniques for regulating the object-relationships of the ego'. Libidinal pleasure is not an end in itself but a means to an end, and that end is a relationship with the object. Fairbairn conceives of libido as a sort of electric current which finds the 'path of least resistance' to the object. For the baby this will naturally take the form of sucking the mother's breast. This may be a pleasurable activity, but its main function is to provide 'a sign-post to the object'; a complete reversal of the Freudian scheme in which 'the object is regarded as a sign-post to libidinal pleasure'. As D. Brown and Pedder (1979) summarise it, 'Rather than an infant seeking gratification of an oral impulse, we have a couple finding satisfaction through a feeding relationship.'

One of the chief interests of British object-relations theorists has been in the quality of early object relationships, and in the effect of these childhood experiences on the capacity of the developing individual to make satisfying relationships with others. 'To be able to love and enjoy, the baby has to be loved and enjoyed' (Sutherland, 1980). This major shift of psychoanalytic interest can be attributed to two main factors (Friedman, 1975): first, the accumulation of findings from direct observations of child development (for example, in Bowlby's work); second, the clinical experience of analysts working with increasing numbers of patients whose problems lie in the realm of 'character disorder' rather than good old-fashioned 'symptom neurosis'. This 'relationship' aspect of object-relations theory brings it out of the purely intrapsychic domain and plants it squarely in the world of interpersonal relationships. In terms which will be familiar to social workers, the focus now is on damaged people who continue to bring about damage to themselves and to others in their adult relationships.

What, then, is the relationship between the 'inner world' of intrapsychic experience and the 'outer world' of interpersonal relations? How does the one influence and interact with the other? Fairbairn (1958) again provides a useful starting point. His reflections on the therapeutic process are relatively straightforward to grasp. He suggests that a person comes to therapy suffering from 'the effects of unsatisfactory and unsatisfying object-relationships experienced in early life and perpetuated in an exaggerated form in inner reality'. This 'exaggerated' internal version of early experience produces what he calls 'the closed system of inner reality', a relatively safe but denuded area of intrapsychic experience where the patient takes refuge from an external world which is felt to be unrewarding or hostile. Thus the importance of the actual relationship between patient and therapist as people can hardly be overemphasised. This real relationship provides 'a means of correcting the distorted relationships which prevail in inner reality'. If this process is successful the patient may begin to respond differently to other people, seeing them for what they really are instead of through the distorting lens of inner experience.

This brief statement about the nature of psychotherapy introduces us to a number of important concepts. The individual's unhappy childhood experience is pictured as providing a particular 'model' (cf. Skynner, 1976) of self-in-relation-to-object which is internalised and which tends to retain its 'exaggerated' or 'distorted' form. This internal model remains largely unconscious and influences that person's whole way of life, particularly their relationships with others. Real-life experience will thus tend to be interpreted along lines determined by this internal view of the world. Fairbairn describes this internal state of affairs as a 'closed system' and sees the aim of therapy as 'opening up' the patient to the corrective experience of a 'real' relationship.

Bowlby's work on attachment theory is closely linked to Fairbairn. Bowlby (1979) stresses the importance of affectional bonds and their influence on subsequent problems. He suggests that present modes of perceiving and dealing with significant people are influenced and distorted by experiences with previous significant individuals, especially caregivers: that is, representational models of previous encounters are internalised, persist and are applied to new encounters. Put another way, individuals anticipate in new encounters experiences similar to those represented by the internalised model. Behaviour is based on what has been taken in from previous encounters.

Thus if experiences have been dominated by separation, or lack of stability and security, characterised by unresponsiveness or threats of abandonment by caregivers, or if relationships have been marked by violence and anger, anxiety in or withdrawal/detachment from relationships is likely as a defence. Defences may take the form of ambivalence: in/out behaviour whereby relationships atrophy; disruption; aggressive or hostile behaviour; or avoidance (a denial of the need for relationships in order to avoid rejection). These behaviours are then reproduced in new relationships. Taking these in turn, social workers may encounter a lack of trust and missed appointments; continual demands and attacks; self-reliance, avoidance of help and/or compulsive caregiving to hide the desire for close relationships and anger about past disappointments (Bowlby, 1979; Skidmore, 1988).

The absence of good enough parenting and a facilitating environment affects an individual's psychological development and produces, therefore, a closed system internally and in external relations. Individuals are less likely to be open to new actions, to form and sustain interpersonal relationships; rather, they will be defensive about new experiences and less confident because of low self-esteem and minimal feelings of self-worth. Rejection, non-acceptance or insecurity leads to withdrawal which promotes further rejection, a vicious downward spiral punctuated periodically by anger which usually only serves to heighten the rejection or insecurity. Conversely, good experiences which satisfy attachment needs promote self-worth, feelings of security and confidence in having needs met, thus leading to an open system of exploration and a benign circle of expression of need finding acceptance and satisfaction, promoting positive interactions and responses, leading to further expressions of need and so on (Fahlberg, 1981a, 1981b).

The relevance of this theoretical exposition to social work is profound. First, it highlights the importance of securing the setting, providing a secure base for work, noting that this care-taking may include limit-setting and safeguarding users (reception into care). Second, it locates therapeutic work in exploring expectations of and behaviour in relationships, in adjusting internalised models of relationships and focusing on the system rather than the individual alone. Third, it suggests the importance of recognising transference in the worker–client relationship (Hamilton, 1987). Fourth, it provides a knowledge-base of child development, attachment and separation, and what to look for in children, especially relevant in cases of failure to thrive and child neglect (Fahlberg, 1981b). Finally, it orientates practitioners towards exploring family dynamics which produce interpersonal conflict or intrapsychic difficulties (such as school phobia). Thus Bowlby (1973) identifies four family dynamic types whereby the dynamic interaction between parent and child based on anxious attachment produces in his examples avoidance of school or open spaces.

Object-relations theory is, therefore, primarily concerned with 'unconscious internal object relations in dynamic interplay with current interpersonal experience' (Ogden, 1983). Put another way, it begins with an attempt to describe the process by which early childhood experience is internalised, and then broadens out to consider how such internalised models may influence, and be influenced by, current real-life relationships. Not surprisingly, the precise nature of this internal structuring of the personality is described differently by different theorists. The more significant areas of disagreement between different variants of object-relations theory revolve around the question of whether 'good' objects are internalised as well as 'bad' ones, and the relative importance attached to unconscious fantasy as against real-life experience in the formation of the internal object world.

Despite these important differences, the following points comprise a broad summary of object-relations theory:

1. What is internalised (or 'introjected') from birth onwards consists not only of 'objects' but also parts of the self in relation to these objects. We are therefore talking about internal representations (or models) of *relationships*, what Sutherland (1963) calls 'repressed relationship systems', rather than simply images of other people. These models are 'dynamic': that is, they 'are alive in the sense that they continue to form new combinations and to have a life of their own in this inner world, within the limited scope of the original information absorbed about them' (Skynner, 1976).

2. These internal models of 'self-object' serve as a sort of 'template' (Sutherland, 1980) by which similar configurations can be created in everyday relationships. A template is a pattern which is cut to the required shape and then applied to the chosen material so that more of the same shapes can be reproduced. Thus, metaphorically speaking, object-relations theory pictures human beings as reproducing their internal 'self-object' patterns in their relationships with other people.

3. The psychic mechanisms by which these processes take place are called 'introjection' (taking something into oneself from the outside) and 'projection' (transferring something from inside oneself on to other people or on to an external situation). Exactly what is projected on to other people will vary, depending whether it is predominantly the 'self' or the 'object' side of the internal relationship which is being projected. This accounts for the way people may suddenly 'switch' from being, say, a 'victim' to being a 'persecutor' within the same relationship.

4. These processes are universal: they apply to all of us. It is a matter of degree as to whether someone's inner world is so 'distorted' (to use Fairbairn's term) that their projections are pathological. Everyone's relationships with other people, especially their intimate relationships, are determined by inner models. At the 'healthy' end of the spectrum individuals can more or less accept other people as they wish to present themselves. At the other end of the scale are those individuals who are so defensively absorbed in their relationships with inner objects that, for them, 'people are not individuals in their own right and valued as such, but are figures to be coerced into the mould of the inner object' (Sutherland, 1980).

Object-relations theory provides a subtle, complex and wide-ranging view of human nature and human behaviour. In particular it begins to do justice both to the 'inner' world of personal experience and to the 'outer' world of social behaviour. It brings psychodynamics out of the 'closed system' of Freudian drive theory and into the more 'open' system of interpersonal relations (Slipp, 1984). In its view of human nature it attaches importance to an individual's earliest relationships with parental figures, and attempts to conceptualise the ways in which this early experience is structured into the developing personality. According to this view, all individuals to some extent are captives of their own inner worlds. Their internal 'models' or 'maps' continue to have a determining effect on their relations with other people. Sutherland (1963) talks of the internal object operating like 'a scanning apparatus which seeks a potential object in the outer world'. In another graphic image, Stierlin (1977) observes that 'inner objects determine our relational course like a gyroscope'. The psychic mechanism called 'projection' has all the force of a cinematic metaphor. It is as if individuals use other people as 'screens' upon which to animate their inner scenarios. Often we project things on to other people which are quite out of keeping with current reality. Hence the confusions, illusions and misplaced passions which constantly bedevil human intercourse. Individuals habitually try to fashion others in their own image, or to get them to confirm a particular image of themselves. The client who said that it took her years to realise that her husband's frequent verbal attacks on her were not really directed at her at all but at 'someone else' was describing this phenomenon exactly. In more technical terms we might say that he was evidently attacking a 'bad' internal object (perhaps of a mother he experienced as uncaring) which he had projected on to her.

McDougall (1986) uses the powerful metaphor of 'psychic theatre' to explore this theme: 'We do not escape the roles that our unconscious selves intend us to play, frequently using other people in our lives today as stand-ins to settle problems of the past.' This image of the individual's life as a series of repeatedly re-enacted 'scenes' from a 'drama' scripted in infancy, into which other people are co-opted as supporting players, provides a compelling alternative description of the day-to-day outworking of internal object relations. In 'healthy' development the internal models are normally continuously revised, so that adaptation and reality sense should, other things being equal, steadily improve with widening experience (Skynner, 1976). Some people, however, cannot adapt to reality and maintain their inner world defensively as a 'closed system', continuing to treat external objects as if they were internal ones.

These themes are crucial to an understanding of 'transference' and 'countertransference' phenomena as well as to many other aspects of social work practice.

Object relations, marriage and the family

Object-relations theory, with its emphasis on the complex interplay between the 'inner' and 'outer' worlds of human experience, has extended itself naturally into the field of marital and family therapy. For the sake of clarity the discussion here will concentrate on two quite accessible papers: Dicks (1963) on marriage, and Skynner (1981) on the family.

Marriage and family life provide settings for the most intense of human dramas. Marriage is the nearest adult equivalent to the original child–parent relationship (Dicks, 1963), the setting in which adults are most likely to regress and to re-enact the dominant themes of their formative years. In his analysis of marital tensions Dicks uses an interpersonal model drawn largely from the work of Klein and Fairbairn. In particular it is a natural extension of Fairbairn's notion that people whose inner worlds are closed systems can only relate to external objects as if they were internal ones. Although Dicks does not use the term 'closed system' it seems natural to apply it to the types of pathological relationship he describes, in contrast to 'healthy' relationships which can be viewed as relatively 'open' systems. Of course we are dealing here with a spectrum of relationships rather than with simple 'types'. It is undoubtedly true that in all marriages (or equivalent relationships, whether hetero- or homosexual) old object relations are worked out with each spouse perceived to a degree as an internal object (Dicks, 1963). In healthy relationships there is enough tolerance and flexibility for each partner to take on the role of dependent child, supportive parent or autonomous adult, according to their respective needs at any given time. Accepting the ambivalence of a 'mixed' person leads to a complementary growth towards individual completeness and enhancement. In unhealthy relationships one or both partners 'require the other to conform to an inner role model and punish them if the expectation is disappointed'. Dicks observes that a great deal of marital conflict arises from the attempts made by one partner 'to coerce or mould' the other one 'by very rigid and stereotyped tactics' to conform to these inner models. It is important to note that even in outwardly disastrous marriages there is often a collusive process in which the partners are unconsciously serving a vital purpose for each other. Sometimes they interlock to such an extent that they become two halves of a composite personality, excluding those elements of their individual personalities which do not 'fit'. This illuminating view of marital interaction takes Fairbairn's (1958) 'closed system of inner reality' and works out its implications in the arena of intimate two-person relationships.

Skynner (1981) provides a description of 'healthy' and 'unhealthy' families which again readily translates into this shorthand of 'open' and 'closed' systems. He views a healthy family as one which is able to maintain 'an accurate perception of reality' through all the vicissitudes of normal family life. In particular it is able to deal effectively with loss, and can adapt to the multitude of demands and changes which confront every family in the course of its life-cycle. By contrast, malfunctioning families tend to cling defensively to their own version of reality or family script (Ferreira, 1963; Byng-Hall, 1973) which, over generations, influences behaviour. These families resist the painful process of change and growth. A sort of three-line whip may then be exerted on all family members to maintain the 'party line': a fixed corporate view of themselves they have come to adopt in relation to the outside world.

Skynner's model of family functioning is a further development of object-relations theory, one that clearly points towards a more 'systemic' view of human personality and interaction (Skynner, 1976, 1982). He sees family life as a complex collective outworking of each individual's internal object relationships within a functioning whole which can best be viewed as a 'system'. Families which function as relatively 'open' systems can allow a wide diversity of individual development among their members. However, in a more 'closed' family system there is a sort of defensive ganging-together to block differentiation and growth, a process which leads to 'the development of powerful projective systems that seek to preserve in unchanging form some past state of relationships, real or phantasied, and to manipulate others into behaviour which will confirm this rigidly-held view of the world' (Skynner, 1981).

This 'systems' view of family functioning will be explored in the next chapter. For the present we can note how readily an object-relations model, with its cycle of introjection and projection, adapts itself from the intrapsychic to the interpersonal in a way that begins to look circular rather than static. First we shall examine the key psychodynamic concepts of transference and countertransference from the same object-relations perspective, and discuss the Kleinian concept of projective identification which provides a crucial link to systems thinking.

Transference

Most social workers are familiar with the term transference, although it tends to be used quite loosely and is frequently misunderstood. Transference is a projection on to the social worker of the client's inner models derived from feelings, images and experiences of previous significant people. The purpose of the projection is defensive and protective, usually to avoid the full implication or impact of these feelings and previous experiences (Skynner, 1976; Blech, 1981).

Transference was Freud's brilliant discovery and it signalled a major breakthrough in his development of psychoanalytic technique. He first discusses the term in any detail in his account of the 'Dora' case (S. Freud, 1905a). Here, transferences are seen as replacing some earlier person by the person of the analyst. The effect is that previous psychological experiences are revived from the patient's past and 'transferred' on to the analyst in the present, either as exact 'reprints' of past experience or as 'revised editions'.

At this stage Freud clearly regarded the phenomenon of transference as a hindrance to his therapeutic work. Later, however, and this was the major breakthrough, he came to see it as a powerful therapeutic tool, and began to distinguish between its 'positive' (i.e. helpful to treatment) and 'negative' (i.e. obstructive to treatment) forms. He introduced the term 'transference neurosis' to describe the way in which the particular configuration of the patient's neurosis tended to be reproduced in the treatment setting in relation to the analyst. This concept is further developed in 'Remembering, repeating and working-through' (1914), where Freud describes the compulsion on the part of neurotics to repeat in action the repressed material rather than remembering it as something belonging to the past. Thus Freud came to view transference as revealing to the analyst in a direct way the precise nature of the patient's neurotic conflict, and he saw the aim of therapy as being to bring this repressed material out of the unconscious realm of compulsive re-enactment so that it could be 'worked through' and then consigned to its rightful place in the patient's memory of past events.

It should perhaps be added that Freud's notion of transference, in keeping with his overall model of psychic functioning, was predominantly a sexual one: the displacement of sexual drive energy from the memory of the original object to the analyst, who becomes the new object of the patient's sexual wishes, the patient being unaware of this process of displacement from the past (Sandler *et al.*, 1973).

It was precisely this element of erotic attachment which had led to the prevailing view in Freud's time that it was dangerous to allow such a relationship to develop between doctor and patient. Freud's greatest achievement was to press beyond this familiar 'danger' and to investigate exactly what was happening.

Since Freud the clinical concept of transference has broadened considerably. The work of Melanie Klein, Fairbairn and others in building up a picture of the internal world of object relationships has furnished a richer conceptual scheme in which transference phenomena may be understood and harnessed to therapeutic effect. Transference (together with countertransference) 'can now be understood as the interpersonal externalisation of an internal object-relationship' (Ogden, 1983). There is also a strong tendency for it to cover everything the patient brings into the relationship (Joseph, 1985), including infantile mechanisms of defence and their accompanying anxieties. Our current understanding of transference also embraces 'the unconscious (and often subtle) attempts to manipulate or to provoke situations with others which are a concealed repetition of earlier experiences and relationships' (Sandler *et al.*, 1973).

Social workers may feel that they are free from such pressures if they do not work in clinical settings. This is a comforting delusion. Despite its technical ramifications in the field of psychotherapy, transference in fact describes a phenomenon which is present to some degree in every helping encounter, and indeed in everyday life. It can reach considerable intensity in a casework situation (Irvine, 1956): for example, when clients feel abandoned by workers leaving or having holidays, or when fantasies or beliefs about what social workers do make engaging with them difficult. Every relationship contains a 'reality' level – at which we perceive others as they 'really' are and respond to them appropriately – and a 'transference' level, at which we have an illusory perception of others, transforming them 'into the image and likeness of an earlier person and a past situation', and responding to them with inappropriate emotion and manipulative action (Irvine, 1956). In any client–worker relationship the worker may thus be subjected to considerable pressure to take on a particular transference role of this kind, to feel and act out what the client has projected. On this model, then, the patient's transference can be understood as an attempt to 'actualise' in the client–worker relationship a particular unconscious relationship with an internal object. Self and worker are given roles. The pressures exerted on workers to act out their allotted role may range from crude attempts at manipulation to very subtle promptings.

Particular pressures operate in helping encounters. Relationships with people in distress and seeking help can be particularly intense, highly-charged encounters. As Steiner (1976) remarks, clients experience some very powerful feelings, impulses and anxieties when approaching someone who appears able to meet their needs:

> What is revived . . . is one of the most crucial relationships in the life of the individual, that between the needy dependent infant and his providing parents. [Consequently] the therapeutic situation has transferred on to it . . . [both] infantile ways of conceiving and coping with experience, and . . . an intensity of response which can give the encounter the life-or-death dimensions which were appropriate to the time when the infant would die if not fed and looked after.

Social workers cannot escape the fact that their deprived and needy clients are likely to approach them with particularly strong 'feelings, impulses and anxieties' arising from their own infantile experience. The full force of what is unleashed may be hard to understand, let alone accept, but transferences provide useful information about the origin and development of conflicts, patterns and scripts, and about the behaviour and character of past significant figures. Social workers may feel that they are doing their best and be dismayed that their clients seem so hostile, or that they remain so demanding or so unappreciative; they may feel that whatever they do clients will find it inadequate or unacceptable; or they may feel cast in a role which is quite different from the way they like to see themselves (for example, unhelpful and useless as opposed to caring). Inadvertently they might raise expectations that they cannot possibly fulfil, so that they are surprised and even hurt by the bitterness of the reaction. It is vital for social workers to understand such processes so that they can deal with them effectively.

Countertransference and Projective Identification

As the natural counterpart of transference, countertransference has had a similar history, at first being regarded as a hindrance to therapy and more recently being prized as 'a most valuable source of information about the patient as well as a major element of the interaction between patient and analyst' (Segal, 1977).

The key emphasis here is the word 'interaction'. Sigmund Freud's (1912) belief was that the analyst should remain opaque, like a mirror, simply reflecting back what was revealed unwittingly by the patient. He regarded countertransference as the therapist's unconscious transference to the patient, a source of interference in the therapist arising from 'the patient's influence on his unconscious feelings' (S. Freud, 1910). The notion established itself that all personal feelings aroused in the therapist should be kept very tightly in check so that they should not distort the therapist's perceptions.

A crucial shift of perspective was signalled by Heimann (1950), who argued that the therapist's own emotional responses to the patient should be regarded as providing vital clues to the patient's internal world of object relations. In place of Freud's 'opaque mirror', she presents therapy as 'a *relationship* between two persons', adding that 'the analyst's countertransference is an important instrument of research into the patient's unconscious'.

This 'interactional view' (Casement, 1985) is vital to our current understanding of countertransference. The following discussion is based largely on Casement's work (1974, 1985) because most social workers will find it readily translatable into their own experience. Other aspects of the debate about countertransference can be followed up in, for example, Sandler *et al.* (1973), Segal (1977) and Kohon (1986).

It is a matter of common experience that clients often have a powerful emotional impact on social workers. In our discussion of transference we examined the client–worker dynamic from the client's side. Countertransference focuses on the worker's side of the interaction, although in reality transference and countertransference may be regarded as interlocking parts of a single interactional system (Symington, 1983). What impulses and feelings are evoked by the client? How does the client expect the worker to react, and what pressure is being exerted to produce that reaction? In sorting out the worker's response we need to make an important distinction. Casement (1974, 1985) divides countertransference reactions into two types: the *personal* and the *diagnostic*. Personal counter-transference is close to Freud's original meaning and describes those reactions which are determined by the worker's own personal history and current emotional experience. For example, Carr (1989) uses the term 'countertransference reaction' in the traditional sense to examine the personal level at which professional workers respond to cases of child abuse, perhaps experiencing a strong urge to rescue the child at all costs, or making an unconscious identification with one or other of the adults. All social workers are subject to powerful unconscious reactions of this type, depending on their own particular personalities and life experience. The more stressful the work, the more pronounced such reactions are likely to be. One female social worker commented that her adolescent clients always related to her as a mother figure, and that she never felt she handled this situation at all well because she found herself reacting to them very emotionally, as if to her own teenaged children. She was clearly acknowledging a problem in the area of personal countertransfer-ence. A further example is given in Chapter 7 of a social worker whose frantic efforts to keep families harmoniously together derived from his own early experience of separation and loss. Such areas of deep personal experience are bound to influence a social worker's responses, particularly in stressful or highly charged situations, and sometimes undeniably distort their perceptions of what is happening. The only way to untangle this process is by self-examination or through skilled supervision. In some cases workers may themselves require therapeutic help.

'Diagnostic' countertransference is different, though it cannot be separated entirely from the more personal kind. It is a reaction which is actively aroused in the worker by the client's projections, so that a worker who is sufficiently sensitive will be able to tune into the particular object relationship which is being projected and 'diagnose' what it is. We can conceptualise this process as the client 'actualising' (Sandler, 1976) or 'externalising' (Ogden, 1983) an internal relationship between self and object so that the worker is cast in a particular role, depending which side of the self–object relationship is being assigned to the worker at any given time. For example, if the client has internalised an early relationship with a damaging or rejecting parent, then the worker might well be cast in the role of this 'bad' object. The worker may then be puzzled to find that 'helpful' work is reacted to as if it is designed to harm or destroy. As a result the worker might actively begin to take on this role, perhaps by getting exasperated with the client and 'forgetting' appointments. Alternatively it might be the client who takes the 'object' role, assigning the role of 'self' to the worker. In such circumstances the situation is turned around so that the worker comes to feel under attack for no discernible reason. This may produce a bewildered reaction in the worker which quickly turns to hurt, then to resentment, and perhaps finally to withdrawal from the case. All too often social workers fail to realise that they have become 'role responsive' (Sandler, 1976) in this way and that they have been induced to act out a role which has been unconsciously assigned to them by the client. Various other metaphors can be used to describe this process. For example, McDougall (1986) elaborates it in terms of 'psychic theatre': the worker is roped into a re-enactment of scenes from the client's inner world. Similarly Byng-Hall (1988) talks about workers being unwittingly 'recruited' into a client's 'life-script'. However it is described, this process can easily propel workers into an unconscious collusion with their clients unless they are able to tune into their own emotional reactions and use their countertransference diagnostically.

The Kleinian concept of *projective identification* adds a further dimension to our understanding of this interactional process. Since it was formulated the concept has been developed in a number of different ways (Ogden, 1979). Kleinian perspectives are clearly presented by Rosenfeld (1987, ch. 8), Joseph (1987) and Spillius (1988), whilst a more critical view is offered by Kohon (1986).

In its original form projective identification describes one of the defence mechanisms associated with the so-called 'paranoid-schizoid position' in early psychic development (Klein, 1946; Segal, 1973). The child is pictured as splitting off in fantasy those 'hated parts of the self' which cause anxiety and pain and projecting them on to the mother in such a way that she becomes 'identified' with them (Klein, 1946). It should be stressed that this defensive splitting and projection is seen as part of normal development, and that it only becomes pathological when it is carried into adult life as the dominant mode of relating to others (Rosenfeld, 1987; Joseph, 1988). In adult life this defensive manoeuvre involves splitting off 'bad' or unacceptable parts of oneself and assigning them to someone else, whilst applying pressure on the recipient to experience the projected feelings or to act out the projected impulses. We all know how difficult it is to work with individuals who split good and bad in this way. They usually attribute all the fault to others, and may lurch from idealising certain people (including social workers) to reviling them. In marriages and intimate partnerships there is often a collusive process of splitting and projection which results in one partner being cast as all bad so that the other partner can feel good inside (Stewart *et al.*, 1975). In families it is very common for a particular member to be designated the bad one, or for the 'good' child to be unrealistically idealised at the expense of the others. Zinner and Shapiro (1972, 1974) have developed this theme, using the concept of projective identification to explore the ways in which adolescent children may be pressurised into acting out their parents' own disowned and projected 'bad' impulses.

Alongside its defensive function, projective identification also operates as a powerful means of *communication*. This theme has been developed mainly by Bion (1962), who also elaborates the notion of the therapist acting as a sort of 'container' for the patient's projections. Casement (1985) again provides some graphic illustration of what he calls 'communication by impact'. Sometimes clients can only communicate an unspeakable inner state by getting the worker to experience it for themselves. Hence, if a worker is made to feel frustrated or humiliated by a client, or is left feeling angry, stupid or despairing, it may well be important to stay with these feelings and to explore whether they represent aspects of the client's own inner experience which are being communicated in this way. For example, a client who has been rejected or abused as a child may, through their behaviour, stir up all sorts of unbearable feelings in the worker, including perhaps a fear of physical attack. In such a case the client is effectively 'identifying with the aggressor' (A. Freud, 1968) and 'abusing' the worker. There may in fact be quite an aggressive or controlling aspect to this sort of communication (Steiner, 1976). As well as personal resilience, workers need good supervision if they are to make creative use of their own emotional reactions in such circumstances, rather than simply feeling overwhelmed by them.

If we believe that childhood themes are constantly replayed and re-enacted in adult life, then it seems natural to look for the origins of these interpersonal processes in the child–parent relationship. Bion (1959) argues that projective identification (by the child) and introjective identification (by the parent) are two sides of a process which together form the foundation on which normal development rests. When a child projects unwanted or unbearable feelings on to a parent, the parent may react in a number of different ways. For example, they may find these feelings unmanageable and immediately expel them. Or they may take them in, identify with them and 'contain' them for the child, perhaps returning them to the child in some more manageable form. It is easy to see how the first reaction could involve both child and parent in a vicious cycle of escalating anxiety and bad feeling, whereas the second reaction might 'hold the situation' (Winnicott, 1954a, 1954b) so that the unmanageable feelings could be made more manageable and integrated into the developing personality. Every parent will recognise this process and will know that if they respond to an anxious or distressed child with matching anxiety or distress, then the situation can frequently spiral out of control. And of course if a parent has no experience to fall back on of being 'contained' or 'held' in this way, or has no one currently who can provide this for them, then they may be impelled to an extreme reaction, such as violence, by the escalating influx of unmanageable feelings from the child.

Helping encounters can be viewed in a similar way; indeed, it might be argued that therapeutic work is more akin to parenting than to any other activity (Lomas, 1987). Sometimes the most helpful thing – perhaps the only thing – a worker can do is to contain the anxiety, anger or grief which is 'spilling over' (Casement, 1985) from the client, in the hope that this may open up the whole process to understanding and discussion, eventually enabling the client to take back what was previously unbearable and work it through for themselves (Rosenfeld, 1987, ch. 8).

To summarise, we can say that countertransference (of the 'diagnostic' type) is the worker's capacity to pick up those different types of unconscious communication from the client and to understand their meaning. The initial impact may well be to make the worker adopt a certain attitude or act in a particular way: to become 'role responsive' (Sandler, 1976). In other words, the worker may be induced not only to experience a particular feeling-state but also to act out a particular role. This may give rise to an uncomfortable feeling of 'being manipulated so as to be playing a part, no matter how difficult to recognise, in somebody else's fantasy' (Bion, 1955). If this process passes undetected it can easily spread beyond the individual worker to embrace the wider professional system, a phenomenon described by Reder and Kraemer (1980) as 'system countertransference' (see Chapters 5 and 7). The importance of projective identification is that it attempts to describe, metaphorically, how disavowed aspects of a client's inner emotional state can be directly and unconsciously communicated to the worker, and how that communication can evoke responses in the worker which may provide vital countertransference clues to the client's inner world of object relationships.

Conclusion

This chapter has traced one line of development from Freud's predominantly intrapsychic model to a more open object-relations model of human functioning which connects the inner and outer worlds of human experience and which begins to do justice to both intrapsychic and interpersonal phenomena. The concepts of transference, countertransference and projective identification help us to identify certain interpersonal processes which have a crucial bearing not only on psychotherapy but on all close encounters, especially those of a helping kind.

2
Defining the theory: a systems approach

The impact of systems thinking on British social work has been patchy. Most recently trained practitioners are probably familiar with the 'integrated' or 'unitary' approach (Goldstein, 1973; Pincus and Minahan, 1973; Specht and Vickery, 1977). This broadly-based 'systems' perspective on social work practice has undoubtedly been influential, though it has not heralded the new dawn so eagerly awaited by some enthusiasts (Evans, 1976). The most dramatic infusion of systemic ideas into social work has in fact come from the family therapy field (Skynner, 1976; Walrond-Skinner, 1976; Selvini Palazzoli *et al.*, 1978; Treacher and Carpenter, 1984; Burnham, 1986).

Defining a system

The word 'system' is widely used in everyday language to apply to a whole range of different things. At its simplest it means 'a set of connected things or parts' (Concise Oxford Dictionary) or a dynamic order of parts and processes which mutually interact (von Bertalannfy, 1968). Whether we are talking about a hi-fi system, a belief system or a system of government, the term 'system' in each case carries the sense of a composite whole which is made up of particular components or elements. These elements can be isolated and examined more closely (for each example, say, an amplifier, a rejection of conventional religious faith or a legislative assembly), but in reality they do not function in isolation. Each of them is intimately tied up with other elements of the same system to form a coherent, functioning whole which 'fits together'. Remove or modify one element, and everything else is unavoidably affected.

Hall and Fagen (1956) provide one of the most widely quoted definitions of a system: 'A system is a set of objects together with relationships between the objects and between their attributes.' 'Objects' here mean the component parts of a system: heart, lungs and blood vessels if we are talking about the cardio-vascular system, or family members if we are talking about a family. 'Attributes' are the particular properties possessed by these objects, the terms in which they can most meaningfully be described. Again the significance of these attributes will vary, depending on the part they play in helping each object to function properly as a component of the system. The 'relationships' bind the system together. The separate components of a hi-fi system are not much use by themselves. However, once properly connected up they become a sound-reproducing system. The 'objects' and their 'attributes' are then 'related' since performance of each stage is dependent on performance in the other stages (Hall and Fagen, 1956). In other words, a system is an organised arrangement of elements, a network of interdependent, interrelated and co-ordinated parts, that functions *as a unit* (Gorell-Barnes, 1985). Its boundary, purpose and the function of its components is defined by the individual observing and describing the system (Gorell-Barnes, 1985).

Many systems appear similar, a phenomenon known as isomorphism (Greek: of the same shape; see Hall and Fagen, 1956). Common characteristics, patterns and attributes are listed below. Closely interrelated, they are separated out only for clarity and convenience.

Wholeness

In living systems every part of the system is so related to every other part that a change in one particular part changes all the other parts and the total system (Hall and Fagen, 1956). This property is sometimes expressed in terms of 'non-summativity': the whole is greater than the sum of the parts, or perhaps the 'behaviour' of the whole is more complex than the 'sum' of the 'behaviour of its parts' (Wilden, 1980). The crucial point about a system is the interconnectedness of its component parts: 'summing up' the parts gives no account of how they stand in relation to each other, and it is the way these *relationships* are organised which gives the system its distinctive quality.

Structure

Living systems maintain a persistent structure over relatively long periods despite interaction between their component parts with the surrounding world (Skynner, 1976). Discrete parts within a system are called *sub-systems*. Each system is also part of a bigger system or *supra-system*. This depends, of course, on where the observer draws the boundary, whether round an individual, a couple, a family, an extended family or a neighbourhood. A family may itself be viewed as a system (containing its own sub-systems), or else as a sub-system of a larger kinship network, or again as the supra-system of an individual.

Boundaries

All living systems have boundaries which mark them off from their environment. The drawing of boundaries is an integral part of the observer's act of observing and describing a system. Boundaries may be physical or psychological. The amount of information transmitted between points within a system is significantly larger than the amount transmitted across its boundary (Miller, 1965). A boundary marks a point of transition where *differences* can be observed in structure, function and behaviour on either side (Skynner, 1976). Boundaries are semi-permeable: they allow some things to cross them (in either direction) but not others. One function of the boundary is thus to restrict the flow of matter/ energy/information to a level that the system can cope with. Sub-systems also have boundaries which mark them off within the system.

Self-maintaining and adaptive capacity

Most living systems are able to react to their environments in a way that is favourable to their continued operation (Hall and Fagen, 1956). Systems give priority to processing information which is needed to relieve a strain, neglect neutral information, and positively reject information which will increase strain (Miller, 1965). In other words, systems have their own built-in mechanisms for adapting to changes in their environment or for maintaining their stability (homeostasis). A crucial notion here is that of *feedback*. This means that 'part of a system's output is reintroduced into the system as information about the output' (Watzlawick *et al.*, 1967). Feedback 'loops' are described as either 'positive' (deviation-amplifying) or 'negative' (deviation-countering). A system's stability or home-ostasis is maintained by negative feedback, which serves to 'correct' any deviation from the 'norm' of the system's current interaction with its environment. In other words, negative feedback operates to keep things as they are. Change is brought about by positive feedback, which amplifies output deviation and thereby pushes the system away from its current stability towards a new state.

Open or closed

Systems are described as 'open' if they interact with their environment, and 'closed' if they do not. All living systems are open in this sense, although some are clearly more open than others.

Open and closed systems

The distinction between 'open' and 'closed' systems lies at the heart of systems theory and may be understood on two levels. First, at the simple descriptive level, 'open' describes a system which is open to and interactive with its environment, and 'closed' describes a system which is not.

Second, at a higher level of abstraction the term 'closed system' refers to the theoretical model upon which classical physics and chemistry were based, and which tended to study phenomena in isolation from their environment. By contrast, open systems exchange materials, energies or information with their environ-ments and cannot be studied as though in a sealed insulated container (Hall and Fagen, 1956; cf. Watzlawick *et al.*, 1967, p.122). Open systems are characterised by continuous activity or a steady state of disequilibrium, their parts act purposefully and structures are adjusted to achieve goals (Evans, 1976). Their composition remains constant despite inputs and outputs, taking in and discharging energy (von Bertalannfy, 1968). Closed systems also have energy but it is locked away, and is unavailable for outside use.

This is 'equilibrium', a state which is essentially self-contained and which tends towards stagnation, becoming static in some kind of end state (Evans, 1976).

In the last chapter we echoed Greenberg and Mitchell's (1983) description of Freudian drive-theory as a 'closed system'. This may now make more sense in the light of the foregoing paragraph. Rather than an open system model, goal seeking and adaptive in response to information, Freud's notion of libido or drive energy is a closed system regulated by conservation of energy (J. Brown, 1964; Wilden, 1980).

The metaphor of open and closed systems can fruitfully be applied to many aspects of human functioning, as well as to theories and belief-systems. It can be used as a sort of shorthand to evaluate the condition of any human system, from an individual to an entire social or national group. For example, an individual who is 'open' to other people, to new experiences and to new ideas, and who interacts productively with the environment, contrasts with someone who (for whatever reason) has a 'closed' mind and who is unresponsive and self-preoccupied. We are likely to consider the 'open' person as in 'better' shape and the more rewarding companion. In the last chapter we looked at Fairbairn's (1958) approach to individual psychotherapy in terms of opening up a person's 'closed system of inner reality'. Similarly, if we look at relationships, some couples clearly have an 'open', lively, creative relationship which thrives on outside contact, whereas others live in a closed world. Their relationship is narrowly circumscribed, feeds entropically on its own internal energy and enjoys little creative intercourse with the outside environment. In some cases the partners may interlock to such an extent that they form a sort of 'total personality', excluding those elements of their individual personalities which do not 'fit' (Dicks, 1963). Such relationships might also be described as either 'complementary' or 'symmetrical' (Watzlawick *et al.*, 1967; Bateson, 1973), depending on precisely how the partners' behaviours match each other and fit together. That is to say, relationships may be characterised by one up/one down (opposite), or by mirror (identical but escalated) positions. The tendency is towards increasing escalation and rigidity of behaviour: more of the same. The result is an interpersonal system which is more closed than open.

In families a similar principle applies. Some families seem to inhabit a world of their own and to be stuck in some sort of time-capsule. Growth and diversification are strongly resisted, and considerable pressure may be exerted upon individuals to conform to family 'myths' or 'scripts' (Ferreira, 1963; Byng-Hall, 1973, 1979, 1985, 1988), or to take on prescribed roles (Zinner and Shapiro, 1972, 1974). The overall effect may be that of fixing family members 'in a timeless, static, frozen pattern' (Skynner, 1981). In a study of families where father–daughter incest has occurred, Alexander (1985) gives a particularly clear account of the essential differences between those families which operate as relatively 'open' systems and those which live at the 'closed' end of the spectrum. She stresses 'informational exchange with the environment' as a key factor in counteracting entropy (the system's tendency to run down into disorder). She also observes that 'openness' has a double dimension: openness to the outside environment (letting new information *in*), and openness within the system itself (letting new information *circulate*). On both counts 'incest' families are found to operate as closed systems. Ausloos (1986) observes that a family's perspective on *time* is another vital determinant of its capacity to absorb new information. In some families time may be 'arrested' so that no new developments take place and there are no adjustments to new situations created by life-cycle transitions (for instance, from childhood to adolescence). In other families things may be incessantly changing, but in such a chaotic way that information circulates too fast to be recorded or remembered. In both cases the system remains closed and entropy increases.

Much the same picture is apparent in larger systems such as institutions or organisations. An organisation, just like an individual, a couple or a family, can get so tangled up in its own internal processes that it becomes more and more closed to the outside world, and less and less effective at performing the task for which it was originally set up. The classic Kleinian study by Menzies (1970) of the nursing organisation within a large teaching hospital provides a compelling psychodynamic account of such a closed system. In social services teams, the stress generated by the work can create a defensive, closed system characterised by conformity to guidelines and procedures rather than discussions about practice dilemmas within social work tasks; the system leads to workers seeking to minimise error rather than acknowledge the inevitability of risk, and to the closing down of communication with staff and users rather than reviewing the position and possible courses of action. Interestingly, some organisational psychologists now take an 'open system' approach to their subject, describing the more flexible, efficient and responsive institutional structures as 'organic' (or 'organismic'), in contrast to the more rigid and self-serving structures of traditional hierarchical bureaucracies (Blackler and Shimmin, 1984).

To summarise: an open system, of whatever size, demonstrates exploratory behaviour, is adaptable, creative, confident, and takes in and acts fruitfully upon new information. There is communication with other systems and between its sub-systems. It allows considerable autonomy for its members. Its boundaries are, therefore, flexible rather than impermeable and fixed. Its face is not set against change.

Applying systems theory to families

The systemic approach, to therapy with families or work with agency systems, is grounded on a number of key principles.

The potential for change

The 'working hypothesis' of the Milan team, whose developing application of systems theory forms the basis of what follows, is that the family is a self-regulating system which holds itself together by, and controls itself according to, rules formed over a period of time through a process of trial and error (Selvini Palazzoli *et al.*, 1978). These rules emerge from all the transactions, together with their attendant feedbacks, which occur within the system and between the system and its environment. The Milan team adopts from general systems theory the proposition that every system has not only a homeostatic tendency to maintain the status quo but also the capacity to evolve and transform itself. Systems are seen as continually evolving and occasionally stuck rather than home-ostatically organised to resist change. In 'pathological' systems the structures governing transactional patterns tend to become fixed, with the result that a closed system develops, characterised by an increasingly rigid tendency compulsively to repeat proven solutions in order to maintain the homeostasis and resist feared change (Selvini Palazzoli *et al.*, 1978). The 'stuckness' derives from the system's continued efforts to apply outdated and erroneous internalised maps and meanings to new situations which require different solutions. Put another way, a stuck family has a script which is too tightly written (Cecchin, 1987; Byng-Hall, 1988). Paradoxically the system's 'solutions' actually inhibit development. If this state of affairs gives rise to symptomatic behaviour, then that behaviour will be moulded into its own distinctive shape by the particular pattern of rule-bound transactions which obtains within that family. On this basis the Milan team's recipe for therapy is deceptively simple: to eliminate the symptoms it is necessary to change the rules (the system's stereotyped ways of organising itself over time) by introducing new information or a different script.

Circularity

This is the pivotal concept of systemic therapy upon which everything else turns. Traditional psychology and social science was wedded to Newtonian physics, usually summed up as one billiard ball striking another; one object makes an impact on another one so that there is an exchange of energy which leads to a particular (and calculable) outcome: A acts on B to produce C. Traditional psychiatry, for example, views the designated patient as the end-point of a cause-and-effect chain which makes that person the locus of a particular pathology. Systems thinking challenges the view that we can understand any living system in such simple terms of linear cause and effect. It sees as illusory the notion that A instructs B or causes B to act in a particular way, or that B's response to A is in any way predictable. It is the system that specifies how it and the components within it will behave. The concept of punctuation is important here. Bateson (1973) talks of 'our curious habits of punctuating the stream of experience so that it takes on one or another sort of coherence and sense'. This is a matter of common everyday experience. We all view things from our own vantage point, from where we stand, and the same sequence of events will be interpreted differently by different people. The problem is that our linear cause-and-effect punctuations tend to be seen as sufficient explanations of what is 'really' happening, and therefore as descriptions of 'the truth' (Cecchin, 1987). The example of the nagging wife and the withdrawing husband is a good illustration of this phenomenon (Watzlawick *et al.*, 1967). From the wife's point of view, her 'nagging' is a reasonable response to her husband's withdrawal. On the husband's side it is clear to him that it is his wife's nagging that makes him want to withdraw. In other words, each partner constructs a particular map of reality or 'blame game' by 'punctuating' the sequence in a particular way. The outcome is a relationship struggle where each attempts to press-gang the other into accepting their viewpoint. An impasse results. Each partner falls victim to the mistake of seeing one part of the 'system' (the other person's behaviour) as 'causing' another part (their own response). Viewing it from the outside we can see that this is a *circular* interaction where each side influences and is influenced by the other's behaviour. The behaviour of each party generates 'more of the same' from the other side, so that the process continues until the cycle is interrupted, perhaps by a social worker who enables a change in the rules of the game and, therefore, in the relationship by taking them outside the interaction.

In systemic terms there is no one 'correct' view. A battle to establish one is unhelpful and should be avoided since it is merely likely to reinforce and escalate fixed views. However, since people habitually punctuate reality in terms of linear cause and effect, it takes a particular effort to tune in to circular relational patterns. The aim is to think in terms of the way things relate or fit together rather than the way things 'are'. This involves an important shift away from ascribing fixed qualities or characteristics to people, a tendency which is embedded in our normal use of language. To describe someone as 'sad' or 'angry' is of limited value unless we know the relational context in which this sadness or anger manifests itself. At an early stage the Milan team adopted the strategy of using the verb 'to show' rather than 'to be' when discussing the emotions expressed by family members. This helped them to steer clear of linear descriptions of personality and behaviour and to maintain a systemic perspective. It does not, as has been alleged (Treacher, 1988), invalidate felt experience, but rather opens up a process for exploration. Saying that someone 'is depressed' or 'resistant' invites a full stop after it. On the other hand, to say that someone 'shows depression or resistance' is more likely to prompt such contextual questions as 'To whom?' and 'In what circumstances?' (Tomm, 1984a), 'What for?', and 'Why now?', thus bringing out the crucial *differences* upon which all useful information rests and the meaning or function of the behaviour for the system.

Following Bateson (1979), information comes from the experience of perception of difference, and interaction between parts of a system is triggered by difference. In order to learn about something we look at it from different angles and we compare it to other things that we already know about. When exploring something by touch we learn more by moving our fingers across its surface than by letting our hand rest on it. 'What we perceive easily is difference and change – and difference is a relationship' (Bateson, quoted in Selvini Palazzoli *et al.*, 1980a). A difference always defines some sort of relationship (or a change in a relationship), and this relationship is always circular (Tomm, 1985). In practical terms, therefore, 'circularity' requires therapists to proceed on the basis of feedback from the family in response to the information they obtain about relationships and, therefore, about difference and change (Selvini Palazzoli *et al.*, 1980a). The aim of the systemic therapist is thus to see family members as elements in a circuit of interaction, and explore the family's circularity by bringing out differences: differences in behaviour, relationships or feelings and beliefs at different points in time. This process forces the family to experience its own circularity and disrupts the fixed attributions and linear punctuations by which it seeks to shape and control its existence. Tomm (1985) sums up this approach with particular clarity:

> By definition a system is always a *composite* unity. It is composed of component parts or elements. What makes the collection of elements a 'whole', a 'totality' or a 'system' is the *coherent* organisation of the components. This coherence depends on reciprocal or recursive (ie circular) relationships between the components. To understand a system is to understand the coherence in its circular organisation. Thus it is the circular connectedness of ideas, feelings, actions, persons, relationships, groups, events, traditions etc that is of interest to the systemic therapist.

Thus, the therapeutic implication is that problems are not confined within the boundaries of individual personalities but are to be traced to their systemic context. The shift is not just from an intrapsychic to an interpersonal model of therapy, from thinking in terms of individuals to thinking in terms of relationships: it is a shift from thinking 'linear' to thinking 'system' (Bateson, 1970). The systemic principle of 'non-summativity' affirms that we cannot get to know the whole by getting to know each of the parts in isolation. The focus must shift from the attributes that particular individuals 'possess', and from the roles they fulfil, to patterns of relationship (Keeney, 1979). Accordingly, people should not be viewed as isolated units but always in a context, in a particular set of relationships in which they operate at any given time. Trying to interpret individual or group behaviour without reference to context invariably leads to the ascription of fixed qualities or attributes, and to the mistake of defining something by what it supposedly is in itself rather than by its relation to other things (Bateson, 1979).

An obvious example is of professionals criticised in recent child abuse enquiries. Blame is attached to individuals, who are defined as incompetent, giving the illusion both of a beginning and a simple solution. The essential greyness, ambiguity and difficulty of the task is underplayed or overlooked. Also ignored are the contradictory messages given by society: workers as failing to protect but too ready to take children away; increasing demands and expectations but inadequately resourced services. The enquiries largely present a reductionist perspective, a partial analysis of the complexity. To unravel how systems descend to the lowest level of functioning, all the issues must be understood and incorporated in attempted resolutions (Ruddock, 1988): staffing levels, resources, societal expectations, training and the relationship between the law and social work practice. To blame social workers and team leaders is easy. To appreciate their position in the system and to afford them help is ultimately more effective. To prescribe additional training or the centrality of the law to practice is to oversimplify, to fail to tackle the connectedness of the many parts within the system.

The techniques devised by the Milan team to investigate this 'circular connectedness' and resist a blame game are *positive connotation* and *circular questioning*. Positive connotation emphasises the potentially positive intentions or aspects of behaviour which is being viewed negatively, thereby altering the family's reality and allowing change to occur without any individual having to admit to being wrong and without blame, badness or madness being attributed to anyone. By focusing in turn on each member of the system, it connects them in a framework of relationships and avoids locking therapists in a factional trap of taking a critical stance against one part of the system (Burnham, 1986; Burnham and Harris, 1988). Consider the example of a parent and child caught in a cycle of criticism and withdrawal. Each blames the other and sees the other's behaviour as fixed and bad. The more the parent is critical, the more the child withdraws, whereupon the more the parent is critical. To break this impasse and enable change it is necessary not just to reframe one person's behaviour, since that would fall into a linear trap of siding with one against another. It is necessary to positively connote each person, perhaps redefining criticism as concern and withdrawal as consideration, and each person as doing their best. It involves changing the conceptual and/ or emotional setting or perspective in relation to which a situation is experienced, and to place it in another frame which fits the 'facts' of the same situation equally or even better and thereby changes its meaning (Watzlawick *et al.*, 1974). Positive connotation changes the meaning people attach to behaviours or interactions in order to free them from being trapped in one perspective and break into the escalation of competing, rigidly held and negatively connoted viewpoints (Gorell-Barnes, 1979), and to render the situation more amenable to behavioural and/or emotional change. Giving a new frame or meaning can have a positive effect, changing relationship patterns and rigid defensive behaviour rather than perpetuating the downward spiral of more of the same, whereby attempts to solve problems become part of the problem.

Instead of questioning individuals directly or focusing on dyadic relationships, circular questioning aims to throw light on the various triadic relationships within the family. It does this in a number of ways, most commonly by asking one family member to comment on, and thus to 'metacommunicate', about the relationship between two others. Other types of circular questions include: questions which encourage the family to translate static descriptions of individuals into connected sequences or patterns of behaviour which occur in the family as a whole; 'before and after' questions aimed at clarifying changes in behaviour or in relationships around some key event; 'comparison' or 'ranking' questions which probe the different reactions of family members to particular issues or events; and hypothetical or future-oriented questions which enlarge the family's frame of reference and draw comments which might otherwise remain inhibited (see Penn, 1982, 1985; Tomm, 1984b, 1985, 1987a, 1987b, 1988; Burnham and Harris, 1988). Such questioning often brings to light a great deal of 'difference' and therefore introduces new information into the system. The information sought by circular questions are the differences in relationships experienced before and after the problem began, the aim being to enable family members to experience the circularity of their system and abandon linear stances (Penn, 1982). With their constant reference to difference and change, circular questions 'undermine the family's belief system by using the language of relationship, not of "what is"' (Cecchin, 1987). They orient the therapist towards exploring the 'systemic connectedness' of the presenting problem, and hence towards understanding why that problem might be necessary for that particular system at that particular time (Tomm, 1985). This method of interviewing does produce change, being a series of interventions which releases the system's potential (Tomm, 1985, 1987b).

Hypothesising

A hypothesis is a supposition or conjecture, constructed from the information available about a particular family, which serves as a starting point for investigation. It is not meant to be 'true' but simply 'useful'; neither more nor less so than other hypotheses. Cecchin (1987) stresses how important it is to overcome the deeply ingrained habit of searching for the one single 'explanation' which will provide the key to what is happening in a particular family. As many different ideas or 'stories' as possible should be generated in order to provide the context for seeing circular patterns and asking circular questions (Cecchin, 1987). In this sense a hypothesis must be systemic: it must attempt to include all the elements of the system and address relationships: what people do and believe, and the meanings by which members perceive and interpret their own and each other's interactions and behaviour (Selvini Palazzoli *et al.*, 1980a). Only by understanding these factors can therapists construct a hypothesis which, whilst remaining plausible, will be sufficiently discordant with that of the family to guarantee the introduction of new information into the system. A good systemic hypothesis serves two practical purposes in the family session. For the therapist it provides a framework for activity, making it easier to stick to the task of tracking relational patterns by focusing on the key questions 'What?', 'Why now?' and 'What for?' For the family it has the important function of introducing new information into the family system, thus countering the family's 'entropy'. Again this bears a close relation to our previous discussion of dysfunctional families as 'closed systems', where the therapeutic task is to 'open' them by introducing fresh information. Of course this only applies if the therapist's hypothesis about the family's functioning *is* new, if it *is* different from the family's own hypotheses about itself. The state of a therapist's hypothesis-making can therefore be regarded as a good guide to therapeutic progress. When unable to develop hypotheses, the therapist may have accepted the family's script and thus have lost a sense of curiosity and become stuck (Cecchin, 1987).

Milan-style hypotheses are not, in fact, 'systemic' in the strict sense because they tend to postulate reasons for the behaviour of certain family members, and reasons constitute a linear punctuation of a circular process (Ugazio, 1985). The real strength of such hypotheses, however, is that, whether they are strictly 'systemic' or not, they are built on formulations of behaviour which are at least *triadic* – that is, involving at least three family members – in contrast to everyday, common-sense explanations of behaviour which are nearly always either individual or at most dyadic in nature.

Neutrality

The term neutrality refers not to the therapist's state of mind but to the overall impact of their activity on the family. The desired outcome is that no family member should be left with the clear feeling that the therapist has taken anybody's 'side' (Selvini Palazzoli *et al.*, 1980a). The point is that therapists who manage to adhere to a systemic approach are likely to perform their task of stimulating the flow of new information in the system without getting drawn into the family's linear punctuations. This means avoiding any overt agreements or disagreements with the views expressed by family members, and on no account delivering moral judgements. The therapists' effectiveness depends on their obtaining and maintaining a different level *(metalevel)* from that of the families (Selvini Palazzoli *et al.*, 1980a).

In his 'revisiting' of the team's earlier formulations, Cecchin (1987) notes that neutrality is often given the negative connotation of aloofness or disinterest. He reframes it as 'curiosity': a healthy, lively, inquisitive and creative stance which accepts nothing and challenges everything, and which empowers the family to rewrite its old scripts and to find new narrative possibilities for its unfolding life-story. The therapist's curiosity invites the family to be more curious about itself. Curiosity helps therapists to be dissatisfied with cause-and-effect punctuations of reality and to look instead for Bateson's (1979) 'pattern which connects'. Instead of getting stuck on 'What caused what?', or on finding the 'true' explanation of something, therapists open themselves to a perspective which 'celebrates the complexity of interaction'.

This position is avowedly 'aesthetic' and part of a therapeutic approach which stresses the importance of 'holism and complexity', in contrast to a more 'pragmatic' approach which 'seeks to reduce phenomena into manageable and practical bits and pieces' (Keeney and Sprenkle, 1982). It compares with Bowlby's (1979) belief that the therapist's task is not to apportion blame but to understand the world as seen by clients, to help them comprehend the extent to which they misperceive what other people do, and to review their models of attachment figures and how they, therefore, respond in current interactions. It compares too with Walrond-Skinner's (1976) admonition that work will be ineffective if all workers do is to transfer one blame game (the family's: it is all that person's fault) for another (the worker's: it is all your responsibility), since this will merely exchange one impasse or battle for another.

This helps to make more sense of neutrality as a clear therapeutic stance. Therapists cannot 'direct' a system to change. At best they can 'perturb' (cf. Dell, 1982) the system in some way, push it off balance, and let it find its own new equilibrium. Many social workers quickly lose patience with this notion of neutrality. After all, how can you remain 'neutral' when confronted by cruelty, exploitation or abuse? A social worker with statutory responsibilities cannot simply 'perturb' an abusing family and then watch with 'curiosity' to see how the system reorganises itself. Perhaps no other point brings home more sharply the gulf that sometimes exists between front-line social workers in area teams or hospital departments and specialist family therapists in clinically autonomous settings. Cecchin offers some answers to these objections, though his tone suggests that he regards the 'social constructions imposed by legalistic, societal and cultural systems' as an unfortunate intrusion into the aesthetic realm of therapy. He concedes the difficulty of acting therapeutically when we have to enforce the law, but argues nonetheless that 'we must co-develop a sense of curiosity that is different from a sense of linear morality' (Cecchin, 1987). Far-fetched as this may sound to many social workers, it does in fact turn out to be good advice. In our experience it is always worth making the attempt to achieve this stance, however impossible it may seem in certain circumstances.

We can draw out some of the issues involved here if we set the discussion in the context of working with a family in which some form of child abuse has occurred. It is commonly acknowledged that the abuse of children affects social workers more profoundly than any other area of their work (see Chapter 7). In Chapter 1 we referred to Carr's (1989) enumeration of the various counter-transference reactions to which professionals may succumb in their work with abusing families. If we accept that none of us is exempt from such deep-rooted personal reactions, then at an unconscious level there is clearly no such thing as a neutral stance. The best we can do is to aim for some degree of professional detachment so that our judgements are not totally determined by our emotional reactions.

The therapeutic concept of neutrality is an attempt to take this process a stage further. It involves accepting and understanding our own personal reactions for what they are, as well as accepting that our colleagues' reactions may well be different. It does not mean being 'neutered' (Burnham and Harris, 1988). It also involves taking full account of moral and legal imperatives. It then proposes that we find an area of our thinking in which we can suspend personal and moral considerations, and put ourselves in the position of each of the other participants in the family drama. In Casement's (1985) terms this means cultivating an 'observing ego' which can view the proceedings from a different vantage point. Through a process of 'trial identification' it may be possible to understand empathically what family members are experiencing. We might also describe this activity in Winnicott's (1971) terms as a form of 'playing'. In systems terms it is a way of trying to introduce more information into the therapy system to keep it open and to prevent it closing down too soon on a single view of 'reality'. This is what Cecchin (1987) is getting at when he advocates a stance of curiosity. Nothing is fixed; no truth is absolute; there is always room for a different perspective. What does it feel like to be this child's mother/this man's wife? What is happening inside the parental relationship? What motivates the abuser? What communication systems have broken down? What information is conveyed by the actual abuse: the form it takes, the frequency of it , and so on? What external pressures are being exerted on the family? What has been, or will be, the effect of the due process of law? Who has been most/least affected by what has happened so far? If it is not just the individual worker but also a supporting team who are actively cultivating this sort of stance then there is a much greater chance that any glimmers of healthy change may be picked up and nurtured in the work.

The charge that therapist neutrality may actually condone oppression or injustice is taken up on a broader front by MacKinnon and Miller (1987), who argue that systems therapists, under the guise of neutrality, tend to overlook the socially-structured inequalities of class, gender, race and sexual orientation. They argue that the concept of neutrality, which is based on a respect for the system's autonomy and its capacity to find its own solutions, can all too easily lead to the abandoning of (or even positively connoting) traditional family 'solutions' which for centuries have reinforced male supremacy at the expense of women and children.

These are valid criticisms, all the weightier for coming from a position which is basically sympathetic to the Milan approach (cf. MacKinnon and James, 1987). We have to admit that systems thinking sometimes operates as though nothing ever 'causes' anything else, and no one in a 'circuit of interaction' can ever be directly responsible for anything that goes wrong. Our own position is that we find the basic notion of non-causal 'fit' (Dell, 1982) a valuable one in that it illuminates a great deal of human interaction and frees us from the common trap of punctuating in terms of linear causalty. If two behaviours are viewed from a linear position, one is seen as causing and one as following from the other. From a systems perspective, however, the behaviours fit together in an interactional system, feeding and sustaining each other. Neither behaviour can be said to cause the other. For example, with a critical parent and withdrawn child, it is impossible and unhelpful to say which behaviour causes which; the behaviours just fit together as a system. On the other hand we recognise that this notion cannot be universally applied without recognising different levels of social, cultural and psychological context. Otherwise we arrive at the absurdity of Maturana's statement (quoted in MacKinnon and James, 1987) that 'power is created by submission': that is, that people who exercise power over other people only do so because those other people are prepared to submit to being controlled. In some situations this is undoubtedly true, but as a universal statement it is clearly a nonsense. It resembles the belief expressed by one of D. H. Lawrence's characters in *Women in Love* that, 'it takes two people to make a murder: a murderer and a murderee', as if a murder can only take place if there is a willing victim. Again there are some sado-masochistic relationships where this kind of dynamic does operate (for example, the relationship between Gudrun and Gerald in the same novel), but as a universal statement about human nature it is totally false. We have to acknowledge that force can be exerted unilaterally in human relationships; that some people are violent, full stop; that victims do not usually 'ask for it'; and that inequalities of status and power are structured into our consciousness as well as our society (Frosh, 1987). If 'neutrality' fails to recognise and accommodate to uncomfortable facts of human nature, then it ceases to be humanly credible or therapeutically effective.

Teamwork and wider systems

One of the best things to emerge from family therapy in general, and from the Milan-Systemic approach in particular, has been a new model of teamwork centred upon the activity of 'live supervision'. The observing team is now an essential part of most family therapy practice, and the lessons learned from this approach are highly relevant to social work training and practice. Typically a family is interviewed by one therapist, or sometimes by a co-therapy pair, whilst one or more colleagues (but usually no more than three or four) observe the session 'live', either through a one-way screen or on television in a neighbouring room. In the absence of such audio-visual facilities some form of in-the-room supervision is normally employed: for example, with a team member sitting in on the therapy session but positioned outside the family-plus-therapist system and taking no direct part in the proceedings (D. Smith and Kingston, 1980; Kingston and D. Smith, 1983). The observing team tries to maintain a position which is 'meta' to that of the therapy system so that they can observe the feedback loops within the family as well as between family and therapist, thus preserving a systemic perspective. They communicate directly with the therapist in the course of the session, either by ear-bug, or by telephone, or simply by knocking on the door to call the therapist out for a consultation. Ideally the supervising team should be working hard the whole time, formulating alternative hypotheses and producing a steady supply of ideas and questions. They are particularly well placed to observe non-verbal communication which provides evidence of the nature of relationships (cf. Watzlawick *et al.*, 1967, ch. 2), and to monitor the impact of the therapist's activity on the family system and the impact of the family system on the therapist. If an intervention is to be given at the end of the session, then this is also very much a team effort and is carefully formulated during 'time out' with the therapist.

Many social workers interested in family therapy, but without such luxuries as video equipment or one-way screens, may feel that systemic work can only be practised with the requisite para-phernalia. Whilst it is undeniable that the pressures of area team social work make it much more difficult to carve out the time and space, let alone the supervision, for such work, family therapy can be practised very effectively with the minimum of equipment. The main requirements are time, space and at least one other committed colleague. Once a basic understanding of theory and technique has been acquired, the actual method of working can be imported into any number of different settings, including clients' homes.

A particular hallmark of the Milan approach is the importance it attaches to the wider systems of which the family is a part: not just the extended family and other social systems, but also the professional helping agencies which form part of the family's ecological network. This is a vital perspective, and it counteracts the tendency in some quarters for the family simply to replace the individual as the locus of 'pathology' (Carpenter and Treacher, 1984). The ways in which different professional systems can become entangled with each other in their dealings with particular clients will be analysed in later chapters. The dynamics of referral from one agency to another are a frequent source of difficulty in this respect. Particular attention must be given to the 'referring person' who is often 'part of the problem', having taken on the role of a 'homeostatic' family member (Selvini Palazzoli *et al.*, 1980b). Another way of looking at this is that an agency may 'triangle in' another agency in an attempt to take the heat out of their own problematic relationship with a particular family (Carl and Jurkovic, 1983). Having a team consultation with any agency wanting to refer a family is one approach (Corden and Preston-Shoot, 1987), together with being alert to whether one is serving some purpose for the agency as much as for the family.

3

Psychodynamics and systems: towards a working synthesis for the person-in-situation

Why psychodynamic theory?

The key factors for effective practice outlined in the introduction are not easy to implement or maintain. What might appear relatively straightforward has an uncanny tendency to become derailed. Workers, service-users and organisations can all, either independently or in their interaction, foul good intentions. Psychodynamic understanding within a broad 'systems' framework helps to clarify these forces. It illuminates individual and group behaviour and the interactions between people. Its contribution lies in the understanding it provides and the intervention techniques which follow. Since the first of these two contributions has been regarded as the more relevant for social workers, we start by examining the value of psychodynamic theory in understanding social work encounters.

Understanding the complexity of human interaction, behaviour and personality

Personal and emotional forces profoundly influence the whole process of working with clients. All human interactions trigger off an immense and complex pattern of personal responses and associations, few of which may enter conscious awareness.

Those not yet born are influenced by those already dead. This apparent conundrum highlights the continuity and complexity of human existence, the link between past, present and future, and acknowledges that understanding the here-and-now is not always sufficient to enable people to change. Both fearful fantasies and previous experiences affect behaviour and can neutralise encouragement, criticism or punishment which are aiming to produce desired change. Unconscious influences or psychological forces, such as defences and needs, may motivate individual and group behaviour. Behaviour is not always rational, which is why social services departments cannot be staffed by bureaucrats/administrators alone (Temperley and Himmel, 1986), and why an emphasis purely on goals and tasks is insufficient. The feelings and subjective experiences of users must be understood. For example, the failure of a contract, to which both parties have openly agreed, may be the result of problems that client or worker experience with close attachments; depression can occur at significant dates, so-called anniversary reactions; small events can trigger responses, often violent, totally disproportionate to the current situation; parents can behave intolerantly and punitively towards their children when they behave as the parents did as children, or they may collude as their children act out their own fantasies or unfulfilled desires; victims of disaster feel robbed of security and previous levels of functioning; clients may be unable to express feelings to workers because of a fear, based on prior experiences, that to do so would shatter either themselves or the relationship.

Particular clients may actually seek to elicit responses which patronise or put them down. Some people, who begin life with low self-esteem and for whom subsequent experience confirms their feelings of worthlessness, may well induce other people (including social workers) to continue to treat them as worthless. This theme is often apparent in transference and countertransference phenomena in client–worker interactions, illustrating that such transactions are never simple and that there are forces at work of which practitioners must be fully aware.

In counselling it is not unknown for sessions following disclosures and effective work to be difficult, even unproductive. This negative therapeutic reaction (Sandler *et al.*, 1973), where work does not proceed and where the worker may even be attacked for the work done, often stems from a client's guilt and anxiety about whether the worker will reject them or will fail to survive the work.

Psychodynamic concepts such as transference, countertransference, projection and defence mechanisms help practitioners understand, and use as information about the work, the feelings behind such defences, those evoked in them and those which clients may have about the worker and the situation. For example, children in residential and foster care frequently attempt to recreate previous relationships which they have internalised. This may lead them to reject the care workers or foster parents. If these processes are not understood (that is, how service-users can unconsciously seek to make substitute care figures repeat the behaviour of parents), adults may act out what to children are familiar family roles of rejecting and angry behaviour (Street, 1981).

Bowlby (1979) has pointed to the significance and influence of early life relationships and experiences on later functioning. Attachment theory provides a framework for understanding the attachment behaviour of children and adults, why change can be upsetting and stressful and why violence takes place more often between family members than between unrelated people (Heard, 1978). Family dysfunction may lie in repeated patterns or myths over generations; life-cycle transitions, such as children leaving home, coinciding also with additional crises and losses; or resentment evoked by interactional patterns based on competition or conflict which leave other urgently-felt needs unsatisfied (Dare, 1979).

These examples reveal how active the past may be in influencing behaviour and understanding, and how influential the meanings and perceptions individuals give to situations are on intentions and current actions. They help us to understand that reassurance frequently does not reassure because it cannot address underlying anxieties.

Understanding the draining emotions in the work

Social workers are on the receiving end of extremely powerful emotional forces. In child abuse cases these forces are obvious, and frequently take the form of aggression or open hostility. In other cases the process is much more subtle and difficult to tune into but just as telling in its effects, which means that retaining a professional role becomes both stressful and difficult. The anger, helplessness, distress and sadness encountered almost daily have to be managed if they are not to live on inside workers and contribute to emotional overload and eventual burn-out. Equally, a worker's response – for instance, to violent and aggressive parents – may in turn affect those parents and the work with them, either by creating an escalation of hostility towards the worker from the parents or by the worker withdrawing from them and their emotions to avoid feeling overwhelmed. Confronted by disturbed and disturbing behaviour, by practice which evokes strong feelings in the practitioners themselves, they must comprehend their reactions if they are not to act them out and if their practice is not to become defensive and closed. They may feel overwhelmed by hate or hostile feelings which, if not understood, may leave them with a sense of failure, guilt or inadequacy. An illustration of the power of the emotions surrounding child protection occurred in a training exercise. Four students were asked to simulate a discussion between two parents and two social workers regarding the outcome of a case conference. They were given details about the family which included marital violence and injuries to wife and children by the husband. These dynamics were mirrored amongst the four students, the marital violence being replayed in an argument between the male and female members of the group which frustrated the task and left the students puzzled, upset and confused until the exercise was talked through.

In another example a client came to the office and vented considerable anger on to a worker he knew well. He had just spent four hours at the local social security office and been refused a loan to meet what he regarded as essential needs. He accused the worker of being useless and uncaring. The worker was left feeling depressed, helpless and hopeless. These countertransference reactions are undoubtedly emotions which the client unloaded by projecting them on to the worker.

In the face of these powerful emotions and the anxiety about what they will encounter and how people will react to their work, procedures alone will not hold practitioners to their tasks. When deep emotions are involved, when ambivalence and conflict are central to situations, retaining an appropriate professional role is difficult (Stevenson, 1986). Both supervision and an understanding of psychodynamics are necessary if workers are not to avoid what is there to be done and seen, if they are to be in touch with their feelings and anxieties, and helped.

Understanding the personal 'hidden' feelings

Not only will psychodynamic concepts illuminate users' reactions and responses to workers, and vice versa, but they also alert practitioners to their own unresolved or hidden feelings. Such self-awareness is important if users are to be enabled to bear the pain of their new knowledge and to be less at odds with themselves (Mercer, 1981), and if work is not to become blocked and ineffective because of practitioners' unconscious reactions, defences or blind spots. This emphasis on self-knowledge and self-awareness does not mean a narcissistic preoccupation or personal therapy but is founded on the belief that personal development ultimately serves both workers and users. Why?

The most important resource available to workers is themselves. Empathy, reliability, warmth, knowledge, skills and genuineness are the cornerstones of practice but they require nurturing. They are not automatic or omnipresent. For workers to remain open, responsive and reflective, concerned for others, sensitive, able to listen and to hear what others are saying, considerable effort and resources are required. Everyone has a shadow side to their personality, hidden parts of the self, which work can trigger and reactivate. Whilst it is tempting to deny this, workers are well advised to recognise this shadow side and, through self-awareness work, to integrate it into their personality and practice.

Workers may find, in working with families, that aspects of the family mirror their own. In work with individuals or families, memories and hurts can be reactivated. In other words, dysfunctions and disturbances in clients and their families can evoke disturbances, past or contemporary, in workers who must work through these if they are to assist others with their difficulties. For example, when talking with an elderly woman about the loss of her husband, a worker found himself paralysed, unable to continue, by feelings evoked concerning the partially mourned loss of his parents several years previously. Increasingly, family therapists are recognising the importance of working on their own material, especially through the use of life-story books and geneograms, to elicit patterns, scripts, conflictual relationships, unresolved dis-appointments and anxieties. This is a recognition, long known to psychotherapists, that a worker's personality and self is a resource which can both facilitate or distort an encounter. The use of self is not unproblematic since the worker's personal past and cultural inheritance can re-emerge in the present, in attitudes, values, prejudices and blocks.

One particular way in which this occurs is the helping profession syndrome (Malan, 1979). Unmet needs and a longing for care are assuaged or defended against by compulsive care giving. This can create considerable stress for a worker when continuous demands hook into the practitioner's own needs (Gardener, 1988) or when devotion to duty fails to bring the hoped-for satisfaction. Unable to say no, for fear of being seen by others as rejecting and unhelpful, for fear of being rejected and of the defence collapsing and the pain of past unmet needs emerging, the worker tries even harder to be more helpful, eventually breaking down.

Another example is how childhood experiences can sensitise workers to avoid or pursue lines of enquiry: for instance, when investigating cases of child sexual abuse. Projecting feelings or scripts, whether or not of hurt, from past into contemporary situations can lead to omission (such as difficulty in considering a parent as a possible perpetrator of abuse), or to commission (such as acting as if one individual *must* be an/the abuser).

Understanding defensive practice and procedures

The impact of these powerful emotional forces may result in social workers, individually and collectively, adopting certain defences. Professional systems may construct a whole network of defensive measures to cope with the stresses and anxieties inherent in the professional task (Jaques, 1955; Menzies, 1970; Obholzer, 1987), quite apart from the more personal defences each practitioner carries around. To cope, individually or collectively, the system may avoid tasks or discourage dependency which is central at times to all relationships, rather than use it constructively. They may deny their own dependency needs by avoiding supervision. When faced with the necessity of taking and communicating difficult decisions, and the anxiety this evokes, especially when exercising statutory authority in child abuse cases, social workers may employ a directive textbook authoritarian approach which discourages the expression of emotions, dilemmas and doubts; or minimise or abandon their authority, assessment and decision-making role in order to be seen as a 'good' person rather than act appropriately and survive being experienced as a 'bad' person.

These personal and organisational defences cannot be scaled down unless social workers feel able to understand and cope with the emotional forces being directed at them.

Intervention

Psychodynamic concepts and theory also underpin a wide range of intervention techniques well known and used by social workers. Psychodynamic formulations have informed family therapy, counselling, marital work, play therapy and groupwork.

Many people, in the face of intolerable stress, turn for coping strategies to defence mechanisms. Designed to avoid pain and conflict or to control 'unacceptable' impulses, they often result in the conflict being expressed in another form, such as symptoms or maladaptive behaviour. If people are not to remain locked in these patterns, unable to change for fear of the consequences, the meaning they give to situations and what it feels like to be them has to be understood and reflected. By a process of ventilation and reflection, interpretation and co-exploration of meaning, worker and client tune into, talk about and unravel the unspeakable, what is hidden or not so obvious, what is not being said and what is avoided, the past and its effects on the present.

The relevance of attachment theory, transference and defence mechanisms to client–worker relationships is central here, first, to ensure the reliability of the social work setting (Chapter 6), and second, to explore how patterns from earlier relationships are brought to and acted out in new relationships. Unless these patterns are reflected back and interpreted as a replay, workers may unwittingly act out a role within them dismissing as resistance, 'badness' or low motivation a use of the worker-client relationship which, through frequent visits, missed appointments, hostility or passivity, reflects anxious or attachment-resistant feelings (Skidmore, 1988).

Their relevance in practice situations is well attested also, especially in grief and loss, bereavement and separation. Thus, when working with an older person on relinquishment and relocation into residential care, focus must be given to feelings about loss of life-style; admission being a prelude to death; anger or, on the part of carers, guilt; and the 'now' feelings after admission, the feelings of helplessness and strangeness. Similar psychological preparation and counselling should occur around reception of children into care: anticipatory visiting; introductions to caregivers; availability of familiar possessions; working through feelings, especially fantasies, experiences of attachments, and anxieties; accepting and interpreting negative behaviour and attitudes, and acknowledging the experience of separation. This combination of counselling, crisis and attachment theories is designed to address the emotional effects of separation. Separation is a crisis experience, evoking grief, anger and anxiety. Anxiety may be reduced by avoidance of denial and reality-based discussion. Grief may be reduced by temporary attachments to dependable, concerned caregivers who must understand the importance of reliability and consistency. Such an awareness from social workers and caregivers helps people to use the new experience with a minimum of distress and anxiety rather than defend against it fiercely, feeling overwhelmed by anxiety and using defences of denial, acting out or withdrawal.

Thus, psychodynamic concepts can make human development and behaviour more intelligible, can open up self-awareness and understanding of the work and can facilitate an empathic social work response (Bandler, 1987). The focus is not just individuals or the past but also relationships, internal and external, and the present. Then and now, inner and outer are connected. Such an understanding can unlock social work transactions, and render work more effective.

Why systems theory?

Social work has been criticised for a myopic, narrow focus, locating problems and pathology within individuals or families and ignoring structural inequalities. Social work has also been criticised for reinforcing such inequalities, rather than counteracting them, by interventions at an individual or family rather than structural level which ameliorate the worst effects of the inequalities without fundamentally challenging them.

The problems brought to social workers are complex and multi-dimensional. Political, historical, cultural and economic systems, besides the psychological, are interlinked and daily impinge on individuals and families, creating, maintaining and exacerbating many of their difficulties which then find expression in psychological reactions. They comprise an influential part of the person-in-situation focus for social workers. Social class and unemployment, for example, affect an individual's health opportunities. Pathology, therefore, does not reside necessarily in the individual but rather in the interaction between systems, at the interface where individual/family and wider systems meet. Systems theory affords this wider view and illuminates how parts interact and influence each other. Assessment, planning, intervention and evaluation must take account of this wider view. 'Why systems theory?' can be simply answered: to highlight the interconnectedness, relationship and dynamic interaction of phenomena, such that intervention at one level affects the entire system. Several examples will illustrate the interrelationship between environmental influences and individual or family behaviour, the connection between inner and outer worlds.

Depression is a psychological state, too often treated by medication, privatising the illness. However, it may be occasioned by public ills: extreme poverty, loss of hope and opportunity, inadequate housing or roles experienced as life-denying rather than life-enhancing. The external world has an effect on and depresses the inner world. Individual unhappiness, even suicide, may follow from social and material deprivation. Consider the case of a client whose life has become painfully limited both personally and materially. He has had a number of eating problems which, psychiatrically, could be viewed in the light of depressive symptomatology. He is angry, lonely and in debt. Some mornings, before daybreak, he steals bottles of milk from nearby hotels. He says he simply cannot afford to buy them. He is becoming increasingly desperate and seems to expect to get caught. His dealings with social security offices and the housing department have become strained, and most people find his aggressive manner difficult to deal with. Now, is his current plight part of his 'neurotic personality', his disturbed personal relationships and his marital breakdown? Is it all part of some essentially self-destructive process? Or is he being forced off the rails by a social system which robs him of status and self-worth by offering him no suitable employment and maintaining him on a weekly pittance which is simply insufficient to meet his needs? We have deliberately polarised these questions, but social workers are constantly caught up in this interplay between the 'inner' and the 'outer' worlds of human experience, between personal or emotional factors and social or material ones (cf. Pearson *et al.*, 1988). In many cases it is difficult to separate out one set of likely 'causes' from another, and social workers may need to direct their interventions at different levels of the 'closed system', mindful of the ways in which internal and external factors interpenetrate and interact.

Inadequate material resources, isolation, a childhood experience of abuse and the restrictions imposed by gender roles may all figure in child care work. The option facing social workers is whether to aim for radical or conservative change, whether to target intervention towards nursery provision levels, housing and economic policies, and how men and women are socialised into types of relationships, or whether to modify and 'tidy away' the worst excesses of society: to confront or not to challenge systems.

The failure of a contract between a social worker and user is not necessarily due to either party to the working agreement. The contract may be frustrated because other systems defeat the objectives (Corden and Preston-Shoot, 1987). The attitude of other agencies; how problems are viewed; 'solutions' thought appropriate; whether or not the professional system meets and has an agreed plan concerning what change is sought and why; the practitioner's experience, social class, relationship skills and gender; extraneous events; all these factors overlap and may affect outcomes.

Older people may be inappropriately admitted to residential accommodation, not because of increasing physical or mental frailty but because the social services department is unable to provide the range or flexibility of services to enable them to live in the community and/or those caring find the experience arouses new (or evokes older) tensions in relationships. These tensions become focused on the old person who provides an all too suitable location for tension which belongs to relationships between other family members but which they avoid by projection. These examples illustrate a number of key principles.

Behaviour, seen in context, has meaning and functions

Processes in many systems will affect individual and family behaviour. Intervening in these systems may change interaction patterns between these systems and families. Thus family assessments should not ignore social systems, for phenomena may remain inexplicable if the range of observation is not wide enough to include the context in which the phenomena occur. To omit the context may result in qualities being attributed to phenomena which they do not possess (Watzlawick *et al.*, 1967).

Public and private overlap and interact

Environmental issues are not secondary. Individuals and families are not necessarily the only target for change. Significant other systems (agencies, neighbourhoods, colleagues, peer groups) may create, maintain or exacerbate difficulties, or influence the outcome of work between social workers and users. A key question becomes what systems should be in focus: political, individual, family, professional network, family–professional? The interaction between individuals/families and these other systems may be the target for intervention, with social workers working at this interface in the role of mediators or advocates.

Social workers are often neither the best nor the only change agents

Other professionals have a responsibility to work for change rather than expect social workers to carry it all. Social workers are often placed under considerable pressure to do something which lets other people off the hook. They take on considerable levels of responsibility rather than locate responsibility where it belongs, in the professional system and/or family–professional network. Social workers have a role in bringing systems together.

Social workers' own agencies may be the target for change

For instance, in the example of the old person above, social workers could press for services which are resource-led not needs-led, user- not provider-sensitive (i.e. services which are co-ordinated, linked and flexible, and felt by users to be appropriate).

Professional networks

These, designed as solutions, can become part of the problem, enmeshed in 'helping' interventions which perpetuate more of the same. Thus, just as families may block individual development and change, so professional systems may block family and professional system change because of conflicting views on the change required and/or the absence of agreed rules for the intervention. Just as family work should focus on the relationships between family members, so the professional system should adopt a similar critical focus and consider the interplay and transactions between parts of the system. A systems perspective affords a more holistic view: an enlargement from individual attributes to those of the situation, from pathology to interaction, from attributions of madness, badness or resistance to relationships between members of a system.

Work with any system, therefore, should consider not only what is communicated between its members but how, and the definitions of relationships (including status and responsibilities) implied within this. It should consider what is not communicated or avoided, and the nature of the communication: are these blocks, for instance, secrets or pressures from other (sub-)systems? Is communication displaced, as family members may blame individuals, or symptoms be used to express feelings, or a third person/agency be recruited to enable two other people and/or agencies to avoid direct communication? Is communication damaged, as in double-binds (Walrond-Skinner, 1976)? Are boundaries permeable and systems open to influence and exchange, or are they characterised by breakdown or rigidity? Such observations will suggest appropriate points to intervene and, as a moving sculpt graphically illustrates, intervening in one part of a system affects relationships in the entire system. The system cannot stay the same.

Social workers must consider, therefore, not simply their exposure to particular users or situations and the effect users and workers may have on each other, but beyond that the whole series of concentric or overlapping systems in which even the smallest social work transactions take place: the dynamics of the team or agency; the influence or pressure exerted by management or other parts of the organisation; the effect of different systems coming into contact and dealing with each other.

Individuals, families and professional systems

These can become locked into a linear perspective; that is, drawn into one punctuation or perception of reality which forms the basis of moral judgements. Typically this is seen in polarised positions where responsibility for problems is located elsewhere. Thus, East blames West and vice versa. Parents and teachers not untypically blame each other for a child's problems, each seeing the other as deficient and responsible (Dowling and Osborne, 1985). A circular systems perspective, however, addresses the patterns, relationships and interactions in which they are 'caught'. Social work itself is a circular process, of assessment leading to intervention and review which informs assessment. Social work's focus is circular and systemic (the relationships between individuals and other systems). Its objectives lie in working for individual happiness and social justice (Vickery, 1974). The two cannot be divorced.

Why synthesis?

Psychological and social problems are interlinked. Each may influence and affect the other. Bad housing may result in depression and will affect an individual's self-perception. Similarly, depression may result in self-neglect and neglect of surroundings. Change is required at both social and individual psychological levels. Change in one without the other will prove short-lived. The search for synthesis and balance, rather than the fruitless debate about the superiority of psychological or social explanations and interventions, is for several reasons an urgent task.

First, especially in contentious or highly-charged areas of work such as child abuse, pressures will be exerted on social workers from many directions, including from within. It is vitally important, therefore, that practitioners make sense of the complex interaction of personal, social and organisational pressures, and look with greater understanding at themselves, service-users, organisational systems and the wider contexts in which social workers and users meet.

Second, social workers encounter a wide range of needs and problems for which no one method or theory of intervention is sufficient explanation or guide through the complexity. Reliance on one method produces a narrow vision, fragments or distorts the reality of users' lives, and courts failure since it oversimplifies reality and misses vital dimensions of problems (Kaffman, 1987). Rather, practitioners need to consider problems from a variety of perspectives and draw from a range of approaches based on a sound understanding of separate theories. A combination of approaches can be extremely effective (Seagraves and Smith, 1976; Kaye, 1986), complementing each other, consolidating and extending the changes achieved by each. For instance, different family therapy models have different strengths: the psychodynamic in working through subjective experiences; the structural in achieving surface change; the strategic in overcoming resistance (Furniss *et al.*, 1983). Flexibility is the key. An analytic style, for example, will be experienced by some as uncaring, disinterested and destructive; by others as respecting independence and self-determination (Malan, 1979; Skynner, 1979).

Third, social work is ill-served by either/or splits. The public–private or individual–social are not polarities but circular interactions. Each interacts with and feeds into the other, for example, women subjected to domestic violence face psychological and environmental obstacles and challenges: living with stress and fear; experiencing helplessness; the difficulties of leaving relationships, especially when a partner is violent; power retained by men through women's economic dependence; the dearth of housing options and inadequate legal protection (Osborne, 1988). Again, in the family life-cycle psychological tasks for each member and environmental influences crucially interact. The psychological tasks for each member interrelate, as when parents and young adults adjust to the latter leaving home. In the developmental stages of the family life-cycle, inner and interpersonal processes are interlinked. Changes in one area affect all other areas. How the world is perceived emotionally, subjectively, contributes to interaction patterns which in turn contribute to how the world is experienced. Both must be considered. The personal and private aspects of experience are linked with the systemic structures of which individuals are a part (Kantor and Neal, 1985). There is, therefore, a need to develop both an individual and social change perspective if social workers are not to re-enact, maintain or perpetuate the problems they encounter.

Fourth, the user–worker relationship must be understood from both a psychodynamic and social perspective if its dynamics are to be appreciated and effective ways forward found. Culture, personalities, organisational systems, social class, theoretical preoccupations, stereotypes and social constructions all impinge on and may adversely affect the relationship. This demonstrates once more that individuals exist in contexts, such as socially constructed gender roles and economic constraints. The contexts affect behaviour and vice versa. Individuals, family and context are inseparable. It is essential, therefore, to consider the context in which a problem occurs, a synthesis missing from much contemporary social work which consists of controlling individuals and families, slotting them into inadequate and inappropriate services tailored not to needs but to economics, and frequently neglecting that society may maintain pathology in families and families in individuals.

Why a synthesis of psychodynamic and systems theories?

Psychodynamic theory has found some apparently strange partners: behavioural therapy, Marxism and ethology. British family therapy has taken shape within an established tradition of individual and group psychoanalysis. Psychoanalytic family therapy, based largely on object-relations theory and utilising particularly the concepts of projection, introjection, identification and containment, continues to prove viable both theoretically and practically (Box *et al.*, 1981; Dare, 1988). Many practitioners find no difficulty with an approach to family work which combines a 'historical' frame of reference with a 'current interactional' one (Dare, 1979). The potential value of such connections lies in their usefulness in understanding and working with intra- and interpersonal conflict, with human relationships. The particular synthesis which is our objective, psychodynamic and systems theories, has much to contribute to the central problems encountered in social work (Yelloly, 1980) since it provides a conceptual framework for understanding and working with the person-in-situation. It links inner worlds with real life experience in its social, political, economic and organisational context, and demonstrates the influence each has on the other. For example, in discussing the ways intake social workers may deal more effectively with stress, Addison (1982) argues that both self-analysis and political action are essential: a focus on workers' own emotions, reactions and behaviour, and on the context, structures and politics of their employing organisations which fail to resource adequately both workers and the work. Dowrick (1983) similarly points to the contribution each theory brings: psychodynamics for understanding the transmission of ideology and explaining individual motivation and behaviour; systems theory for understanding the context, the individual and family's place in society and the effect of this on them. Psychodynamic theory directs practitioners to the importance of subjective and emotional experiences, and systems concepts to interpersonal relationships and the overall context.

However, can such connections be sustained? It is widely thought either that these two explanatory approaches are antithetical and contradictory, or that connections will merely produce a fudge rather than a model which can make sense of the complex interaction of personal and organisational pressures that is social work. The view that the difference is too great to bridge is usually founded on an outmoded understanding of psychodynamic theory. This still equates psychodynamics with instinct theory, linear causality and the discovery and working through of early repressed trauma, and ignores the development of object-relations theory which bridges intrapsychic and interpersonal phenomena by stressing individual–environment interaction and exchange, meaning and subjective experience (Cooklin, 1979; Zawada, 1981). So where do these approaches converge?

1. Both work at the interface where the internal world is externalised and the external world is internalised (Dare, 1981). The perspective is less on people possessing symptoms than on problems existing between people (Dare, 1988), or between self, internal objects and external reality.
2. Both view symptomatic behaviour as having both an expressive and a defensive meaning, purpose and function: it expresses conflicts whilst simultaneously defending against relationships or feelings. The defences carry a cost; there are consequences for all involved, but especially for the symptom-holder.
3. Both approaches attach importance to the concept of developmental stages, and both search carefully for the particular point in an individual's or a family's life-cycle where change has become problematic or where the prospect of change is feared or resisted.
4. Both approaches employ hypotheses: formulations aimed at understanding processes and experiences within and between people which are circular. That is to say, individuals are inseparable from the environment which facilitates or frustrates them, and from the wider systems which impinge on their lives.
5. Both approaches emphasise the importance of boundaries, which should be age-appropriate and neither too loose nor excessively rigid.
6. Both regard symptoms as the best adaptation to events possible at the time and argue that, under stress, redundant solutions or

repetition compulsion will be evident in behaviour. Both seek to identify and change these acted-out patterns or defences, the origin of which may be repressed and not remembered, by bringing out the underlying feelings at the point where change became or is becoming problematic.

7. Both approaches seek to free service-users from their 'stuck' positions by concentrating on here-and-now transactions, illuminated by history where this helps to understand the present. In psychodynamic work there is a special emphasis on the transference, which focuses attention on the ways in which significant past relationships are reproduced in the present relationship between client and worker. Myths and rules in systems produce similar repetitive patterns of interaction.

8. Both approaches aim not only at symptom reduction but also at systemic reorganisation, intrapsychic or interpersonal. There is an attempt to identify what is being avoided, and solutions are sought which feel congenial to service-users and which have a meaning for them. Since change is commonly resisted at some level, some increase in anxiety may be necessary for movement. One approach may work more with the unconscious and one with external systems but each sees both as a reservoir of past experiences which exert considerable power. A rearrangement of the meaning given to these experiences and of the relationships they have inspired becomes the focus of the work. Fact is differentiated from fantasy and 'the problem' gives way to a focus on family interaction and/or individual/ family relationships to the worker and the work (Holmes, 1985a, 1985b). Interventions or interpretations are used, not as true statements but as metaphors, to provide alternative frames of reference, encourage behavioural change, and extend or change the meaning given to experience or actions (Lomas, 1987).

9. Both approaches value a meta or internal supervisory viewpoint (Selvini Palazzoli *et al.*, 1978; Casement, 1985): a standing-back to monitor the process and review the work, to avoid enmeshment and collusive participation in complex dynamics and emotional pressures such as projections (which tap into the workers' own material) or appeals to their expertise (which activate their desire to be helpful). Holding a meta or supervisory viewpoint helps workers to avoid becoming part

of the problem, to examine how they may be seen by the system
with which they are working, to comprehend complex dynamics
and to consider possible interventions.

Clearly, both approaches are struggling to address the same basic
problems, even if they are approaching them from different angles
and drawing different boundaries around their field of observation
and intervention (Obholzer, 1987). Psychodynamic theory emphasises change intrapersonally and in relationships between inner
objects, centres on intrapsychic defences and may, at times, have
underestimated the influence of systems on individual development
and self-realisation (Willi, 1987). Systems theory works for
interpersonal change and focuses on interpersonal confusion and
miscommunication as the origin of problems (Arden, 1984; Lomas,
1987). The two approaches can be taken as complementary rather
than divergent since they work for change at different systemic
levels. They may view human phenomena through different lenses
and attune practitioners to different features of the presenting
situation. They may use different conceptual frames but both are
explanatory metaphors within which symptomatic behaviour can be
'reframed' (Holmes, 1983, 1985a, 1985b). Together they provide a
wider reference and more flexible method of working. However,
what is the potential value of such a working synthesis for social
work practice?

   First, it is still possible to hear social work discussed in terms of
Newtonian 'billiard ball' mechanics: a worker intervenes in a
situation in such a way that a clear outcome is produced, like one
billiard ball striking another. Davies's 'maintenance mechanic'
(1985) is representative of this approach. However, current
psychoanalytic wisdom and contemporary systems theory both
suggest that no such simple view of human interaction can really
stand up to scrutiny. There is no such thing as a worker simply
'acting upon' another person or intervening in a situation without
becoming part of a complex interactional dynamic. As soon as
worker and client meet they become a system which is subject to the
same internal forces and shares the same characteristics as any other
system. There are many possible ways of conceptualising this
process. From our own chosen models we can think in terms of the
simultaneous and circular interactions between client and worker
(cf. Keeney, 1979) which constitute the systemic 'force field', or in

terms of the recursive projection–introjection processes upon which transference and countertransference phenomena are based. Either way the picture is the same: social workers are constantly on the receiving end of powerful emotional forces, and their own equilibrium may be quite seriously disturbed. What is needed is a working structure which helps practitioners not only to survive their immersion in the client–worker system but also to make sense of it and to function creatively within it. In more dynamic terms they require a structure and support in their work which enables them to withstand and 'contain' the intense pressure of their clients' projections and needs. If they can 'tolerate' the countertransference pressure of having intense reactions stirred up in them, then there is a greater chance that their work will help people change (cf. Carpy, 1989).

Second, both sets of theories highlight that there is always a greater complexity to human phenomena than we are aware of at any given moment. When workers confront an individual client, couple or a family, they are presented with a particular segment of their lives. On the basis of their own life experience, personalities, theories and current feelings, workers form an impression, make a 'punctuation' and establish for themselves a particular view of what is going on. Psychodynamics tells us that all sorts of unconscious factors will be at work in this process: that defensive organisations will be activated, that projective and introjective processes will be operating, and that transference and countertransference phenomena will strongly affect everyone's perception of 'reality'. The more emotionally charged a situation is, the stronger such forces will be. Systemic theories tell us that the simple causal hypotheses that we all automatically resort to, such as 'this child is getting into trouble because her parents are neglecting her', should always be viewed as small 'arcs' in a larger 'circuit' (Tomm, 1984a). There are always at least two sides to every situation. By shifting our focus; by trying out in our minds different explanations; by empathically putting ourselves in the place of each family member in turn; in such ways, as well as by monitoring our own input and trying to gauge its impact, we can expand the scope of our work and keep our 'curiosity' alive. This is not to deny that at times workers are obliged to intervene decisively on the basis of limited information. Even if acting in a statutory role it may still be possible to cultivate a sort of 'observing ego', or to construct with the aid of a colleague a 'supervisory viewpoint' (Casement, 1985), a meta position which helps workers not to get so totally caught up in the 'action' that they lose their professional vantage point.

Third, the importance of good training and supervision or consultation should be obvious. Both approaches depend for their efficacy on good training and continuing supervision. Despite their different emphases, both approaches use supervision experientially to improve learning and stimulate personal growth.

Finally, both psychodynamic and systemic approaches attach prime importance to 'the pattern which connects'. In his own discussion of transference Bateson (1979) talks about 'the patterns and sequences of childhood experience' which are built into every individual and which recur in our daily experience. The whole of therapy is concerned with helping people to free themselves from the repeating patterns of past experience which impose themselves upon the present with such an iron grip. Object-relations theory examines these patterns in terms of our inner models or maps of ourselves in relation to significant others. Psychoanalytic therapy functions on the premise that these inner configurations emerge dynamically in the transference. Family therapy targets the 'stuck' patterns of belief or behaviour which can cause individual or interpersonal distress. Social patterns also cause hardship and distress, and social workers need to be attuned to 'pattern' at many different levels of seriousness and complexity. The repeating patterns of symptomatic or antisocial behaviour in particular individuals or families; the patterns of social or emotional deprivation which are passed from one generation to the next; the familiar pattern of a particular type of case, or the familiar sequence of a process like grieving; the reproduced pattern of disturbance afflicting a professional team, which seems to 'mirror' the clients' own disturbance; all these patterns, and many more, are part and parcel of social work practice. In our view a combination of psychodynamic and systemic approaches provides a broader and more flexible model with which to examine the whole range of social work practice. To emphasise one at the expense of the other is to miss a vital dimension. The two perspectives need each other. Social work needs both. The combination helps social workers to span more effectively the inner and outer worlds of personal and social experience, and to accommodate the intrapsychic, interpersonal and socio-political within a broad 'systems' perspective. It offers a unique perspective on the patterning of human feeling and behaviour, although ultimately, of course, 'the pattern which connects' is the pattern of our common humanity, and at best our theories are only as good as the people who use them.

4

Criticisms, myths and parodies

Even if psychodynamic and systemic approaches can be linked coherently and applied fruitfully in combination, what is the relevance of this for social work? Many social workers question the usefulness of anything to do with psychotherapy in their work and, whilst there is a growing acceptance of family therapy techniques among social workers in a variety of agencies (Treacher and Carpenter, 1984; Burnham, 1986), many are deterred by the jargon in which it couches itself and the clinical settings in which it habitually operates. Both approaches, therefore, have appeared to be precious activities with little relevance to social work.

This chapter will examine the caricatures, myths and stereotypes commonly applied, often on the basis of extremely limited understanding of what the approaches entail, to psychodynamics and systemic family therapy. The problem with myths and stereotypes is the ease with which they become legend. Partial truth is dressed up as factual analysis and presented as absolute, exclusive belief. As such, they earn an enduring quality, whilst their partiality distorts, indeed contaminates, opinion and the possible contributions of their subject.

Whilst sympathising with the common wariness among hard-headed practitioners of anything that seems precious or self-regarding, or which seems intent on looking for underlying psychic causes instead of responding to people's 'real' needs, we feel that these are parodies and misapprehensions of the psychodynamic and systemic approaches which must be countered. This forms part of our argument that the case for training social workers in the knowledge and uses of both is overwhelming (Temperley and Himmel, 1986). This chapter is an attempt to separate fact from fancy. We are not suggesting that criticism is inappropriate, or indeed that all criticism has been invalid. In fact, one problem for social work has been its uncritical borrowing and acceptance of ideas. However, some criticisms have reflected hostility and underlying rejection rather than a balanced appraisal.

The 'bad press'

A typical assault is that mounted by Brandon (1987). He depicts psychodynamic social casework as dead and buried. His is a mocking attack, humorous but ill-suited to scholarly debate. Gill (1988) is similarly critical, being totally disillusioned with Freud and dismissive of family therapists for allegedly omitting empirical evidence for their observations, descriptions and abstract notions. Gill commits familiar errors. Psychodynamic work is assumed to be solely about the unconscious which is dismissed as irrelevant, rather than with what is observable. However, as Malan (1979) demonstrates, psychodynamic theory deals in observations, feelings and behaviours which people would often rather not believe about themselves. Gill also ignores the developments of psychodynamic theories alongside Freudian theory and the revisions of Freud's beliefs. Neither does family therapy omit a search for evidence for the usefulness of hypotheses prior to interventions. Gill's criticisms reveal not faults in models but an absence of in-depth theoretical and practice understanding. As so often, what is criticised is only a pale shadow of the theory and of what each has to offer in practice (Pearson *et al.*, 1988).

Wootton (1959) criticises what she regards as the pretentious façade of psychodynamic casework which emphasises some aspects of a user's situation at the expense of ignoring others. She urges a reappraisal of the claims made for this method of work and of how social workers conceptualise their work. Sheldon (1978a) concludes that the psychodynamic approach is irrelevant both as a model of social influence and as a basis for counselling. Brewer and Lait (1980) lampoon social workers for clinging ineffectually to half-digested psychodynamic notions whilst ignoring the allegedly more effective and empirically more testable behavioural techniques. Butler and Pritchard (1984) give short shrift to psychodynamic and systemic approaches to mental health social work. Finally, Baird (1989) accuses proponents of Freudian theory of pursuing bogus wisdom and having faith in something that is silly, sickly and consisting only of air. Such swingeing attacks appear fundamentally ill-informed and hysterical.

Fortunately, several 'correctives' stand out. Yelloly (1980) argues that, whilst the concepts and language of psychodynamics make the task of understanding difficult and have more relevance as a framework and knowledge-base than as a practice technique, the negative assessment awarded to it has been exaggerated. Its important contribution lies in its perspective on people and their problems. Criticisms of both approaches have obscured their value and, in the case of psychodynamics, thereby misrepresented casework. Yelloly illustrates that casework never was a version of psychotherapy. Its goal was less insight into unconscious feelings than an understanding of frustration, guilt, anxiety and other tensions, together with exploration, clarification and the identification of current behaviour patterns at a conscious level. This was coupled with an emphasis on effecting change in a social situation, partly through the medium of the worker–user relationship which was central to any techniques used and which could itself contribute to change and growth.

Ellis (1978) argues that the importance of sociology should not invalidate psychological explanations but only any narrowness of explanations used. Ellis cautions against exclusive reliance on Sigmund Freud, pointing to the shortcomings of his work, but equally warns against wholesale rejection of Freud and the psychodynamic approach since both have much to offer social work practice, to understanding the complexity and personality of human beings and to self-understanding.

What the criticisms overlook and the correctives provide is the importance of balance and the potential value of psychological work with individuals and families alongside efforts to increase material resources or effect social change. However, what is the reason for the bad press and the hostility? Psychodynamic theory, in particular, illuminates profound and painful truths, the darker side of feelings, personality and behaviour, which people prefer to conceal in the shadows. Psychodynamics is concerned with the primitive which lurks behind, but often emerges through, the civilised to challenge what people like to believe about themselves. Anger, envy, aggression and guilt are its focus. This amounts to a narcissistic wound (Malan, 1979; Yelloly, 1980). In addition, the complexity of the observations and the language in which they are couched makes their relevance and applicability initially hard to grasp. Freud did not always offer evidence for his ideas and, in common with many theoreticians trying to establish propositions, campaigning zeal may have resulted in an overstated case (Kaffman, 1987). More recently, Freud's change of mind about the veracity of his patients' disclosures of sexual abuse, his abandonment of the so-called 'seduction theory' (Storr, 1989), has not helped his popularity. Perhaps, also, both approaches have been applied from a base of inadequate understanding and training.

The myth of psychoanalytic domination

The psychodynamic influence on social work is sometimes thought to have amounted to a take-over. That there was an influence is unquestioned but even that strident critic, Wootton (1959), concedes that social work's surrender to Freud was neither unquestioning nor complete. Whilst there were social workers who practised a form of intensive psychotherapy rather than psychodynamic casework, and whilst there has always existed a temptation to 'wild analysis', to make psychodynamic interpretations inappropriately, the extent of its influence has been exaggerated (Specht and Vickery, 1977; Yelloly, 1980). The more sociological approach, which predated it in social work, was never lost (Irvine, 1979).

This is not to deny that some practitioners may have neglected the broad perspectives of social work and discovered in psychodynamic theory a resolution of their inability to change social and economic structures by turning their impotence into a focus on individuals, thereby privatising public ills (Bailey and Brake, 1975); it is, however, to question the extent of any take-over and to reassess and restate the value of its knowledge: the focus of psychodynamic work on life experiences, anxieties, conflicts and interpersonal relationships, where appropriate, alongside emphasis on practical and situational factors.

The myth of ineffectiveness

Psychodynamic psychotherapy is ineffective. That view, popularised by Eysenck (1952, 1965), has not gone unchallenged (Malan, 1963,

1973; D. Brown and Pedder, 1979; Bloch, 1982) on the grounds of the complexity of psychodynamic change and the difficulty of defining outcome criteria which do justice to the subtlety of the human personality; his interpretation of the data; an inherent bias towards behaviour modification; and the diversity rather than unitary nature of psychodynamic psychotherapy. These authors conclude that psychotherapy can have positive effects, especially when there is a clear rationale, an explicit and agreed objective, and focused transference-related interpretations. There is, therefore, no reason to discard psychodynamic formulations or methods.

Social work has not escaped criticism that it is ineffective. However, once again, the criticisms may have been exaggerated and misdirected against the theoretical model. Sheldon (1986) is undoubtedly right in claiming that social workers often achieve unspectacular results with their amalgam of psychology, counselling techniques and sociological thinking but is this due to the theories themselves? Unrealistic or vague objectives, poor evaluative designs, a failure to acknowledge discrepancies between worker and user objectives or methods of achieving agreed targets, and an inadequate description of, or holding on to the nature of, the intervention can all disrupt both the work on counteracting personal and social inequalities and the process of evaluation itself (Corden and Preston-Shoot, 1987; Preston-Shoot and Williams, 1987). Add to this the arguments that comparisons with behavioural techniques are unsympathetic to psychodynamic approaches and that the organisation of welfare services renders major social change through social work impossible, and the disappointing results may be seen differently. Moreover, there is evidence which suggests that psychodynamic work can make a difference (Moyes, 1988), especially in marital and parental functioning (Mattinson and Sinclair, 1979) and where target problems cannot be clearly identified (Pearson *et al.*, 1988).

There remains a clear need to know more precisely what works in what situations for whom, and to retain a clear focus around small objectives rather than entertain unrealistic aspirations of major individual or social change. We outlined various known key ingredients for success in our introduction. In our view, social workers need to evaluate their work more consistently. Models are available for this (Preston-Shoot and Williams, 1987). They need to specify what they might mean by working with the person-in-situation, to define their objectives concretely and to retain a clear articulation of and grasp on the chosen methods of intervention. They must encourage society to re-examine its expectations of social work, rather than collude with unrealistic, often contradictory, demands.

The unscientific myth

A frequent complaint is that psychodynamic theory is not provable and ascribes unconscious motives or resistance to its critics who are thereby dismissed. The claim of psychodynamics to be a theory is regarded as weak because it is not refutable however much it may explain; it has built-in defences against disbelief; and it is not testable (Sheldon, 1978b). Psychodynamic interpretations are seen at best as inferences.

This view misunderstands and misrepresents psychodynamic theory and therapeutic language. The view risks the error that what cannot be measured or systematically proved is invalid, untrue or does not exist. First, there is far more evidence than generally assumed. Although criticised for being inferential, psychodynamics deals in observable behaviour (Malan, 1979; Yelloly, 1980). Transference occurs in everyday life and the evidence is overwhelming both for the existence of unconscious mental processes and the phenomenon of the return of the repressed, the disguised expression of feelings which an individual has been avoiding (Malan, 1979). Many psychodynamic concepts can be demonstrated as valid, and analysts are not reluctant to discard those found to be unsatisfactory on the basis of research and clinical experience. Malan (1979) and Bowlby (1979) use psychodynamic concepts as hypotheses about the dynamics and development of personality, employing clinical experience and research methodology to test their usefulness, and to confirm or refute their value as formulations.

Second, psychodynamic theory is not concerned with explanation, prediction and control so much as with interpretation and assisting self-reflection (Pearson *et al.*, 1988). It is a semantic rather than a scientific activity (Rycroft, 1968). Rather than the truth or falsity of interpretations, right or wrong answers, comments are more or less useful ways of understanding and describing behaviour. Psychodynamics deals in meanings which cannot be verified or disproved. It is a conversation centred on a curiosity which begins with questions, then produces hypotheses and interpretations which may create more questions. The acid test, therefore, is its ability to help people discover or rediscover the meaning of their own lives which enables them to explore and act purposefully. This paradigm, of allocating meanings to behaviour and interpreting meaning (the humanistic mode of enquiry), is of a different order from a paradigm which emphasises measurement, objectivity and prediction of outcome and seeks to explain fact (the scientific mode: Home, 1966; Leonard, 1975).

Language and theories are metaphors; they are attempts to clarify phenomena which cannot be described precisely, as if they were physical objects. Basic concepts such as transference and projective identification should be treated not as the 'scientific' statements they are sometimes mistaken for but as metaphorical attempts to interpret the meaning of particular clinical phenomena. There is no such thing as 'the unconscious', only unconscious mental processes in a person (Arden, 1986).

Problems arise when practitioners, perhaps because uncertainty is too difficult to live with, lose sight of the metaphorical nature of theories and of the language which underpins them. Concepts then appear mechanistic, more like a depersonalised description of engineering work than an exploration of the human mind, and are treated as if they are 'things' existing in their own right. This process, called 'reification' (Latin: 'to make into a thing'), sees experiences and ideas regarded more and more as fixed entities or objects. Concepts become preserved and sacrosanct as if necessary for theoretical identity, security and orthodoxy (Watzlawick *et al.*, 1967; Selvini Palazzoli *et al.*, 1978). To counteract this, some therapists have tried to confine their descriptions to what can be observed, substituting the verb 'to seem' for the verb 'to be'. This is not, as Treacher (1988) suggests, scientific arrogance or an invalidation of felt experience. Rather, to say that someone seems sad rather than is sad is to invite enquiry and thereby avoid reifying the experience.

The dangers of mystification: the problem of language

Perhaps for justification to oneself and to others, every profession invents its own language. Some are easier than others to decipher.

Nonetheless, therapeutic jargon is a common complaint besides being an apparently obligatory initiation into the rites of a model and a supposed requirement for entry into professional status. Rather than clarifying any distinctive contribution, words too easily mystify, muddle and obfuscate. This can have the unfortunate effect of burying some very good ideas. Technical language is substituted for perfectly good, ordinary words, such as 'object' for 'person' in object-relations theory, with the result that theory deters all but the most committed, seems removed from real people and, therefore, may seem inapplicable or dangerous.

Social casework, psychodynamic theory and family therapy have all employed grandiose terminology and jargon. Its removal is an urgent challenge since the misplaced complexity obscures practice and its dilemmas (Timms and Timms, 1977). What sense and direction emerge for social workers from assessment criteria which include the extent of narcissism and the quality of an individual's libidinal relationships (Hollis, 1958)? Neither is contemporary social work immune: what is meant by social work support, the person-in-situation configuration (Hollis, 1970), assessment or the aim of increasing users' self-confidence? This lack of clarity makes it difficult to know what to do or when to stop. Psychodynamic social work developed a pretentious language possibly as a defensive façade (Wootton, 1959), which was so off-putting that it diverted attention from worthy efforts to develop a psycho-social approach to casework practice, to try to bridge the gap between those methods which focus too exclusively on intrapsychic experience and those which reach for social solutions without any consideration of personal dynamics. This balance between 'internal' and 'external' factors has remained a crucial focus of debate within social work practice, and has been a recurring theme in this book. However, the language used should elucidate rather than obscure the subject matter. Technical terms are necessary but practitioners should aim to control their jargon rather than be slaves to it.

Some of the basic concepts are themselves difficult enough, but the language in which they are presented and the diverse uses to which they are put frequently cloaks them in a further layer of impenetrability making understanding difficult. Therapists are apt to misuse borrowed terms and to distort the original specificity of concepts like transference, resistance and countertransference such that they become devalued, the more so when applied by professionals on the basis of second-hand sources rather than first-hand knowledge (Sandler *et al.*, 1973). This is the problem of multiple meanings whereby concepts lose clinical precision and it becomes unclear whether one professional knows what another one is talking about. Theory should simplify not complicate practice, and illuminate rather than obscure personal experience, individual meanings and relationships. Convoluted and vague language is antipathetic. Practitioners are uncertain what is proposed or how to proceed.

We might add that there is a vital connection between language, understanding and action. How we listen to people, how we engage with them, how we interpret to ourselves their speech and behaviour, how we communicate with them both verbally and non-verbally about our own understanding of them and how we process the complex 'feedback' from these interactions; these are some of the complex links in a delicate chain which can so easily become twisted or broken. The language used by social workers with users can often appear to come from a different world, a different sphere of discourse. It may seem a middle-class technocratic language full of coded references to professional values, bureaucratic procedures and statutory obligations which makes no perceptible effort to embrace the user's world, their belief system or language. Passive, bemused and monosyllabic, users accept the judgement handed down to them. Practitioners chalk up another disposal.

A challenge, therefore, for practitioners is to sort out their language in order to ensure that the 'reality' they are framing in any given interview is a shared one with the user (see Day, 1985). The language of social work is frequently our language, maintaining mystique and power imbalances rather than empowering clients to be fellow citizens. What social workers understand they mean may not be what users believe is conveyed to them. A challenge, therefore, is to ensure that language is enhancing communication and user-participation in the work rather than providing a way of avoiding clear statements.

The myth of the presenting problem

This is the most familiar parody of the psychodynamic approach to social work. The practitioner allows the electricity to be disconnected whilst 'discovering' family relationship difficulties and latent problems. The manifest content, the presenting problem, is set aside or devalued; the 'real' problem is investigated. Moreover, such practitioners are seen as interested only in inner worlds and not material difficulties. Thus Wootton (1959) lampoons the urge to penetrate behind the presenting problem to the something deeper that is supposed to lie beneath, criticising the arrogance of claiming to understand service-users better than they understand themselves. Emergencies and socio-economic problems are not accepted at face value. Practical problems are deliberately disregarded in favour of an emphasis on psychological issues.

Indeed, Mayer and Timms (1970), in their research into dissatisfied clients, found that service-users complained that social workers ignored their financial plight and sought information about family and marital circumstances which seemed irrelevant to the clients. They concluded that to offer psychological help without satisfying at the outset a client's material needs is to fail to deal appropriately with their problems, which often include a struggle for basic survival and profound financial anxieties. Whilst a material approach will never be a panacea, and whilst there may be psychological overtones to or consequences of material difficulties, Mayer and Timms argue that social workers should not be blind to clients' economic realities.

Ironically, this caricature remains alive when social workers, as a gatekeeping defence against overload, can be only too willing to accept the presenting problem as a straightforward request. Thus, although the traditional criticism is that material problems are reinterpreted at an emotional, deeper and historical level, now the number of demands and the pressure to achieve immediate, tangible results in order to overcome images of ineffectiveness means that other problems are not elicited (Prodgers, 1979). Deeper needs are ignored because of organisational defences. Stereotyped solutions, primarily based on practical provisions, are designed to keep work out, to 'gatekeep' (Addison, 1982). However, if services become provider- rather than user-sensitive, problem-focused rather than need-focused, they may miss what is not so observable. It may require time and trust as well as skill and sensitivity in offering services and counselling before an old person is able to acknowledge and discuss their deteriorating physical and mental health. A young mother with five children aged six and under described herself as overwhelmed. Home help, family aides, section 1 money, nursery places and social work support did not reduce the disorganisation. Whilst overwhelmed financially and practically, the young mother was also overwhelmed emotionally, especially by feelings from having been sexually abused as a child. The social worker required understanding, time and trust before the young mother could allow these feelings to emerge. Concentrating on the practical alone would have resulted in 'more-of-the-same' social work with the practitioners redoubling their efforts before (possibly) abandoning the young mother with failure.

Another example is the marginalisation of social work with older people. The image is that it is straightforward and requires only practical services, when it really demands the same social work skills and contains the same practice dilemmas as other areas of social work. Nonetheless referrals are often responded to by type of practical service required. The problem is 'solved' by the provision of material resources, running the risk of losing sight of the person, their experience and the context behind the referral (Day, 1985). The presenting problem may be the only solution an individual or family could find, or a defence against acknowledging a problem, as for example when an older person refuses services for fear they will result in residential care. Alternatively, people have images of what agencies will do and may present problems which they perceive fit the agency's purpose. There are, therefore, two problematic polarities. The one elevates the psychological, the other stresses the provision of material resources and gatekeeping. In either case, the user's needs can be distorted. What can be salvaged from this position?

Whilst some clients were clearly puzzled and surprised by social workers' insight-oriented methods and whilst the workers paid insufficient cognisance to cognitive factors (beliefs, thoughts, opinions and culture) and erroneously interpreted as anxiety clients' termination of contact (Mayer and Timms, 1970), others welcomed the worker widening out the discussion and found workers' responses to their comments meaningful. The Mayer and Timms study did not invalidate psychodynamic, insight-oriented practice; rather, it alerted practitioners to the serious consequences which follow from neglecting the user's perspective. Concerned curiosity (Cecchin, 1987) ensures open rather than closed practice. This means exploring possibilities rather than having a dogmatic, rigid adherence to the 'correct approach'. It means working with a family's concerns, but also being ready to widen discussions if there are other needs to consider, other possibilities, feelings and meanings. The choice is not between material/resource provision or psychological exploration as a means of problem-solving: both may be needed if social workers are not to become part of the problem.

The 'only intrapsychic' myth

We hope to have clarified by now that psychodynamic theory is not concerned only with intrapsychic phenomena to the exclusion of interactional patterns between individuals and external reality. Instead, it focuses on relationships and interactions, and how these may be internalised as pictures available for subsequent recall and use. Thus attachment theory is concerned with goal-directed, proximity-seeking behaviour, whereby interpersonal experiences are internalised as pictures of needs met or not met, this picture being reproduced in interpersonal interactions in a circular process. The actions of one individual cross the boundaries of that individual's personal space to that of another, forming a communication system between people (Symington, 1985). There is no such thing as an individual. Instead of Freud's reliance on psychic energies and instinctual drives, object-relations psychodynamic theorists direct us to the tension of relating inner and outer reality to the influence and effect of parental behaviour on attachment-seeking behaviour, to the here-and-now of an individual's problems, to present conflicts, coping mechanisms and interactions and to an interpersonal dynamic (Heard, 1978; Yelloly, 1980).

The split between intra- and interpersonal is a false divide. Individuals often project unwanted and disowned feeling-states on to others. Parents may project disavowed aspects of themselves on to their children. Individual pathology has to be understood in terms of interactional family and social processes. The use of an individual for distance regulation or for deflecting conflict between two others, whereby one individual becomes unhelpfully triangulated, or the observation that family relationships can become oriented around what is required, avoiding other types of relationships for fear of calamitous consequences, confirm that individuals and their behaviour can be best understood not simply as a function of their personality but of their membership of a group and their interaction with the people in this group (Blackwell and Wilkins, 1981). Thus, psychodynamic theory is not concerned solely with an individual but with interactions between individuals and the conflicts, misunderstandings and patterns which can result. From here it is a short step to focusing on the interaction between individuals and societal systems, where individual behaviour may be a function or consequence of relations with these wider systems rather than an incidence of pathology or inadequacy.

Another myth arises here, namely that psychodynamic theory is only concerned with the past and its correct interpretation, with the there-and-then not the here-and-now. Malan (1979) is characteristically forthright. People seek help for current conflicts, sometimes with a background of long-standing difficulties. Whilst both may originate in the past, it is not always necessary to make such links. It may be sufficient to work through the current conflict. Understanding present conflicts does not depend on restructuring the past although it may be enriched by this (Lomas, 1987). The past repeats itself in present behaviour. Interpretations about the past are more speculative than those about the present. The past is only relevant as it influences today, as it reveals behaviour patterns in the here-and-now, and enables individuals to get in touch with important emotional history without intellectual escape into the past (Skidmore, 1988).

Social workers should be careful not to invalidate the past. Reminiscence work, life-story books and geneograms are not examples of a preoccupation with the past but a recognition that, by identifying the effect of past experiences on present perceptions and behaviour, such work can facilitate change in here-and-now patterns, and enable the development of attachments and behaviours not possible before.

Imbalances of power

The sexist bias of psychoanalysis and systemic therapy

Freud admitted that he found the sexual life of the adult woman 'a dark continent for psychology' (S. Freud, 1925). His theories about female sexuality, encapsulated in concepts such as penis envy, have found little favour with a modern generation more attuned to feminist awareness. The charges most commonly brought against Freudian psychoanalysis are two-fold: first, that women are viewed by Freudian theory as biologically inferior to men: and second, that the therapeutic practice of psychoanalysis is too often employed in the service of reconciling women to their subordinate role. Many people, therefore, still reject psychoanalysis *in toto*, apparently unaware that a great deal of constructive reappraisal has been undertaken since the 'great debate' on female sexuality in the 1920s and 1930s, when prominent figures such as Ernest Jones, Karen Horney and Melanie Klein took issue with Freud on a number of key issues (Wieland, 1988).

Taking an overview of this post-Freudian reappraisal of female sexuality and of women's role in society, we can perhaps discern three broad trends. First, Freudian theory has itself been reinvestigated from a feminist perspective, notably by Mitchell (1974, 1984), and has yielded a vital contribution to our understanding of women's psychological and social oppression (cf. Pearson *et al.*, 1988). Second, the whole development of object-relations theory (beginning with the work of Melanie Klein) has shifted the gender focus away from the father-dominated Oedipus complex (the period when Freud considered sexual identity was formed) and has pushed it back into the earliest pre-Oedipal period, where the key relationship is that of a dependent child and a nurturing mother. It is in this earliest phase of human development, according to object-relations theory, that an individual's psychic structure begins to take shape through a cyclical process of projection, introjection and identification. Feminists have followed Klein (1928) in rejecting Freud's phallocentric view: that is, his use of boyhood as the model for the sexual development of both boys and girls (Mitchell, 1984). Gender differences are now included in the 'structures' which are internalised at this early stage (Eichenbaum and Orbach, 1982; cf. Frosh, 1987, ch. 7). We should add, however, that object-relations theory in general is still open to criticism. Whilst the theory does not require that the principal attachment figure has to be the mother, in its expression it frequently mirrors the patriarchal culture which assigns child care predominantly to women. It tends to attribute all psychopathology to some sort of maternal failure (Greenberg and Mitchell, 1983). In particular, Winnicott and Guntrip are taken to task for 'romanticising' the mothering role, or attributing 'salvational' properties to it (Frosh, 1987).

Third, the practice of psychoanalytic therapy has been used very effectively by feminists as 'a means of understanding and undoing people's acquiescence in their oppression' (Sayers, 1988). The broader discussion of this theme is well articulated by Frosh (1987, ch. 8), who argues that object-relations theory provides a means of understanding how each of us internalises the prevailing power structures of our patriarchal capitalist society, and that psychoanalytic therapy provides an extremely effective tool by which to uncover and 'interrogate' these internalised structures.

It is in the field of therapy that feminist work in the past decade has been hailed as 'the growing edge within psychoanalysis' (Pearson *et al.*, 1988). The setting-up of the Women's Therapy Centre in London in 1976 marked the beginning of this movement (Eichenbaum and Orbach, 1982), and a rich variety of therapeutic approaches – from Freudian to object-relational to Lacanian – can now be seen in the published work of feminist psychotherapists. To take some recent examples: Sayers (1988), using a mixture of Freudian and post-Freudian theory, argues that women occupy a 'contradictory' position between surrendering to their social subordination and resisting it. Traditionally they have reacted to this conflict by retreating from the real world into an illusory world of neurotic disorder. Psychoanalytic therapy is presented as an effective means of reversing this process and enabling women to carry their struggle for personal autonomy back into the real world of human relationships. This whole area of what women need (as opposed to what they will settle for) is addressed by Dana and Lawrence (1988) in relation to eating disorders. Building on earlier work (Lawrence, 1984), the authors make telling use of psychoanalytic insight to relate the inner world of a woman's psychic experience to the outer world of social conditioning. In their quest for the meaning of symptomatic behaviour they view a disordered style of eating as a metaphorical expression of the sufferer's need for, and capacity to make use of, emotional sustenance. Therapy is itself presented as a nurturant relationship, an attempt to give women what they need but feel unable to take in (anorexia) or hold on to (bulimia). This nurturing of thwarted or repressed emotional need is a cornerstone of the feminist therapy movement (Eichenbaum and Orbach, 1982).

In a comprehensive feminist critique of the family therapy movement, Goldner (1985, 1988) argues that family therapists have adopted an abstract systems theory stripped of connection to the larger social field. She examines the historical process which has led to women being identified primarily with child care and concludes that, far from being dysfunctional in any pure systemic sense, it is the product of two centuries of social conditioning. Gender, she says, belongs at the centre of family therapy but has been invisible for too long and urgently needs to be 'retrieved'. Hare-Mustin (1987) argues that both psychodynamic and systemic approaches to family therapy are marked by gender bias, the former exaggerating and the latter ignoring gender differences. She argues that gender has had a negligible influence on the development of family therapy despite its centrality to how the world is viewed and organised. For her, the concept of therapeutic neutrality is questionable since all therapists have their own internalised values about male and female attributes and roles. There is obvious validity in the criticism that family therapy and systems theory has ignored social constructions of gender and inequalities in society which discriminate against women. However, there is evidence that family therapy is now addressing attitudes, behaviour and social and economic systems which reflect the paternalistic organisation of society. It is beginning to challenge family members' assumptions about how they organise their relationships (Christophas *et al.*, 1983; Pilalis and Anderton, 1986; J. Williams and Watson, 1988). It is asking practitioners to scrutinise and reassess their own value bases, family scripts and gender attitudes as an important prerequisite to challenging inequalities in families and society and empowering individuals in their own families and social relationships.

The ethics of therapeutic approaches

When, if at all, are professionals justified in imposing or reaching for change? Where is the line which divides abusive or coercive practice from a justifiable therapeutic approach? What limits should be set on effectiveness? Social work is not free from such ethical dilemmas.

Psychotherapists and family therapists stress the importance of ethical practice: the duty not to cause harm; the obligation to identify indicators and contraindicators for particular therapeutic approaches; the importance of assessments, especially in psychotherapy of an individual's strengths, resources, capacity to tolerate stress and painful feelings; and the availability of people for support. Therapists are warned not to idealise technique above caring, to consider the possible effects of their interpretations, and to beware of an urge to dominate masked as a wish to heal (Malan, 1979; Lomas, 1987). Accordingly, paradoxical interventions should not be used frivolously or haphazardly but should be based on an evaluation of the degree of resistance to change where there are covert, long-standing, repetitious patterns of interactions which have not responded to traditional, direct interventions which should always be tried first (Papp, 1980; Reder, 1988). Paradox is regarded as inappropriate when more structure and control from the therapist is required (for example in cases involving violence, sudden grief and attempted suicide: Mortell, 1981). Interventions must not be existentially threatening since suggestions which ignore the humanity of the recipients and are blind to the potential meaning of their behaviour and to their experience can have catastrophic results (Kaye, 1986).

Nonetheless, some family therapists and social workers appear particularly uneasy about the ethics of some interventions and interpretations. Treacher (1986) criticises systemic family therapists for using covert techniques at arm's length, for retaining power and for appearing removed from the world of the family and impervious to peer and user criticism. He accuses therapists of keeping the family passive and attempting change through omniscient pronouncements in which the family is seen as an object. In another article he argues that positive connotation is demeaning and critical of families (Treacher, 1988). Whan (1983) is equally critical. He believes systemic therapists manipulate and deceive families, disregarding the notion of respect for persons. He argues that they assume power without consent and challenge the social work principles of user self-determination and involvement in decision-making about the work of change. He particularly objects to the idea that clients do not necessarily need to understand the approach. In sum, the critics perceive trickery, insincerity and manipulation.

Since all methods of intervention may, in some sense, be regarded as manipulations, the question becomes how to use methods in the best interests of individuals and families. The onus is on professionals to demonstrate this best interest requirement. Practice is unethical when it cannot demonstrate this (Corden and Preston-Shoot, 1987).

Clearly positive connotation and paradox, like any techniques, are open to abuse. If used without an understanding of their power or as slick techniques, if applied indiscriminately or without connection to the family's objectives and views on acceptable change, then practice slips into the unethical. However, the power imbalance in the helping encounter may be modified through explanations about how the therapists work and by the use of working agreements involving principles of consent to the work. Additionally, if positive reframes and paradoxes are regarded as invitations to curiosity, different meanings or perspectives which reflect the 'stuckness' or conflicts in a system and an understanding of why individuals behave as they do – their 'because clauses' (Reder, 1988) – they invite, but do not require and cannot force, change.

Social work principles are important and ethical practice is essential. Less empowering are rituals to be followed at all costs. Must individuals and families *always* know the hypothesis or understand the intervention? What value should be given to openness if an intervention is more effectively absorbed when its impact is not reduced by discussion (Skynner, 1979)? What are the ethics of more of the same which seems to characterise much long-term social work? What are the ethics of not using paradox, when other interventions have failed, and of not, therefore, possibly opening up a new dimension of experience, a new way of perceiving things? Part of the problem may be that professionals are trained to think diagnostically not operationally, to show concern, care and support regardless of whether or not this helps people to change (Cade and Southgate, 1979). Consequently, principles become ritualistic scripts which, rather than protecting or enabling service-users, may disadvantage them because professionals have abandoned their responsibilities to work for change. Professionals have a choice: to allow patterns to continue as they are or to do something different which helps people change in a direction they wanted when earlier solutions failed (Bruggen and O'Brian, 1987).

The conservative caricature and the myth of the missing social dimension

Systems theory, it is argued, promotes a consensus view of society, is intolerant of conflict and is conservative. Despite the wider view of problems its perspective affords, it shuns the social in favour of individual and family pathology and problems. The social structure is not addressed (Pilalis and Anderton, 1986; Treacher, 1986). Psychodynamic theory, too, is regarded as supporting the existing socio-economic order. Hollis' psycho-social approach (1970) almost totally ignores the social side of the equation, such that Wootton (1959) argues for putting the social back into social work and the situation back into the person-in-situation. Economic difficulties and inadequate housing, not personal failure or misconduct or early childhood, she charges, cause poverty.

However, systems theory can be used radically to challenge the oppressiveness of resource systems (Bailey and Brake, 1975). Depression is not necessarily an intrapsychic conflict but may be a response to social frustration (Hartman, 1969). A family's behaviour may reflect not simply its internal dynamics but also its relationship to other social systems which may maintain or exacerbate the problems (Coulshed and Abdullah-Zadeh, 1983). Systems thinking should place the family in its context of wider systems where, indeed, efforts regarding change may need to be directed (Kingston, 1982).

Neo-Freudians argued that cultural factors were more salient than biological ones in individual development (Bloch, 1982), whilst Bowlby (1979), criticising Freud for elevating hereditary over environmental factors, believed that much ill-health and unhappiness was due to environmental influences and the absence of opportunities for individuals to fulfil inner needs. Both family therapists and psychotherapists assert the need to explore the effects on individuals and families of socio-economic and cultural factors, of external stresses (Winnicott, 1965; Will and Wrate, 1985). The personal and social, inner and outer, are considered together since life experiences, economic and political systems and feelings all contribute to personality development; since dominant modes of thought and behaviour are introjected by individuals through the family; since stereotyped roles – for example, gender roles – entail personal and political conflicts requiring solutions at each level as each level contributes to distress (Dowrick, 1983; Dana and Lawrence, 1988).

Why then, if psychodynamic theory is sharply critical of the existing order (Kovel, 1976b), and if a consensus view of society is not logically inherent in a systemic approach (Evans, 1976), are the theories assumed to be conservative? Are they conservative or have they been applied conservatively? We believe the latter to be the case.

As with social work, theories can be interpreted and used conservatively or radically: to support dominant versions of how things are and should be, or to challenge socio-economic and value assumptions. Indeed, both psychodynamic and systems theory argue for the non-necessity of what is but, like social work, have been tamed, stripped of their visions of radical change, and turned into a focus on individual transformation in order to promote the dominant socio-economic culture (Kovel, 1976b). Maybe social workers and therapists have problems being radical (Cypher, 1973) or perhaps the dominant political and economic structures are too powerful to challenge effectively. It is not the theories that are inherently conservative, therefore, but the context in which they are used which promotes a consensus view. Consequently social workers do not challenge the domination of economics over effectiveness but tailor assessments to what is available rather than present a full account of an individual's risks, needs and required resources and place the responsibility for decision-making where it should rest, with managers and politicians.

Why has this happened? How have these theories come to be used to support rather than challenge the status quo, to ignore the social? Frosh (1987) provides one answer by demonstrating how dominant power structures and values are internalised in infancy, thereby prolonging society's present form through individuals' unconsciously determined expectations. If practitioners do not engage in awareness work, socially constructed and internalised attitudes towards gender, age, race and disability will permeate their practice. Through not having examined their own cultural inheritance, they will be unable to identify and challenge the assumptions around which others have structured their lives or the constructions those with power place on family life, caring, unemployment, mental health and distress.

Kingston (1979), in a penetrating analysis, observes that individuals and families are more accessible than organisations and supra-systems to intervention. Thus systems theory often stops short of relating individuals and families to the wider context. Organisations hold sufficient power to deny their own pathology and to provide legal authority to intervene in the lives of families but not agencies. Moreover, local authorities are funded and controlled by politicians which further restricts the power of change. It is difficult to maintain a critical edge to practice, retain assertiveness and vision, mobilise people without power and resources, challenge values and structures, and avoid sliding into ritualistic agency practice.

Networking (Dimmock and Dungworth, 1985), self-directed groupwork – where group members set the goals of the work (Mullender and Ward, 1985) – and family-agency system work – where it is acknowledged that agencies may be maintaining problems (Dowling and Osborne, 1985) – are all useful 'correctives' to locating pathology within the individual or family. However, facilitating community action against structural inequalities still remains less likely than a form of community social work which remains service-oriented, directive and controlling (Butcher, 1984). As Dowrick (1983) demonstrates, whilst systems and psychodynamic theory argue that conflict is inevitable at micro and macro levels, social work encourages the capitalist status quo where human and economic value are directly equated.

Finally, the theories themselves do not deny the possibility of real conflict. Whilst there may be a consensus in a family about maintaining a 'solution', this does not mean the absence of heartfelt issues and genuine conflict. Even if the system needs a symptom as a homeostatic mechanism against feared difference, power differences will exist, some members will have the power to oppress others and there will be real conflict between parts of the system (Kingston, 1982). This is why, in families, members may disagree violently and yet remain fixed in one 'solution'.

Conclusion

Our aim in challenging these myths has been to argue for a more considered, reflective attitude rather than dogmatic closure by advocates and critics alike. We believe that psychodynamic and systemic concepts have a practical relevance and that social work requires both. The private and the public interact with each other. Social workers may have to intervene at each level.

5

Social work and society: downward spirals and double-binds?

We have argued that the value of psychodynamic and systems theories lies in the framework they provide for understanding themes, patterns, events and defences, and in the practice techniques through which this understanding may be applied. In this and subsequent chapters we intend to demonstrate the validity of this viewpoint, beginning here with social work's interaction with, and relationship to, the larger systems within which it is located: social services organisations, public and societal expectations, and the political context. Social work is located within a social, psychological, economic and political frame or context which frequently appears to render social work an unloved and challenging (if not impossible) profession. This chapter is an attempt at a meta view, an examination of how social work's complex psychological, political, organisational and social inheritance affects practitioners, and how they might intervene and practise strategically in it, using the contribution which psychodynamic and systemic thinking can make.

The focus will be on the organisations, systems and structures which influence social work and within which social workers work. The chapter will examine the processes, reactions and dynamics which block effective functioning and which create defensive practice. For example, the concepts of 'open' and 'closed' systems, and 'basic assumptions' (Bion, 1961) can be used to pinpoint some of the processes within professional organisations where considerable energy becomes tied up in intraorganisational stresses and conflicts to the detriment of the professional task.

The Barclay Report (Barclay, 1982) commented that too much is expected of social workers. Unrealistic expectations are projected on to them, followed by strident complaints when these expectations are disappointed. Working in social work is becoming increasingly stressful. The mounting responsibilities in child abuse, society's expectations, the media and public condemnations which follow tragedies, and financial constraints which curtail training opportunities and resources; these and other factors are de-skilling social workers. Not only are social workers and service-users put at risk, but social work has become the recipient of, and receptacle for, displaced public anxiety (Holdaway, 1986).

This chapter is a recognition that one task for social work is to understand and then intervene in its location (Evans, 1976). Key questions therefore arise. How may the processes described above be understood and, on the basis of awareness, how might social workers intervene effectively in these processes? If practitioners are not to be shaped and de-skilled by structures, what contribution can psychodynamic and systemic thinking make towards helping to understand these phenomena, especially public anxiety about and expectations of social work? What guidance do they give to social work about how to respond?

Macro and micro contexts

From a macro to an individual micro perspective the world in which we live is riven with conflicts, divisions and tensions. It is unpredictable, uncertain and fundamentally unsafe. Nations have constructed an enormous capacity to destroy each other and themselves. A struggle for power and domination characterises much human interaction. Tragedies in football stadia, the destruction of aircraft by bombs and by structural failure, and the loss of life through human error all serve to underline how tenuous is the hold on existence. The environment is dangerously abused daily, such that the survival of the planet as we know it is increasingly being called into question. Images of interpersonal relationships have been shaken by the emergence of the Aids virus and child sexual abuse. The reassessments and questioning which these phenomena demand do not come easily or painlessly. Geographically and by class we are a nation divided in terms of health, culture, housing, poverty, life expectancy and employment. Despite legislation, divisions and barriers continue to exist through discrimination on grounds of race, gender and age. Attitudes cannot be legislated away. Equally sinister, and displayed in the growing concentration given to child abuse at the expense of other social services user groups, human value is increasingly being equated with political influence or pressure and economic value. Questions are asked regarding whether local authorities can justify expenditure on social work services to older people, people with physical disabilities or mental illness or to people with health-related difficulties, such as terminal illness. Increasingly, social services are becoming equated with statutory work alone, but here too inequity resides. Child protection legislation is enacted swiftly and implemented immediately, unlike that relating, for instance, to people with disabilities. The Disabled Persons Act (1986) required a private member's bill, and its cost implications account for its only partial implementation.

Considerable numbers of people continue to exist in bed-and-breakfast accommodation and/or to experience on-going poverty. The physical and emotional effects of such experiences set up a cycle of deprivation and call attention to the urgency (for example, in child protection work) of addressing structural inequalities and deprivations alongside other intra- and interpersonal needs. Continuing deprivation and disadvantage, particularly the feeling of impotence, of being unable to have an impact or effect, destroy people physically and psychologically. The responses are many and varied: withdrawal into despair and alienation, sometimes called anomie; protest; criminality; depression. Emotional carnage is omnipresent and has a multiplicity of origins and effects.

At the micro, intrapersonal level there exists the potential for violence and expression of raw emotion within each individual, the potential to abuse oneself or others. The abuse and neglect of service-users in institutional or residential care highlights the brutality to which individuals can succumb, and the complex interaction between individual, interpersonal and structural phenomena in the onset and maintenance of dysfunctions.

Bowlby (1979) has argued that the fundamental needs or drives within the human personality are those of survival, protection and belonging. The unpredictability and uncertainties of human existence may, therefore, be seen to threaten these basic needs or drives, with the result that individuals and groups employ defences to protect themselves against the painful, threatening aspects of their existence (Hinshelwood, 1987).

Until recently, a defence of symmetrical escalation has been employed by the superpowers in relation to their arsenals for 'protection', a closed system where each activity was interpreted as a threatening act and met with a counterresponse of greater force.

In response to tragedies and disasters, rather than staying with the pain and acknowledging feelings such as impotence and uncertainties, there is more usually a flight into activity where reflection is squeezed out because it is painful (Hinshelwood, 1987). Feelings are either denied or externalised by a search for control and for rational explanations, by scapegoating, and by idealisation of 'solutions' to provide 'as if' security and control of human personalities and processes. The illusion of omnipotent behaviour is thereby created.

Enquiries into the deaths of children in care or known to social services are examples of this phenomenon. It is rarely acknowledged that supervision and monitoring cannot prevent tragedy, or that human personalities are capable of extreme deception. Individual workers are blamed rather than the structure of service provision analysed, including the inadequacies and uncertainties within the law relating to child protection (Lyon, 1989; Braye and Preston-Shoot, 1990). The illusion is created that training and procedures will provide solutions. The reality of social work practice is denied.

Denial operates at many levels, intra- and interpersonally. What is denied is the shadow, the depths within the human personality. For instance, greed is denied and projected on to claimants who are then negatively labelled as scroungers. Unwanted parts of self are projected on to others whose 'madness' or 'badness' is then reacted against as if it belongs to them. Hostile or destructive impulses are deflected by projection on to an outside enemy (Jaques, 1955). People become objects. The reality of their experience and their individual feelings are denied and parried. The rhetoric is of homogeneous groups: the elderly, the disabled, the homeless, the unemployed. Difference is denied because to acknowledge it is felt to threaten one's own position and security.

People 'ignore' what they do not wish to see in themselves and in society. Child sexual abuse, and now the abuse of old people, have been denied or the victims blamed, as in rape cases, to protect an image of 'not us; we are not like that'. People in dominant and powerful positions may experience unease and guilt if they acknowledge basic structural inequalities in society or basic human impulses and needs. Thus individuals are blamed and scapegoated to maintain an illusion. For example, abusing parents are blamed for not being good enough rather than society examined to see how it denies parents a chance to be good enough (Jordan, 1982). Dominant groups promote ideologies designed to appeal to and satisfy their basic needs and drives (Dowrick, 1983). The current political vogue for so-called Victorian values is in fact an authoritarian attempt at self-preservation, to protect position and power at the expense of less powerful groups, mainly women, children, unemployed people and members of ethnic minority groups, who carry the split-off, denied and projected emotions and troubling images of the dominant groups. Recent legislative moves against homosexuals may be regarded as one such example being dramatised. In essence, the system is closed and not amenable to different inputs.

Child abuse

To illustrate some of the dynamics described in the previous section, and to provide an example of locating experience in a framework rather than reacting to it, we have chosen the subject which dominates social work and consumes most of its energies: child abuse.

The capacity for violence exists in everyone. It is easier to see this potential for abuse, and the deception, deceit, abuse of power and exploitation which can accompany it, in others than in oneself. It is easier to deflect this pain, to project the unwanted 'bad' parts of oneself on to others and then react against them, as a defence against anxieties of contamination and fragmentation. Raw, shadow feelings are denied and projected on to 'abusers' and 'abused', whose essential humanity and felt experiences are ignored. The primitive urge then becomes not to understand but to tidy away. Abusing parents are therefore seen as different from other parents rather than as being at one end of a spectrum of parenting distress which affects every parent (Gorell-Barnes, 1979) and which is affected in large measure by structural inequalities and historical family experience. Seeing individuals as bad and beyond understanding represents a closed system since these very individuals are denied the opportunity of making an input, of conveying their experience, their feelings and the rationality they have retained.

Social work has become one mechanism for this 'tidying away'. Social work acts as a relieving container, protecting society against disturbing impingements, allowing it to believe in its own good by heaping troubling images or contempt on to one group, and passing its expectations of solving these problems to another, the social workers (Jaques, 1955; Hinshelwood, 1987; Lask, 1987). As a result social work has become caught in a downward spiral (see Figure 5.1).

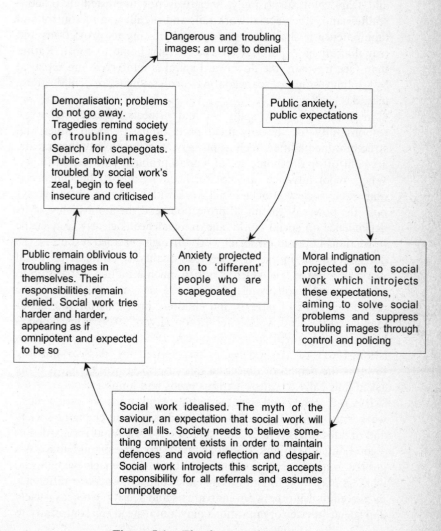

Figure 5.1 *The downward spiral*

Social work provides a protective script to enable society to avoid troubling situations and thoughts (Byng-Hall, 1988) and to leave illusions about individuals and families unchallenged. This script is designed to avoid the calamities of abuse and tragedies but also the calamity it is feared will follow from acknowledging impotence in controlling the destructive forces of the personality (Braye and Preston-Shoot, 1990). Thus social work is a 'solution' for dilemmas and fears. Not surprisingly, society is not interested in practice realities and, when social work fails and the illusion of control and omnipotence is shattered, society is left facing its projections and troubling images. Parts given away return home to roost. Rather than face the pain, the downward spiral is reinforced and replayed by dramatisations, scapegoating professionals or child abuse inquiries.

In this way society splits off and projects on to social work responsibility for the unwanted parts of itself. Social issues and structural inequalities, such as poverty, and the anxiety they create, are split off and become social work's problem and responsibility. When major advances are not forthcoming and its dependence is unmasked, society attacks social work with a fervour which betrays both the power of the initial projections and the ambivalence of its dependence on social work. The ambivalence is clearly seen in the restrictions imposed on social work through curtailed resources, the decision not to invest in three-year qualifying courses for social workers, and the law which is not so much a unified instruction to social workers, conveying great powers, as a tension between the respective rights of parents and children, providing an ambiguous mandate for social work intervention (Lyon, 1989). This ambivalence is not surprising for it contains a basic assumption (Bion, 1961) of dependence, characterised by passive hostility towards the person or object, in this case social work, that is being asked magically to satisfy various needs and longings.

It is as if society and social services organisations are asking social workers to change individuals and families without changing society and organisations (Pilalis and Anderton, 1986). What is regarded as a good outcome differs. Everyone may agree on less child abuse as a desired outcome but not on how it should be achieved. Social workers may wish to aim for systemic change, to make a difference in the relationship between individuals and society, whereas society and social services organisations may aim instead for conformity to established, dominant norms and values. This latter view, and the powerful injunction to tidy away and individualise or privatise problems which accompanies it, is embedded in legislation which restricts social workers to a legal mandate to intervene in and change families and individuals, not agencies or social and political systems (Kingston, 1979). Focus is diverted away from social, economic and psychological inequalities, from society's failures, to social control. Social work becomes enmeshed in an individual/ family model of dysfunction. Dominant values and comfortable images are maintained. Yet even this mandate, as observed above, is severely curtailed because of ambivalence about dependence on social work. Not surprisingly, therefore, the potential solution, social work, can become part of the problem.

A further difficulty for social workers is that the projections themselves are split. Society is unclear what it wants from social work and how it wants to deal with its guilt and the challenges to its comfortable images. There is a split: should abusers be treated or punished? Should the approach be liberal or punitive? This is overlaid with tensions between outrage against abusers and concern about false accusations against adults, between protecting children and parental rights, between children as the property of parents and children as citizens with rights. All sides believe they are right and the drama is acted out at societal and political levels, mirroring a similar drama which is often enacted in families. Responsibility, despite contradictory expectations, is ultimately off-loaded on to social work which is caught in a double-bind: damned if it does, and damned if it does not.

The final vicious circle for social work here arises from society's expectations and 'needs' fitting with the helping profession syndrome carried by many practitioners: their need to be helpful and caring, either as a means of receiving love and/or of denying their own negative feelings of anger, hostility and despair which can be projected on to others and worked with there. Thus, the danger is that society's expectations fit with and reinforce a need in practitioners to be wanted, to prove themselves and social work. The result can be overcommitment, burn-out and failure, a closed system in which workers and society reinforce each other's behaviour and perpetuate the problem. In systemic terms, this relationship is complementary: each fits with the other's require-ments. A closed system is established in which each party expects the other to satisfy their unacknowledged needs. This takes us into the relationship and dynamics between social workers and society, and between social workers and their employing organisations: how they act upon each other and cope with anxiety about the work.

Social workers and society

In family work and family therapy, family dysfunction often centres around insufficient or contradictory communication and the absence or rigidity of boundaries (Leicester Family Service Unit, 1981). The problematic relationship between social workers and society similarly centres around boundaries and communication: what is or is not communicated and how.

The boundaries, instead of being sufficiently flexible to allow exchange of ideas and information and yet sufficiently strong to provide stability and identity, alternate between being too rigid and too permeable. When too rigid, no exchange or influence is possible. Rigid boundaries are often observable when social workers seek to influence social services and government policy. The decider sub-system seems unamenable to input. When too loose, and here it is when policy-makers seek to influence social workers, the outcome is control of social work whose separate identity is lost. The result can be chaos, as an example illustrates.

Immediately upon publication of the Cleveland Report and the initial government response regarding parents' rights and the use of place of safety orders, a social services department issued fresh instructions on procedures for investigating child abuse referrals. The use of place of safety orders was to be strictly controlled. The instructions were issued without any consultations with other agencies involved in child protection and without any discussion with social workers and court officers. In responding to the injunctions to safeguard parents' rights, the position of abused children and their siblings was overlooked. In particular, the difficulties children have disclosing sexual abuse were under-estimated, especially the accommodation syndrome: the pressure on children from abusers not to disclose or to retract earlier disclosures. Social work's professional identity – its knowledge, values, practice and theoretical base – was lost. Only following difficulties arising from operating the new policy, and feedback from social workers, was the department able to consider in a less defensive way the implications for itself of the issues arising from the Cleveland crisis.

The relationship between society and social work is also characterised by insufficient and contradictory communication. Let us take insufficient communication first. Expectations of social work are unclear. For instance, the Beckford Report (1985) did not clarify how social workers are to judge which cases involving high-risk factors require immediate action to remove children and which do not. Nor did it clarify whether, therefore, social workers should remove all such children just in case. The shades of grey present in many child protection cases are denied. What is or is not good enough child care has not been confronted by society, and neither has the absence of good predictors of violence or 'rock-solid' indicators of high risk. Since expectations are, therefore, unclear and vague, the potential for inappropriate social work responses is considerable. The social work response in Cleveland is deemed to have been inappropriate but what are social workers to do in the face of medical evidence and/or disclosures and/or society's demand that children be protected, especially considering the fact that the absence of disclosures does not mean that abuse has not taken place?

Second, regarding contradictory communication, it is impossible to escape the conclusion that social workers, particularly in child abuse, are confronted with a double-bind, required both to protect children and yet not infringe parental rights. The dilemmas inherent in this are denied, as is the difficulty of finding any 'right' answers in an environment which frequently contains hostility, complexity and unpredictability.

This analysis of insufficient and contradictory communication has four consequences for social workers' roles (cf. Blackler and Shimmin, 1984). First, it results in role ambiguity: what is expected is unclear and contradictory, complex and diffuse. Of the eight available action orientations open to social work (Whittington, 1977), society gives dominant emphasis currently to a formalistic orientation as a basis for action. Rules, procedures and statute, organisational requirements and compliance dominate. However, even rules and statute require interpretation but public and social work expectations about what will be interpreted may differ.

This leads to the second consequence: role conflict. In addition to the formalistic orientation mentioned above, several other approaches are currently in vogue: the economistic, emphasising value for money and prioritising; the defensive, emphasising avoidance of complaints; control, stressing reform of transgressors; and the orthodox-expert, stressing client 'need', protection and adjustment, where the client possesses the problem. Social workers, however, may wish to stress other action orientations, particularly the interventionist-expert paradigm which emphasises consciousness-raising and client rights, and the service model which highlights client demands and satisfaction (Whittington, 1977).

In addition to the tensions created by divergent action orientations, centred on 'Who is the client?' and 'What are the objectives?', there are three major practice dilemmas (Braye and Preston-Shoot, 1990): who makes the decisions – professionals or agencies, professionals alone or in partnership with users, social workers and/or other professionals; what informs the decisions – needs or resources, economics or humanitarianism, legal duty or professional knowledge and values; and what the purpose of the decisions is – care or control, rights or risks. These practice dilemmas are central to all social work, creating a tension which it is difficult to balance, and anxiety which it is difficult to handle. Practice based on dogmatic, rigidly held and polarised belief systems is not uncommonly the outcome.

The third consequence is role incompatibility. Ruddock (1988) has warned of the system which compromises social workers' competence and professional standards, too often allowing them to descend to the lowest level of functioning. The crisis-oriented environment is neither the most effective nor economic response. Resources are allowed to dictate to needs, with consequent inappropriate placements. The theory of good practice and reality do not always coincide. Social workers are given inadequate resources for the job and are too often overloaded whilst simultaneously deprived of effective supervision, empathic support and on-going training. This again reflects society's ambivalence.

The fourth consequence is role insecurity and vulnerability. We have already pointed out how social workers can engage in compulsive work, having introjected society's needs and injunctions not to fail. Equally, the absence of confirmation, validation and affirmation has resulted in social work internalising negative projections from society, based on disapproval, rather than positives based on acceptance and approval. Low morale and feelings of inferiority, unworthiness and anxiety are the result. The danger is that social work, in its practice, then reacts to actual or imagined rejection or disapproval with identity diffusion, self-fragmentation and diminished self-esteem. That is, its professional judgement, core values and theoretical and practice knowledge – its sense of self – are lost (Feldman, 1982). The example of one department's response to Cleveland, given above, is an illustration of this phenomenon.

Additionally, this insecurity and vulnerability comes from anxiety which emanates from the uncertainties inherent in social work: what goals? Whose goals? How to achieve them? What effects will intervention have? When should the rights of one party give way to those of another? The level of responsibility carried by practitioners also creates anxiety and insecurity, especially as the role is regarded ambivalently, if not with hostility, by members of the public. The final source of insecurity and anxiety comes from social workers' proximity to service-users who, especially in child protection and mental health cases, may exhibit severe disturbance and physical or verbal aggression. Strong feelings, pain and conflict are part of the job and social workers cannot help but be affected by them, whatever coping or defence mechanisms they employ. To witness or anticipate destructive tension, rejection and conflict produces stress, anxiety and feelings of vulnerability (Mattinson, 1975). The resultant vicious circle or closed system (Figure 5.2) demonstrates how social work can become enmeshed in a 'game without end' where the now urgent need is to communicate about the communication, to assume a meta position and focus on the system.

As Figure 5.2 illustrates, the result is stress, tension, reduced job satisfaction and diminished self-confidence. A closed system of fearful, defensive practice is created whereby social workers are dehumanised and de-skilled. Their urgent task is to distinguish what belongs to them, and to recognise rather than act out this vicious circle. Under this pressure, social work has lost sight of its boundaries and of realistic levels of its responsibility for change. Social workers rarely say who they cannot help and have, therefore, become scapegoats when things go wrong. To the degree of responsibility taken and introjected by social workers can be attributed much of the burn-out and malaise currently evident within the profession.

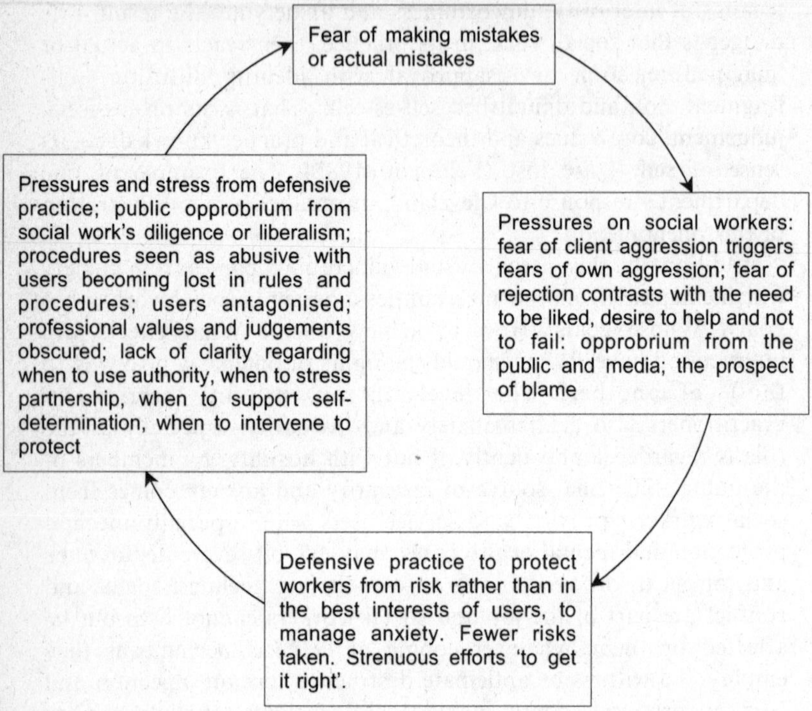

Fear of making mistakes or actual mistakes

Pressures and stress from defensive practice; public opprobrium from social work's diligence or liberalism; procedures seen as abusive with users becoming lost in rules and procedures; users antagonised; professional values and judgements obscured; lack of clarity regarding when to use authority, when to stress partnership, when to support self-determination, when to intervene to protect

Pressures on social workers: fear of client aggression triggers fears of own aggression; fear of rejection contrasts with the need to be liked, desire to help and not to fail: opprobrium from the public and media; the prospect of blame

Defensive practice to protect workers from risk rather than in the best interests of users, to manage anxiety. Fewer risks taken. Strenuous efforts 'to get it right'.

Figure 5.2   *A vicious circle in social work*

Social workers and their organisations

The organisation of social services reflects society's ambivalent attitudes towards social work and its users. It also reflects the anxiety experienced by social workers who have evolved particular structures (procedures, ideologies of need, office arrangements) within which they can shelter. Organisations may thus be viewed as socially constructed defence mechanisms. These defences are designed to protect the members of an organisation from the anxiety and stress evoked by the work, and they have a determining effect on how that organisation functions. There is, therefore, a reciprocal process at work in the organisation of social services: both society and social workers seek to satisfy their needs through organisational structures. These formally created social institutions provide ways of working that satisfy the defensive needs both of the individuals who work in them and of society as a whole (Hinshelwood, 1987).

Before looking in more detail at both sides of this two-way process, which can of course be viewed as a single interactional system, it is important to consider the pioneering work of Menzies (1970) and what it contributes to our understanding of social work organisation. In a classic psychoanalytic study, Menzies investigated the nursing staff of a large London teaching hospital. She had been called in as an outside 'consultant' to address the chronic anxiety and high staff turn-over among the nurses. Her analysis of the situation is a Kleinian one in the tradition of Bion (1961) and Jaques (1955). Basically, she argues that stresses within the nursing organisation need to be understood at both the individual and collective level. At the individual level primitive anxieties, deriving from the savage world of early object relationships, are aroused by the stressful nature of the nursing task (exposure to physical damage and death), and these anxieties give rise to primitive splitting and projective defence mechanisms which are aimed at evading the anxiety rather than defeating it. This, of course, is largely an unconscious process. What then happens collectively, over time, is that these primitive defences are incorporated into the structure of the nursing organisation so that they become in effect 'institutionalised'. This means that the entire 'social system' of the nursing staff operates as a defence against very powerful and deep-rooted collective anxieties. Once established, this defensive system becomes an objective reality which then controls the ways in which the professional task is performed and which is extremely resistant to change. It sets the scene for every new entrant to the profession and may impede their personal development and psychic integration.

Menzies examines in detail some of the day-to-day manifestations of such a defensive system, highlighting such phenomena as the splitting of the nurse–patient relationship, detachment and denial of feelings, the attempt to eliminate decisions by ritual task-performance, and avoidance of change. Clearly much of what she says can just as easily be applied to other professions which expose themselves to human suffering (cf. Menzies Lyth *at al.*, 1988). We shall explore some of the social work equivalents of these defensive patterns below.

The effect of organisations upon workers

Looking first at how society and social welfare organisations act upon social workers, several themes may be identified.

Control of social workers. We have already illustrated society's dependence on social work and the ambivalence attached to this reliance. This ambivalence finds expression in the organisation of social services. A first characteristic is rigidity and conservatism which betrays a fear of creativity, innovation and change (Lomas, 1987). Agencies are designed hierarchically, for stability. Rules, hierarchy, bureaucracy and procedures are strongly emphasised, to contain dissent and to produce passive practitioners. Whilst some stability is essential, the absence of openness to change and flexibility, to curiosity about the effectiveness of services and impact on the workforce of delivering such services, promotes not stability but 'stuckness', demoralisation and an inability to meet new demands. Practitioners are pulled down by, sucked into and ultimately collude with organisational practices (Preston-Shoot, 1989). Discrimination against certain user groups, inappropriate placements born of a shortage of resources or even a failure to observe minimum statutory obligations (such as child care reviews) are accepted as social workers' professional assessments are compromised by what agencies will provide.

Moreover, perhaps for fear of the feelings which might emerge and disable the organisation, there is a marked reluctance to consider the needs and feelings of practitioners. The human element involved in service delivery is denied. Despite calls to humanise welfare organisations, to attend to process as well as outcome (Douglas *et al.*, 1988), maintenance needs of staff continue to be overshadowed by the demands of the tasks. This is reflected in decreasing training opportunities, continuing complaints about the adequacy of supervision beyond monitoring the performance of statutory obligations, and such practices as level three staff being expected to manage with reduced supervision or residential staff being asked to work alone and without training with sexually abused and/or aggressive children. This is tantamount to abuse of staff (Preston-Shoot, 1988). Organisational priorities have become skewed for fear of either being unable to complete the task or getting it wrong. In this way tasks are emphasised at the expense of staff care and development. The stress on practitioners cannot be seen as organisations are playing out a defence mechanism on staff. Organisations are defending against uncertainty, insecurity and the volume of responsibilities required to be met with diminishing resources. The experience of workers remains unacknowledged whilst sweeping claims continue to be made for what agencies can do: more and more with less and less. A feared calamity, that of not being able to complete the task and unleashing powerful emotions from public and/or staff, is avoided by means of this required relationship.

An example of this process is how managers manage departmental reorganisations. Rational explanations predominate. Despite the loyalty, shared culture and feelings invested in working groups to be found in teams, surfacing in resistance to or unease about change, this attachment behaviour is rarely acknowledged and worked through. Any reorganisation will involve staff in a mourning process, and will provoke distress, uncertainty and fears about survival and ability to cope. These feelings of anger, despair and adjustment, associated with loss and change, must be acknowledged and worked through if an effective workforce is to be created.

Control of users. We have already seen how what users may expect from organisations depends in large measure on which action orientations predominate. Despite working concepts such as contracts (Corden and Preston-Shoot, 1987) and approaches to defining the work which place users at the centre of deciding 'what, how, why and when' (Mullender and Ward, 1985), the emphasis on partnership and/or user self-direction is by no means widely or consistently practised. Organisations are still predominantly service- not user-led, resources- not needs-led. Rather than providing services as of right, the area of social services is becoming increasingly residual, necessary only where other forms of care, usually by the family, have broken down or are unavailable. This emphasis on containment and limitation permeates organisational procedures and structures: ideologies of need, reception area arrangements, lack of publicity about services available or even lack of consultation about the type of services needed. Perhaps for fear of opening the floodgates to demand, procedures and structures are fashioned as defences against such anxiety.

Control of the work. Ideologies and working practices are used to control the work and the anxieties evoked by it. Volume is controlled by problems and tasks being interpreted through ideologies of need (G. Smith and Harris, 1972). Services may be limited and justified on the basis of economics rather than efficiency or effectiveness. Need may be similarly limited by being defined not by service-users but service-providers, and by being filtered through moral terminology (are users deserving?) and procedures emphasising strict eligibility criteria (are the causes of this need justifiable? Are the resources available?)

Ideologies and working practices are also used to 'control' the anxieties evoked by the work. Office arrangements may be designed to achieve withdrawal from users and their emotional world. Procedures may be used to provide an illusion of proper order, whereby the rational is elevated above unconscious processes to sustain the myth of being in control and having the answers, when the realities of human nature and of practice might suggest otherwise.

The effect of workers upon organisations

Turning to how social workers act on the organisation to cope with the anxiety of work, again several themes can be identified. Some of these processes, adopted by practitioners to counteract insecurity and impotence, are also used by entire organisations to provide 'as if' security. This, in fact, restricts effectiveness, acting as a massive defence structure to fend off anxiety, doubt and uncertainty, and to cope with the collective anxieties of the organisation's members (Jaques, 1955; Menzies, 1970). The themes are set out below (M. Williams, 1966; Mattinson and Sinclair, 1979; Addison, 1982; Reder, 1986).

° Delusional certainty: for instance, children always tell the truth rather than children have a right to be believed.
° Directive authoritarianism: expertise and positional authority are emphasised, and the expression of emotions is avoided.
° Adhesion: doubts and alternatives are not considered. One path is followed exclusively.
° Bureaucratic rigidity: tight control is emphasised rather than innovation, creativity or curiosity. It is designed to eliminate

human error and ensure that risk-taking is minimised. There is little discussion about the work.

° Safety first, positive or negative defensive practice (Harris, 1987): everything is investigated and several types of investigative procedures are used; removal into institutional care may occur even though inappropriate; rehabilitation may be deferred; weekly visiting without clear reasons for such frequency and even though this may increase client feelings of inadequacy, raise the likelihood of worker burn-out, and limit the effectiveness of the work because interventions are not given time to have an effect. Cases are rarely closed. Too much, too soon, for too long are the characteristics of involvement.

° Distance: people are placed in categories, usually by type of service. Presenting problems are worked with, other needs being ignored to prevent workers feeling overwhelmed and to enable them to cope with the emotional effects of the work. Practical services and stereotyped solutions/approaches are employed.

° Reaction formation: hostile feelings, fear, anxiety are denied and translated into a placatory, 'nice' position.

° Deflection: the authority role is avoided, central issues are not confronted, positive feelings are emphasised.

° Projection: clients are seen as hostile, aggressive, non-motivated or manipulative, to enable workers to retain acceptable concepts about themselves and their work.

° Escape into management or training.

° Denial of expertise: other professions or agencies take over roles such as therapeutic work with abused children and their families.

° Arrogance and 'as if' omnipotence: often masks denial by workers of the work's emotional effects on them.

° Cynicism and flight out of social work. Alternatively, a retreat into a paranoid position of suspicion where bad feelings are projected, often into management, and then attacked for being unhelpful (Jaques, 1955). Management may mirror this by blaming social workers, its own projections creating a symmetrical relationship. Alternatively, management may adopt a complementary position by placating practitioners.

These defences should be regarded as understandable responses to anxieties whose sources are felt to be beyond control (Jaques, 1955). They do, however, make change difficult if they are not confronted.

Only by confronting them will practitioners eventually be able to tolerate and deal more effectively with the anxieties evoked by the work. That is because defences, to remain effective, have to be escalated and individuals eventually reach a point where this is no longer possible, certainly not without great cost to themselves. Failure to confront these processes leaves practitioners with a treble dose: the anxiety evoked by the work; the anxiety caused by the tension of having to maintain and escalate the defences; and the lack of work satisfaction inherent in the operation of these defence systems (Braye, 1978).

It should be clear, therefore, how social workers and their organisations, ostensibly established as solutions, may become part of the problem. Equally, social workers cannot avoid failure. Procedures, however exact and tight, will not necessarily prevent abuse or tragedy. The human element cannot be removed from social work or from its interaction with users. Tragedies will not be prevented by being regarded solely as examples of human error or individual deviance. What, then, can practitioners do? How might they survive and intervene more effectively in this scenario?

Survival and intervention skills

Social work is enmeshed in dense, complex issues around power, struggles for domination, values and rights. It is regaled by all shades of opinion. However, in the debate about what social work is and should be, social workers have largely been victims and reactive rather than central and proactive (Rojek, 1986). They have been blown hither and thither, as if rudderless. Social workers must reclaim the central ground and, in particular, point out the difficulties they currently face. Rather than providing 'as if' reassurance, they must urge a major rethink and clear mandate from society (Parton, 1986) ; this should not be a further tightening of procedures or redoubling of efforts or contradictory expectations, which will merely perpetuate a spiralling of more of the same without end, but a recognition that, if social work is to become a force for change, debates need to be resolved. Additionally, social workers may usefully adopt a meta position in relation to their own dilemmas and ask future-oriented questions (Penn, 1985). The future is not yet set. Thus, what type of service does society want and can social work best provide? This approach requires social workers to avoid blaming and to positively connote or define society's dilemmas and present responses. It requires one or more hypotheses for the present position and questions which direct attention to the anxieties and defences used against them. Such an approach encourages a meta position, opening up dialogue and potentially new solutions to contemporary problems or dilemmas. It emphasises curiosity rather than a headlong rush into solutions.

This approach requires that social workers, rather than accepting double-binds, vicious circles and projections as given, step outside the frame and, from a meta position, review their dilemmas and name the game. Rather than perpetuating the game, such a manoeuvre enables social workers to recognise the dynamic interrelationship between social work, social services organisations and society, and to understand what society repudiates and projects on to them (Blech, 1981).

Returning to the two figures presented above, it does not matter where social workers intervene in the circular interactions. A difference begets a difference. The system cannot remain the same following an intervention. The objective is to create an open system, based on inputs and communication about interactions, rather than to maintain a closed system where social work either fits with society's requirements (a complementary relationship) or vies to establish a relationship on its own terms (symmetrical interaction).

The message is that social work must refuse to accept the terms of the game dictated to it (Treacher, 1986), examine its interactions and maintain manoeuvrability. Two groups of strategies, which overlap, suggest themselves.

Organisational strategies

The avoidance of self-sacrifice. Social work has exaggerated grossly its ability to effect individual and social change, a characteristic not uncommon in emerging or insecure professions. Yet, although unable to achieve many of the changes desired by itself or society, social work has retained such objectives and inhabited unrealistic aims and roles, often as vaguely defined as the problems for which solutions are sought. Negative results have produced not curiosity and questioning but redoubled efforts. More of the same will not effect change.

Social work cannot achieve change alone, especially social change which requires entry into political processes. Social work must avoid sweeping claims. It must broadcast its limits: what it can and cannot influence and affect. It must not be afraid to identify reorganisations as modifications because of financial constraints rather than claim them as changes towards better services. It must verbalise the limitations placed on its work by political values and limited resources.

Clarity of role and recognition of the limits of responsibility. Social workers must say what is possible with the resources available, what they can do and what they need to be able to work effectively. Reclaiming realism is an urgent task. Social work cannot solve alone mental illness, poverty, inadequate housing provision or deficiencies in welfare provision, or the effects of any of these. By not defining how much responsibility social work can realistically be expected to assume, by accepting all referrals and by not defining who cannot be assisted when, social workers have become easy scapegoats for all failures, and allowed society to maintain its myth of being a caring culture. It is a substantial contribution to burn-out.

The answer is not always to try harder but rather to communicate the nature of the task. The answer is not to try to meet all needs or answer all questions but to delineate what can be achieved and what tests of outcome are acceptable. Disappointing results must be framed in their context to avoid increasing defensiveness (Malan, 1963; Sheldon, 1986). Responsibility must be placed where it belongs: to management belongs the responsibility for prioritising and deciding action; to social workers belongs the responsibility for assessment and recommendations; to users belongs the responsibility for change. Social work can facilitate change but cannot make change happen. Thus it is to a family and not to social workers that one might pose the question (Mason, 1983) 'What do you think needs to happen in order that members of a case conference do not have to be so concerned about you?' The process is one of disentangling vast expectations.

It is into social, political and organisational arenas, therefore, that social work should take fundamental questions about social welfare services. Again we take child care as our focus but the same questions must be debated about the role, especially regarding statutory intervention, of social services in relation to older people and people with mental health problems or learning difficulties.

1. What risks can social workers take? This question is currently avoided by scapegoating professionals.
2. Given the limitations of the accuracy of professional judgement and of the state of knowledge, and given the inevitability of risk and uncertainty, when should social workers intervene?
3. What do we mean by a child's welfare?
4. What are acceptable standards of parental care?
5. What is seriousness?
6. How should the tension between rights and risks, care and control, parents' rights and childrens' rights, economics and effectiveness be resolved?
7. Should resources or needs shape service provision?
8. What are acceptable standards of service provision? are the risks which follow from workers and services being overloaded and underresourced acceptable?

Intervening in organisations. Social workers must analyse and challenge their organisations, especially when they feel invited to overturn or abandon their professional judgement or to make decisions other than on the basis of their professional knowledge, skills, value and/or theoretical base. It is easy to become submerged into role rather than struggle with it. However, social workers must retain and advertise criticism of agency policy when it de-skills them (for example, by not providing training or adequate supervision); when it compromises professional work and assessment (for instance, by endorsing inappropriate placements); when there are no resources to meet assessed needs; when hierarchical boundaries are such that people are inaccessible, physically or emotionally. Social workers must refuse to be marginalised and compromised, otherwise the effects on them will mirror those of service-users who are amongst the most marginalised members of society. This involves staying meta to the system: identifying the predominant operational culture or action orientations in the agency; retaining professional assessments; identifying problem systems; retaining curiosity and asking awkward questions. In other words, rather than simply carrying out agency functions, it means being a change agent with the agency as the target system. It involves putting feedback into the system, especially to managers and politicians. It represents an attempt to keep the system open rather than colluding with defences inspired by the context of practice. For example, in a debate on social work in health care, a senior manager stated that social work services to some client groups could no longer be justified. Social work, in our view, should not be making such decisions but rather be identifying needs and asking politicians and society why these needs cannot be met. In another instance, senior managers denied any shortage of foster placements, blaming social workers' incompetence for any difficulties. One office's response was a memo to the director (from the team to avoid any scapegoating of individuals as a management defence) positively connoting his concern for good practice in finding substitute carers and, therefore, listing every example of difficulties in finding foster homes and each instance of an inappropriate placement.

Locating social work in the system. In case conferences, social workers are only one party to decisions. In much work, especially child abuse, other agencies and factors join with social work to form a system. Presenting a systems view provides a more complete picture. For example, in addition to the practice dilemmas inherent in social work, the ambiguity of present child care law (Lyon, 1989) and the training and status differentials between social workers and other professionals (especially medics) complicates interactions in child protection work.

Central to each of these strategies is an educative role. Social work cannot control people. More resources, lower caseloads, induction programmes for new employees, team away-days to review progress and set objectives, and staff involvement in planning services will not prevent tragedies but will improve practice (Zastrow, 1984; Thoburn, 1986). Expectations must be realistic; society's projections must be given back.

Social workers, if they are to sustain their commitment, need hope, motivation, validation and realism. Stress must be recognised. Managers carry the reponsibility of considering emotions, process and dynamics alongside the task. For this they will need outside consultants who can provide the holding necessary when feelings are expressed and who can enable staff to identify more effective ways of coping with the anxieties, emotions and projections involved in the work.

Individual strategies

Reflection. The work and dynamics of organisations touch every practitioner. Rather than defend against such feelings by repression, denial or projection, social workers must be enabled to acknowledge and deal with the feelings and anxieties if they are to avoid demoralisation, 'stuckness' or burn-out. Practitioners should go meta and use their internal supervisor (Casement, 1985) to ask themselves questions about their work and its effects. Thus: what is happening? What part am I playing? What parts am I being invited or expected to play? What do I feel about this? What might I do about this? Why am I visiting now/so often? What are my goals? Will this intervention facilitate or frustrate achievement of my goals?

Coping. Again, social workers can usefully focus on key questions: what can I change out there/in me/in my agency? Who can help me? What positive reframes can I find for what is out there/in me/in my agency? How will I know when I am feeling defensive, what will be its manifestations and to whom can I talk about it? Social workers, to remain effective and to hold to their task, must express uncertainty and anxiety when they feel it (for instance, feeling intimidated by violence or its prospect). Equally, they must be enabled to define their tasks and purposes realistically, to fulfil what they can fulfil rather than to aspire to what cannot be achieved. They must be enabled to say 'no' and to work with any need in themselves to be helpful. Their responsibility must not be allowed to become unlimited.

Action plans. These are useful for reflection and positive individual and/or collective, personal professional and/or work decision-making. The model given here can be used in relation to any focus including training, supervision, direct work with service-users, self and team functioning (Preston-Shoot and Williams, 1987).

Step 1: What is my current situation as regards...?
Step 2: What is my desired situation as regards...?
Step 3: What are my objectives?
Step 4: What is my plan? How do I intend to achieve my objectives? What tasks and timescales are appropriate?

Step 5: How will I know that I am making progress towards my objectives and desired situation? What indicators will be useful?

Step 6: Who else do I want to involve and how?

Step 7: When and with whom will I review and reset my action plan?

Social workers are human beings and have a right to be good enough. Based on an awareness of their location in a wider context, social workers must communicate openly and challengingly with themselves, their managers, users and the public.

6

Making sense of social work tasks

This chapter will apply psychodynamic and systemic concepts to clarify dynamic processes in direct work between social workers and service-users. Dynamics, if not identified and understood, can be destructive since they are likely to be acted out rather than used as information on how to proceed. In a meeting to allocate places in an elderly persons' home, a team leader had four urgent referrals for the one available place. Each social worker, on presenting their assessment, was heavily criticised for ineffective work: for failing to explore fully options other than residential care; for emphasising a user's wishes above needs, or both above available resources; for overinvolvement rather than dispassionate evaluation. The workers felt angry, confused, distressed and de-skilled. What were the dynamics being dramatised here? Confronted with an impossible task and feeling unable to leave the field by communicating the difficulties to senior managers, the team leader used denial and projection as defences: denial of the anxieties evoked by the situation, and projection of 'bad' feelings about the task on to social workers where the 'badness', in the form of inadequate assessments, could be more safely challenged. The team leader thereby accomplished the task of allocating the one available place by accommodating to the situation and identifying with senior managers such that he was more aggressor than victim. The defence, however, was counterproductive, creating distance between social workers and the team leader, and uncertainty about how to undertake assessments for Part III accommodation.

The power of dynamics is frequently illustrated in child protection where the emotions elicited in or encountered by social workers can impede their use of authority. When investigating non-accidental injury, how many social workers have not struggled to outline the reasons for their presence and the extent of their powers and statutory obligations to parents? How many have not, on occasions, steered the conversation into safer waters for fear of the effect on them or on their relationship with clients? Whether a defence in aid of survival or accommodating to the power of the abuser, it illustrates that dynamics can prevent change and sabotage effective work.

For some individuals or families social work has become a way of life, a ritual. Long-term support has failed to produce change and appears aimless, lacking any methodology or rationale for the structure and content of the work (Smale, 1983).

These observations permit one conclusion. Social work can either become part of the problem or part of the solution; a mechanism for homeostasis and more of the same, or for change. Without conceptual frameworks social workers are more likely to maintain or exacerbate problems rather than contribute to solutions.

Referral games

Some referrals to social workers are ambiguous and vague. On whose behalf the referral was made, whether the 'client' was aware of the approach, and the exact nature of any difficulties seem unclear. The referrer's solution is, however, very apparent: social work intervention, immediately. Not that the referrer is always clear about what this may achieve; it is just a solution. If social workers are not to become entangled and embroiled in stories and inflated expectations, and to lose thereby some leverage to influence systems and achieve change, they must recognise and understand 'referral games', where games are interactions played according to rules, including a rule that 'forbids' discussion of the game, and which can only be ended by stepping outside them.

A psychodynamic frame enables practitioners to respond to the referrer's defences and anxieties, and to recognise the threatening nature of change and the resistances which can, therefore, ensue. Working systemically enables practitioners to maintain manoeuvrability by considering who the client really is, illuminating the dynamics and context behind the referral, and deciding where and how to intervene on the basis of this information and understanding. It is the context which gives a referral meaning. The focus, therefore, shifts from the subject of the referral to a systems view where the referrer's perspective is but one definition. This approach, by focusing on and possibly intervening in interactions between referrer and referred, helps social workers to avoid becoming triangulated (sought as an ally by one against the other, or by both to stabilise and 'save' their conflictual, unstable situation: Carl and Jurkovic, 1983).

Three games involve dynamics between an individual or family and a referrer; three centre on an individual; one concerns dynamics between an individual and family system.

Game one: this case/my need is really urgent

Obviously some referrals must be responded to immediately. However, information contained in others may not support the pressures for immediate action which accompany them. Yet practitioners feel pressurised into accepting uncertain, vague work for prompt attention. What dynamics are operating here?

Referrers and users may feel it necessary to exaggerate the importance of a referral in order to secure a service, often by using 'dangerous' labels: this client is at risk; this situation is worrying (Coulshed and Abdullah-Zadeh, 1985). Exactly who is at risk from whom or what, or why the situation is so concerning or urgent, or what social workers are expected to do and whether users want their involvement may all be unclear. However, acting on the basis of such labels is difficult to avoid.

Alternatively, the referrer may frame the problem as urgent either to deny their anxiety or 'stuckness' with their role in the situation, or to avoid confrontation entering their relationship with a client. The referrer may feel him- or herself to be the loser in the individual/ family–referrer system and be wanting to recruit a social worker to 'save' or 'strengthen' their position. For instance, a health visitor repeatedly referred a mother, without her knowledge, for social work support. Mildly mentally handicapped, she had two children about whom the health visitor had become 'concerned' because their father, once very involved in child care, had left the home. Unable to see the mother for several weeks, the health visitor insisted that social workers should investigate this 'worrying situation'. This illustrates how practitioners, confronted with their anxiety, can minimise an individual's strengths and maximise pathology, and how, in referring on, practitioners can maintain problems or escalate situations because of their inability or unwillingness to confront dynamics between themselves and their clients.

Key questions to ask are: at risk from what? Whose urgency? Who has the problem? Why the referral and why now? What does the 'client' want and what do they perceive the referrer to be concerned about? For whom are the problems more acute? (See Blech, 1981). Such questions enable social workers to clarify risks and needs, to communicate an understanding of the referrer's difficulties, to frame their work and concern in wanting to refer on positively, and to suggest tasks which may not involve allocation to social workers. The questions help to avoid network confusion. They identify where the referrer is in relation to the user, and open up the possibility of sharing anxiety and perspectives, where possible with referrer and user present together (Mason, 1983).

Game two: you are the expert

Social workers have particular expertise and statutory duties. For instance, courts may request social enquiry reports or place adolescents on supervision. However, attributing an expert position to social workers may be a defensive device. The referrer may be seeking to avoid responsibility, perhaps for resolving their anxiety or 'stuckness' in a situation, an agenda which they may not share either with the social worker or the suggested beneficiary of social work intervention. The referral is sometimes accompanied with an implicit invitation: 'see it my way'. In accepting such a referral the social worker may find the referrer suddenly uninvolved: change becomes the responsibility of the social worker. Alternatively, social workers may be asked to mediate in problems between referrers and individuals/families, to stabilise conflict or diffuse stress in the guise of wanting change. It is not so much change that is being requested as the avoidance of anxiety or conflict in the referrer–user system. The danger here is that social workers can become triangulated and part of the problem they are treating, either by taking on and acting out the clients' conflict with the referrers, allowing users to sit back, or by struggling to effect change in the user system, allowing referrers to opt out and preserve their position within the user system (Carl and Jurkovic, 1983). In each scenario users and referrers divert and avoid their conflict by routing it through a third person/agency. The social worker is recruited to 'protect' the user–referrer relationship, just as a 'problem child' may be used to 'rescue' a marriage by diverting attention away from it. Needless to say, the social worker makes no progress despite expending considerable energy.

On accepting such referrals social workers may initially be greeted then disqualified by referrer or users or both, and ultimately defeated and scapegoated (Selvini Palazzoli *et al.*, 1980b). As Bion observed (1961), dependence on an individual or institution is often ambivalent, quiet or open hostility accompanying requests for a specified intervention. This is especially probable where the referrer provides stability, a homeostatic prop for the user system and where social workers, if they refuse to accept a similar script, will find themselves split off as the 'bad' professionals, the referrer remaining the 'good, helpful' practitioner. To illustrate this phenomenon, a health visitor, who had supported a mother of four children for several years by visiting several times a week, referred the family for 'support'. When the social worker began to work for change with the family, especially in relationships between the mother and step-father and between them and the children, the health visitor and parents formed a coalition against the social worker and actively sabotaged the work. Taking over, effectively ignoring the context of the referral and the resources, difficulties and relationships within the user–referrer system, will not unblock that system and enable it to change or to accomplish its necessary work but rather further de-skill it or confirm it in its present form.

Game three: I am the expert

These referrals are characterised by defensiveness, denial and projection. Typically, the referrer is stating: 'I know what the situation is, it is this...', or 'the real problem is...'. Thus, a school may refer a child because of underachievement and truancy. The school blames the parents who, when interviewed, blame the school (Dowling and Osborne, 1985). Each side seeks to recruit the social worker as an ally. Each is convinced of the correctness of their linear perspective and cannot see the need for a social work assessment. Required action seems obvious to them: change the other party.

If social workers approach such referrals systemically, their focus is on process as much as content, on identifying vicious circles whereby the actions of one (sub-)system feed into and escalate the actions of another (sub-)system. So, the more a parent criticises a child for being withdrawn, the more that child withdraws, so the more that parent criticises the child for not communicating. If, however, social workers accept the referrer's perspective, their responses may ignore the 'client's' perspective and trap them into working at a content level defined by the referrer. Questions to ask might include: how obvious is an older person's need for residential accommodation, as referred by the doctor? What else is in the picture?

In these three games the referrer is, in some senses, the problem. Seeking a particular response, the referrer taps into social work's defensiveness or introjection of dominant expectations projected by society. Social workers can, therefore, find themselves taking on work when they could more beneficially intervene in the referrer or referrer–user system.

Game four: help me – don't stop

Some users present problem after problem. They are frequent callers. When closure is discussed or work terminated, their anxiety increases, new problems are presented or old difficulties return, and there occurs regression to a less independent level of functioning. This behaviour may represent an acting-out of past attachment experiences, a clinging to assuage fear, a defence in effect against the fear of disintegration (Lomas, 1987). The social worker appears to provide a holding function. Acknowledging and working with these feelings becomes important, therefore, if users are to develop a sustaining sense of self which is not dependent on the holding provided by social workers (Skidmore, 1988).

Game five: help me – if you dare

Some users' experiences of attachments will have left them feeling ambivalent or insecure in close relationships. They may believe that they were or are acceptable only if 'good'. Some will, therefore, strenuously attempt to split off and repress their 'negative' feelings, or will project their 'bad objects' on to others and react to them there. Others will deliberately emphasise these aspects of themselves to test the social worker's commitment. Examples of this phenomenon are clients missing appointments, raising anxiety, or showing antipathy and ambivalence. Vulnerability (in the form of important and usually hidden fears and feelings) is projected on to the worker, who is left feeling impotent. This feeling is what the user experiences but dare not acknowledge. Once again, acknowledging the process of scripts from past attachments being transferred on to the social worker is crucial if progress is to be made in forming an effective helping relationship.

Game six: help me – don't you dare

For some individuals a dominant motive is to avoid attachments by withdrawal or compulsive self-reliance. Having experienced attachments as dangerous, they seek to avoid any repetition of rejection or feelings of worthlessness, and will expect social workers to interact with them as if a mirror image of past caregivers. Thus the transferred attachment dynamic here is one of avoidance or resistance against a close relationship. Appointments may be kept erratically or the positives of the relationship denied. The individual's behaviour may invite rejection or be rejecting. They may dismiss the work and worker as valueless. Failing to appreciate this dynamic may lead workers to attribute negative qualities to these individuals, such as 'resistant' or 'unmotivated', and to respond accordingly, thereby confirming the individual's perception of relationships.

The withdrawal, or compulsive self-reliance, acts as a solution which the individual will be frightened of abandoning. It may be a solution to a fear of being harmed or of being harmful. Either way, closeness will be both longed-for and feared, making for in-out behaviour in relationships. Two approaches to this dynamic may prove helpful: first, acknowledging and reflecting upon the transference (discussing, for instance, the person's history and how this may be shaping present behaviour); second, especially where this reflection does not shift the person's perception of the worker, a deliberate prescription of no change in order to overcome resistance to change (Cade, 1979; Cade and Southgate, 1979). If the individual co-operates with the prescription, they demonstrate some control over their behaviour when they may previously have denied this; if they change, difference has been achieved.

Within these three games users seek from social workers the consistency, care and reliability which others have not provided whilst, sometimes simultaneously, expecting no difference in this new relationship and, possibly, 'punishing' social workers for (or attempting to press-gang them into) repeating the failures of past care-givers. In that sense, users are attempting to transfer or reproduce scripts whilst practitioners are endeavouring to enable the creation and working through of corrective scripts.

Game seven: cure him/her, or, resolve this 'one' problem

This final game relates to dynamics operating within the individual–family system. Consider the apparently straightforward request from a family for residential accommodation for an elderly relative, or a family who insist that moving house or receiving one child into care will resolve everything. The implicit message is 'do not change us'. The dynamic operating here is 'detouring the conflict' by means of triangulation. Conflict is avoided and denied by the recruitment of a third person or issue as the source of the difficulties. Thus, this game is frequently accompanied by the injunction 'don't you dare' since, if the problem is resolved, the detoured avoided issues will become more exposed. The system believes that it cannot survive without the function of distance or conflict regulation provided by the third person or issue. Hence, a family having demanded that one 'problem child' be received into care is very soon likely to demand that child's return home or to produce another problem in order not to have to focus on the avoided feelings and relationships. Consequently, some practitioners use paradox to overcome the resistance to change which accompanies this game, and to avoid a power struggle over problem definitions between them and the family (Papp, 1980). Key skills are to engage everyone in the individual–family system and to explore the context and interactions behind the referral.

Key questions in the analysis of dynamics underpinning referral games become:

* What is the problem?
* What does the problem trigger or suppress?

* Who referred and why? What is the position of the referrer in the referred person's system (Selvini Palazzoli *et al.*, 1980b)?
* Why is the problem a problem? Are individuals or agencies overreacting to ordinary life-cycle developments (Coulshed and Abdullah-Zadeh, 1985)?
* Who is it (most) a problem for? Whose urgency?
* Why now (anniversary reactions; life-cycle changes)?
* Where does the problem reside? Who has the problem? In which system and why?
* How is the referral made? What might that suggest about the referrer and the referred system?
* Who most/least wants change?
* What is the referral for? What does the referrer want? What role is being offered to a social worker? Is it appropriate for social workers to take this on? What could the referrer do?
* Is the referrer stuck (no resources, poor supervision, anxious, a homeostatic prop in the user-system)?
* Is the referral being accepted because of statutory obligations and pressure, or because it is viewed as appropriate (Reder, 1986)? If the latter, what definition of appropriateness is being used?

This analysis enables social workers to formulate hypotheses about the referral and the situation. These provide early guidance on whether, where and how to intervene.

The helping encounter

Offering and seeking help evokes emotions, triggers memories and behaviours, and creates pressures for both users and workers which influence them either towards or away from effective work. Accordingly, an interactional view (Casement, 1985) is required of the professional–client relationship. The encounter is very complex, involving a two-way unconscious communication between both parties. It is, in effect, a co-evolving system involving transference, countertransference and projective identification. How and why does a worker develop a particular feeling or attitude towards a client, or a particular belief about them? What forms of communication cross the gap between client and worker, in each direction? How does change occur? The way worker and client interact with and combine in this system and become part of it will determine how it will develop and change.

The worker's perspective

Think about defences, transference and countertransference. One principle of systems theory is that 'you cannot not communicate'. Every communication contains communications about feelings, the content and the process which may or may not accord with each other (Watzlawick *et al.*, 1967).

Before service-users encounter social workers, much will have been communicated and interpreted which will influence attitudes and approaches to subsequent contact (the ease of locating the office, the reception area, staff attitudes, interviewing facilities); all these convey messages about the extent to which departments and staff are open or closed and defensive. Equally, practitioners will inevitably communicate much about their process as they explore the content of a referral. In particular, pressures of work can create closure: practitioners adopting specific strategies to reduce the volume of (or emotional experiences evoked by) the work. Rather than being open to inputs from users, workers construct a defensive, closed system based on one or more of five strategies (M. Williams, 1966): first, control, a directive, authoritarian approach where staff emphasise expertise and discourage emotional expression. Solutions are prescribed and applied with little concentration on users' feelings; it is a matter-of-fact approach.

Second is withdrawal, where staff emphasise procedures and an intellectual, textbook approach rather than use of self. Third comes the strategy of replacing challenge, confrontation and use of authority with being liked and developing positive, friendly feelings. Next there are pressures of work and feelings of responsibility which interact circularly with feeling drained, each reinforcing the other. This becomes reflected in anxiety about dependency. The result can be reliance on short-term work and underplaying the importance of attachment rather than acknowledging the need for a secure base responsive to users' needs and sensitive to their feelings if they are to relinquish dysfunctional behaviour patterns (Bowlby, 1979; Skidmore, 1988). Equally, social workers may assume unrealistic levels of responsibility, doing things for users rather than creating a facilitating environment in which change may occur. Both responses emanate from social workers' anxieties about making a mess, or defences against demands and unremitting need. Each can render social work part of the problem unless they are recognised and resolved.

The final defensive strategy is to prescribe solutions without fully defining the problem. Paradoxically, being helpful is not always helpful (Crowther, 1988) if practitioners are so preoccupied with how to help, with solutions, that action is contemplated before assessment is completed. This certainty, 'knowing' a situation even before it is explored, may arise from a worker's need to be perceived as helpful, to be liked or from discomfort in the job. It may spring from avoidance, arising out of the countertransference of emotional or behavioural reactions to material, or from a wish to avoid experiencing emotions which may be triggered by proximity to a user's feelings and problems. A user's pressures for immediate answers or stereotypes about case situations may produce it. Each is an illustration of closure. The last, 'as if' familiarity based on assumed similarity with previous situations, demonstrates the dangers of preconceptions which encroach upon openness to individuality and an acceptance of difference and otherness in others (Casement, 1985). If workers succumb to the pressure to provide immediate answers, often presented as an appeal to their expert knowledge, users (and referrers) may be further de-skilled. Their confidence, self-worth and belief in their ability to exercise control and influence over their lives may be undermined and they may fail to find solutions or directions which feel authentic to them. Curiosity and exploration are replaced by impositions. Alternatively, the appeal to workers' expert knowledge may be a device to neutralise it. Succumbing to this, workers may find themselves incorporated into the system, their manoeuvrability lost. Staying meta with remarks such as 'Who can say, what do you think?' gives workers more information about attitudes, beliefs and dynamics within the system. Providing or suggesting solutions prematurely can leave users baffled, uncertain of how they have been reached. They may inhibit users from describing their feelings and situation and, indeed, leave them feeling defeated and deflated, more distant from rather than closer to social workers (Casement, 1985).

Premature solutions can result in less useful interventions, usually practical as opposed to emotional, or frustrate progress as action will have preceded agreement on problem-definition.

The maxim should be to hurry slowly, allowing users or referrers to describe the situation before identifying the target system. This is what Reay (1986) calls reflective open practice: each problem is unique, no problem is taken as given. The problem is to define the problem. This requires openness: not retaining one hypothesis, however useful it may seem, but exploring other possibilities; not closing areas or feelings down by reassurance or denial but addressing dynamics such as those in the worker–user relationship. For instance, a male social worker working with a woman who has been sexually abused must acknowledge and explore the transference relationship (power, gender, boundary and attachment dynamics) rather than give immediate reassurances or deny the presence and influence of such issues in the helping encounter. Reassurance rarely reassures. Moreover, it may be a counter-transference response, an urge to make something better and to avoid exposure to painful areas rather than to 'stay with it'.

The users' perspective

In every communication there is information about content and process. Besides looking at what is manifest, it pays to consider what is not so obvious.

Past experiences of or stereotypes and fantasies about social workers, stigma, gender, social class, race or age; these can all influence how users approach social workers. Initial presentation may be dominated by here-and-now anxieties:

1. vagueness, from 'Dare I tell you?' to 'What will be the effect on me?';
2. flooding the social worker with information, a reflection of feeling overwhelmed;
3. demands for action, a response to conflicting feelings the user cannot resolve;
4. guilt or shame about 'need', prompting the user to decline further appointments.

Equally, initial presentation and subsequent responses to social workers can be governed by behaviour devised as a solution to previous stressful relationships and now applied inappropriately. To use systemic phraseology, it is a redundant solution. Defences such as rationalisation, splitting, or idealisation and accommodation to the social worker's suggestions may be designed to minimise pain, fear and loss. Put another way, the behaviour may be based on feelings that calamity will result or hidden feelings emerge, intra- and/or interpersonally, if users abandon the assumed 'required' relationship and seek to negotiate a relationship felt by them to be more congenial by confronting their own fears and anxieties and the behaviour of other people with whom they are in relation. If social workers are to enable users to integrate these feelings and modify scripts, as well as to facilitate effective work on the content of the referral, these dynamics must be worked through. For example, users often believe that cases are closed or workers leave because they, the users, are bad. They may even expect to be left on the basis of previous attachment experiences. Rational explanations alone, concerned with having completed the work or workers having obtained promotion, will not defuse these feelings.

A systems view

A systems view suggests a circular rather than a linear perspective on causation. Referrals are usually presented as the problem residing in one location or person. As such they promote the illusion of a beginning. For instance, parents or teachers refer a 'problem child'. However, rather than being the cause of problems, the child's behaviour may be an attempted solution: how to be or survive in their family and/or school systems, their behaviour representing the best adaptation which seems available. Again, an individual experiencing marital difficulties is also under stress at work. Which is cause and which effect will be difficult to establish with any certainty. In any case, intervening in one area will mean that the circular pattern cannot stay the same.

Circular causality is preferred because, in the functioning of systems, one part cannot be understood separately from the others. Each influences the behaviour of the others, so what information social workers collect depends on whom they ask. Punctuations of events, of where things began, will be different according to where people are located in the system. The problem, therefore, resides more in interactions and differences of punctuation or perspective, whether intrapersonal (internal object relations) or interpersonal (between different sub-systems).

Intervening with the 'problem person' alone leaves essential relationships and systems dynamics unchanged. It is a more-of-the-same solution, treating symptom not systems, and may actually prevent change. Arguably, this is why delinquency programmes are so unsuccessful, why recidivism and reconviction rates are high, or why the treatment of depression by antidepressants fails so often to produce a sustained cure. Sadly, the approach is seductive: something appears to be done. It may shield agencies from difficult work and protect society from uncomfortable truths. Equally, failure can be blamed on recalcitrant users and ineffective professionals.

Framing and addressing problems interactionally requires, first, that social workers monitor their own reactions to and roles in a situation. What roles are they being press-ganged into or led away from? What does the situation trigger in them? What problems or issues does the problem create for them? What information does this convey about the situation and about possible responses? Counter-transference reactions are useful information about situational dynamics and are only blocks to effective intervention when unrecognised or ignored.

The use of geneograms, life-story books, reminiscence work and network maps enable social workers to identify members of the system and pertinent themes, patterns and alliances, and to link people into their historical and social context, their strong attachments and conflictual relationships. Such visual aids can powerfully demonstrate the strength and nature of contacts, for instance, or the existence of belief systems carried through several generations, or the dysfunctional nature of too permeable or too rigid boundaries between family members or between a family and wider systems.

Convening referral meetings, family meetings and family–professional system meetings will quickly illustrate the position of individuals and agencies, the nature of their relationships and the roles they play, and the contribution of each system to the maintenance of the difficulties. Such meetings, by obtaining everyone's views on the problems, avoid the danger of colluding with one person's definition of the problem, or with the projection of problems on to one individual. Equally, social workers are less likely to become trapped into being 'omnipotent' saviours, or triangulated between users or between them and other agencies. Rather, such meetings enable social workers to answer why they are involved, for what purpose, how others define their involvement and what others expect of them (Coulshed and Abdullah-Zadeh, 1985; Corden and Preston-Shoot, 1987). Convening the systems also activates the support systems which have resources to assist the user-system. It reduces the likelihood of these support systems acting out disagreements or conflicts or of the user-system splitting professionals into 'good' and 'bad'. It engages everyone in the change process. Social workers may, therefore, more easily retain realistic levels of responsibility by involving others in clarifying problems, expectations, goals and acceptable levels of change, and not become locked into omnipotent frustration where everything seems 'down to them'. Everyone is engaged in clarifying the purpose of the referral, the dynamics within the problem situation, and how and where to intervene (Gorell-Barnes, 1980; Dungworth and Reimers, 1984; Pottle, 1984). There is less likelihood, therefore, that social work will hold back change and create long-term chronicity by shielding others from their responsibility for change and by creating a system where the more social workers help, the more others become de-skilled, demotivated and passive, as if they have no resources or skills (Selvini Palazzoli, 1985).

Several skills facilitate this process of taking a systems view within the helping encounter and convening referral and family–professional system meetings: first, pushing for clarity and specificity, for example: 'What do you mean by problem? Why is this a problem for you?' A useful technique is to 'go one down' at this point. Thus: 'Forgive me, but I do not understand; what is the problem?' Second, workers should recognise in their analysis that their own system may be part of the problem, requiring them to intervene in their own agency. The third skill is to stay meta, not assuming sole responsibility for change and defining purpose of involvement clearly. For instance, if social workers are met with denial, they could ask potential users what they believe other people to be concerned about and what they can do to make these people less concerned. If working with people experiencing depression, they could look for change beyond the individual to wider family, social, economic and political systems. Finally, practitioners should explain the rationale for this approach, in terms of what it clarifies, and positively frame any queries as helpful concerns about work which may need to be undertaken. This may enable workers to move beyond objections to this approach which are founded on an image of social work as a helping profession, which is obliged and duty-bound to accept all requests for intervention as they are framed by those making them.

Assessment

There exists the illusion of the true, correct assessment. This omniscient fantasy and expectation, whilst comfortable for the public, threatens to disable practitioners, inhibiting and stultifying a process which can only be more or less useful and which must be creative and rigorous. In pursuing these objectives, psychodynamic and systemic approaches inform both content and process. Psychodynamic theory sheds light on the process of assessment, on dynamics within the problems being addressed and within the worker–user relationship. Systems theory illuminates the inter-connectedness of systems and how circular patterns maintain and escalate behaviour and interaction.

Assessment: engaging

This opening phase is characterised by separateness: possible reservations about engaging, and anxiety about how one will be seen, how much to disclose and how others will react. There may be an ambivalent dependence: users wanting guidance or assistance but feeling strange and, perhaps, suspicious. They may, therefore, test out the social worker's understanding, reliability and concern, whilst also exploring what is required within the relationship. These are crucial preliminaries, akin to forming and norming in groupwork (Tuckman, 1965). If work is to proceed from a secure base (Bowlby, 1979), a relationship of trust must be established. This experience will also be filtered through other experiences of caregivers, including social workers, which may obstruct seeing this social worker as trustworthy. Such transferences, based on trying to make the present caregiver fit previous experiences, may produce defiant or rejecting behaviour and/or excessive demands. These attachment experiences must be recognised and assuaged if the fear underpinning them is to be diminished and users enabled to move on.

The first step is to elicit the user's preconceptions about social work, social workers and past experiences of help. Seeking help will arouse anxiety and curiosity, perhaps also feelings of shame, guilt or fear of disapproval. Users may feel apprehension about the effect on them or workers of disclosing problems: 'They will take my children away; they will abandon me.' Such feelings may produce defences: comedy; anger; silence; complaints; suppressed fear or criticism, often revealed by users criticising themselves or displacing criticism on to other workers or comparing professionals (Casement, 1985), accommodating to the power and wishes of the worker. These defences must be explored, otherwise they will result in a closed system, one incapable of tolerating the healthy expression of emotions or of modelling interest and acceptance.

In challenging such defences, either directly or by 'going one down' and phrasing comments generally ('In my experience people often...'), workers should assess what attachment behaviours they are encountering, indicate how individuals relate to them, and openly discuss users' feelings about social workers and requesting help. A useful exercise in which to engage jointly is sentence completion, beginning 'I think...; I feel...; I imagine...'. Alternatively, social workers can enquire directly what users fear might happen in this or other relationships if they expressed their feelings or entered into a relationship with them.

The second stage is to clarify why the contact is occurring. This scene-setting may, especially in statutory work, require social workers to elicit users' views on the compulsory nature of the interaction, including the extent to which users see themselves as clients, and to specify boundaries: what is/is not negotiable; where power and authority lies and under what circumstances it may be used; what the legal position and decision-making process is. If subsequent practice is to make sense, this clarity is important. It provides a degree of certainty which may help to minimise defensive behaviour. It acknowledges power issues and relates the worker–user encounter directly to the network and systems which underpin it. It opens up the possibility of combining a statutory role with therapeutic work.

Third, since users are often uncertain what to expect in terms of confidentiality and ground-rules, and since they often feel a planned approach to be missing (Corby, 1982), social workers should describe how they work. Confidentiality can easily trap the unwary. Concerned about not eliciting all the relevant information or about losing a relationship with users, social workers may agree to keep details confidential. They may, thereby, become enmeshed in secrets or dysfunctional alliances, or triangulated as part of a dyad with information about that dyad or a third person, and lose leverage and manoeuvrability. More helpful therapeutically, and necessary in relation to statutory work where information often has to be shared within the professional system, is a position where workers retain the right to share information with the user-system and professional system when it is therapeutic and/or necessary in relation to their duties to do so (Wendorf and Wendorf, 1985).

These procedures are designed to keep the worker–user system open. They centre on holding, predictability, reliability, accessibility and limit-setting (Skidmore, 1988). They are key elements in providing secure caregiving, with the social worker as the facilitating environment in which, ideally, change may occur (Winnicott, 1965).

Assessment: what work?

If problems are poorly defined, work is likely to be ineffective. Equally, an overelaborate assessment is likely to obscure rather than clarify. What is required is a formulation, informed by theoretical knowledge and practice wisdom, which, at the minimum level of complexity necessary, satisfactorily describes risk factors and people's needs, and suggests possible interventions. These may be questions to ask, tasks to set and/or courses of action to implement. In seeking such clarification, everyone in the system under focus must be included in the data collection and eventual hypothesis which will inform the intervention.

Key questions, both to ask and/or deliberate upon, are helpful in pursuing specificity and formulating assessments which begin with 'In this situation...' or 'For this person...', such as: what is the problem? What is happening? How would you put it? How is it a problem for you? For whom is it a problem? Why is it a problem, what maintains it and what is avoided as a result? Why now? What do you mean by problem? What is your explanation? Who agrees/ disagrees with this explanation? When was the problem noticed? What else was happening then? Did this happen in your own birth family? What solutions have been tried, and with what result (Pottle, 1984)? Who usually deals with the problem, why, and what do they do? What do others do in response? What do people believe will solve the problem? What change do people want? What change will they settle for (Lask, 1980)? Who agrees/disagrees on this? What are people hoping for from the social worker? What would happen if the social worker could not provide this (Reder, 1986)?

One objective is specificity. If people say they have tried everything, what have they tried and with what results? If adjectives such as depressed are used, what is meant, what does the individual do? The approach is similar to ABC (antecedents, behaviour, consequences) and FINDS (frequency, intensity, number, duration, sense) as used by behaviourists (Curnock and Hardiker, 1979) to pin down observable behaviour, how people react to it, and how this reaction may provoke more of the same behaviour. What will be informative are differences between members within the system, the consequences of the problem, what is avoided (tasks, conflicts, problem areas, types of relationship) and what is gained, and how people react to this process of exploration and clarification. For example, the problem may serve a function of regulating distance between people. Alternatively it may be a displacement from another issue, aiming to reduce anxiety by focusing on a less threatening problem.

To make sense of what is said, how, and what is avoided or seems missing, an understanding of defence mechanisms will prove helpful:

1. denial, keeping from awareness facts or feelings;
2. projection, feelings put on to another individual or situation;
3. displacement, feelings about one person or problem detoured on to another as in scapegoating;
4. splitting: this may take the form, interpersonally, of keeping one person good and one bad, to avoid distress. For instance, children of separated parents may hold a good image of the absent parent to avoid anger and pain about being abandoned

or separated, and/or anxiety about whether they are loved or good enough. Intrapsychically, it may reveal itself as compartmentalisation. Good and bad experiences, and the feelings associated with them, are kept divided, as in sexually abused children who sometimes split themselves into different personalities. One client presented a 'bad Barbara' who acted out her angry and hurt feelings, and a 'good Barbara' who tried to live her life and relate to others as though she had never been abused.

The emotional atmosphere often provides clues to what defence mechanisms are operating (for example when it seems incongruent with the seriousness of the problems being discussed). The life-cycle points reached by members of the user-system may be relevant, especially if several members face developmental changes concurrently, with the result that the system is struggling to adjust (Dare, 1979). Symptoms may have the effect of preventing or delaying transitions to new types of relationship.

History shapes individuals. The influence of early life experiences on later personality development has been clearly documented. Memories of significant life events may be triggered by contemporary experiences (for instance, social workers who recall 'forgotten' incidents when they themselves were abused during their investigations of current child abuse). Historical experiences may produce life scripts which individuals attempt to replicate or correct (Byng-Hall, 1985) and which give meaning to interaction, symptoms and behaviour. History, therefore, may provide important clues. Initial experiences are internalised, where they then shape belief systems and affect subsequent expectations and approaches to relationships (Dare, 1979). Thus, victims of abuse or neglect may reproduce relationships where they are victims or, to accommodate to and avoid confronting feelings about the original abuse/abuser, where they identify with the aggressor and initiate abusive encounters. For instance, a seven-year-old boy, shortly after being sexually assaulted by a male neighbour, began undressing children in the school toilets, demanding they touch his penis and sexually abusing them. In play therapy he could express his rage and confusion which he had been unable to verbalise and which he had defended against by identifying with his abuser.

How emotional themes and conflicts were handled in an individual's family of origin may therefore prove very relevant.

These themes and conflicts, stories and scripts, are central to everyone's experience: sexuality, gender roles, proximity and distance in relationships. They affect how individuals think about, feel and behave towards each other. They take social workers into assessment of communication and relationships in families and other systems.

1. How are roles and tasks allocated? Is this distribution felt to be satisfactory by those involved or is it the result of power relationships and gender inequalities (J. Williams and Watson, 1988)?

2. Is communication blocked, displaced or damaged (that is, characterised by secrets, symptoms or double-binds: Walrond-Skinner, 1976)? Is communication direct or indirect, masked or clear, ambiguous, encouraging or contradictory? Do individuals engage or become discouraged and switch off?

3. Are boundaries flexible, rigid and impermeable, or diffuse? Are individuals enmeshed or disengaged (Minuchin, 1974)?

4. Are rules and expectations clear, predictable and age-appropriate? Are people stuck in one set of rules and expectations or can the system accommodate change? If stuck, what maintains this?

5. How is conflict and intimacy handled: is it suppressed, expressed, avoided, or appropriate (Sein *et al.*, 1987)?

6. What defence mechanisms are operating here?

7. Are children overburdened with the unlived life of their parents, with parental images (Fordham, 1969; Lomas, 1987), and consequently unable to separate in order to form their own identity? Child abuse may result when parents, intolerant of their own failings and needs when they see them replicated in their children, 'attack' these split-off, disowned and projected parts of themselves. In such instances, social workers should work with the hurt child in the parent since these repressed childhood experiences return and resurface in ambivalent parenthood and will not be amenable to change offered through encouragement or control alone. The same idea can be used to explore the common phenomenon of adolescent 'acting out' (Zinner and Shapiro, 1972, 1974). Parents sometimes re-enact with their children, through a process of projective identification, the conflicts and tensions which they

themselves failed to resolve at a similar stage with their own parents. Thus parents who have had a rather repressed teenage period might unconsciously spur their adolescent children into rule-breaking behaviour. This enables the parents simultaneously to adopt two gratifying stances: both a covert identification with the rebellious child against the strict parent, and an overt alignment with the strict parent of their own teenage experience (in effect 'identifying with the aggressor'). The parent's own unacceptable and largely unacknowledged rebelliousness or delinquency is thus projected on to the child and attacked, but also secretly identified with and encouraged. Thus, an intrapsychic conflict between impulse and prohibition within the parent is transposed and acted out within an interpersonal conflict between parent and child who come to represent the opposing forces. When the child colludes with the parent's projections, because in some way it suits them to take on such a role, this 'fit' produces a tight interactional system.

Assessment: think patterns, circles and triangles

The questions just listed orientate practitioners towards identifying patterns of interaction: themes, sequences, repetitions, alliances, triangles and circular relationships. On the basis of these formulated hypotheses interventions may be devised to release new patterns of behaviour. Thus Bowlby (1973) identifies four family typologies where either an adult or child believes that something dreadful will happen to themselves or to the other person, as a result of which adult and child engage in specific behaviours (leading in Bowlby's example to school phobia) to combat the fear. In marital work, Elkaim (1986) uses both systemic and psychodynamic concepts to understand and unravel the reciprocal double-binds which operate in many closed system dyadic relationships. Each member of the couple operates on two levels of personal agenda: an 'official programme', an explicit request for a change in the behaviour of the other person; and a 'map of the world', an internal blueprint for the behaviour of both self and other which derives from early experience. When the official programme and map of the world are at odds with each other, the subject is caught in a double-bind.

In some relationships both partners are caught in a bind, and their binds interlock to form a reciprocal double-bind in which the behaviour of one (covertly) stimulates more of the same (overtly) unwelcome behaviour from the other. This takes us into the realm of symmetrical and complementary relationships, vicious circles characterised by mirroring or one-up/one-down behaviour which escalates within its own rigidity (Watzlawick *et al.*, 1967).

The relationship between internal map and external reality may be applied intrapersonally as well as interpersonally. Individuals construct internal models of their life experience and then apply those models in their day-to-day relationships (Stierlin, 1977). Their 'openness' as individuals depends on the extent to which they can update and adjust their internal maps in the light of feedback from current experience. There is a constant struggle to bring the internal map and external reality into harmony, or sometimes to impose the former on the latter (as in transference).

These conflicts, whether intra- or interpersonal, are often exhibited in triangles (see Figure 6.1: Malan, 1979; Hyde, 1988). The key is what is avoided: anxiety, a feared calamity to self or another, or a dreaded situation. Behaviours or relationships are used to minimise these possibilities. The defence against the anxiety or calamity is the required behaviour or relationship. The anxiety may be a feared calamity or hidden feeling, that is interpersonal or intrapersonal. What is eschewed is this hidden feeling or a different relationship (Malan, 1979; Hyde, 1988). For example, a sexually abused child accommodates to the abuser and abuse and remains in a required relationship for fear that confrontation and disclosure will result in calamity, be that separation or the acting-out of threats by the abuser. The same child may defend by denial against the hidden feelings of anger, disgust and terror, being anxious or fearful that otherwise these will erupt and damage. As another illustration, an emotionally abused child may use as defences reaction formation, turning anger or fear into seeking to please, compliance or clowning; turning against the self, as in resignation, numbness, hopelessness and low self-esteem; anxious attachment, shown in watchfulness, anticipatory avoidance and clinging, in order to assuage anxiety; and/or obsessionality, using rituals as a means of controlling a hostile world. Each defence is inspired by an environment where the child felt under attack. This unsafe environment is also internalised and becomes an inner persecutor which influences the child's world

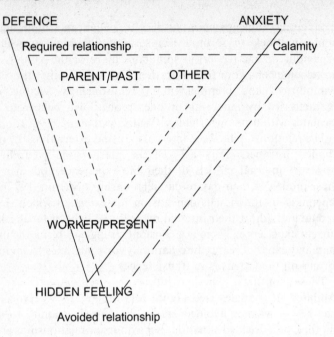

Figure 6.1   *Triangles*

view. This may operate even after the external threat has been removed. The defences are designed by the child to limit the threats to him- or herself and to contain the anxiety about the threats they face. Psychodynamic therapists intervene by interpretations moving towards the hidden feelings or avoided relationship through defence and anxiety. Systemic therapists will, through interventions, aim also to enable the formation of different forms of relationship previously assumed to have been unsafe (Byng-Hall, 1985). Both approaches seek to enable individuals, families and other systems to articulate their beliefs, fears and assumptions, since these affect how they live and behave, and to modify their behaviour so that it reaches towards their ideal situation rather than reacts against or accommodates to their dreaded situation (Heard, 1974).

In finally answering the question 'What?', social workers can use circular diagrams to demonstrate how the problem and behaviours interlink and reinforce each other. At each point there will be a 'because' clause (Reder, 1988), an explanation delineating the meaning or function of a problem or behaviour, whether that is accommodation to an abuser because of an imbalance of power, or missed appointments because of distrust of close relationships, or detoured conflict to maintain homeostasis and to protect individuals against conflict or feared change. Thus, in answering the question 'What?', light is shed on 'Why?'. For instance, a family were referred because the parents were insisting that their son was difficult to control, even though neither teachers nor a psychiatrist could find anything wrong with him. The mother had a history of depression, requiring occasional admissions to hospital. The husband presented himself as the stronger parent. In tracing relationship patterns in this family, it emerged that husband and wife were locked in a complementary interaction: the wife saw herself as depressed and needing to be cared for; the husband was seen as the carer; both were resentful and dissatisfied with, but unable to change, the nature of their relationship. The wife was frightened to relinquish her 'sick role' in case her husband would leave whilst he was afraid that, without the role of carer, his wife would find him deficient and reject him. To avoid focusing on their dissatisfaction, their conflict had become detoured through their son who behaved as if to order, to demonstrate that only his father could control him because his mother was ill but that his mother's presence was necessary to prevent his father from losing his temper and physically abusing him (see Figure 6.2).

Intervention

Change will not be achieved if social workers project on to users their need to be helpful and deal with the need as if it was over there. The helping profession syndrome, exhibited in visiting too frequently or without defined purpose, and in undertaking every task on behalf of clients, will undermine users and, ultimately, frustrate the changes sought. Neither will change occur effectively if social workers introject wholesale, uncritically, the responsibility offered to them by society. Responsibility for change lies with users. Social workers cannot force change. They can only create the conditions whereby such change is possible. Moreover, a necessary precondition for psychological intervention is the meeting of material needs (Kovel, 1976a) and consideration of how the

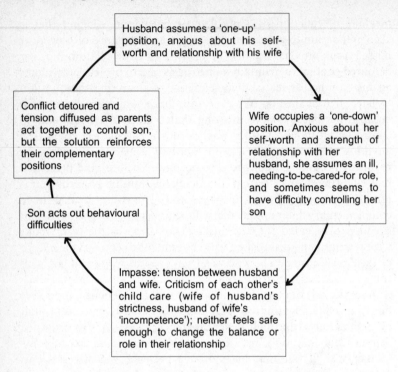

Figure 6.2　*Circular reinforcement*

economic and psychological are affecting and influencing each other. Change will not occur if social workers become locked in battles over cause and effect, or how to define the problem. In the family example given above, the social worker, anxious to 'rescue' the wife from her sick role and the son from his 'deviancy', 'told' the family that the wife was not ill and neither was the son delinquent. Needless to say, the family resisted this redefinition by failing to keep appointments and by recruiting other professionals who might accept their script. Rather than engaging in disputes about 'the real problem is...' the social worker would have been better advised positively connoting everyone as a prelude to tasks or paradoxical prescriptions and injunctions, thereby enabling change because it would not involve loss of face or having to admit error.

Interventions should include everyone in the system, even if only by exclusion, clearly stating what is expected of them. Members of the extended family, such as grandparents, may be crucial to the change process, especially where focus is on boundaries and roles. Equally, other agencies can also undermine the change effort and their co-operation or involvement may have to be obtained and clarified.

Interventions which promote 'more of the same' should be avoided. For instance, if a task-centred approach has not proved successful, another approach may be indicated, depending on the information about possible blocks obtained at this point. In another example, a widow had made repeated enquiries over several years about admission to Part III accommodation. Each time social workers had visited and given information. Each time they recorded that the condition of her house was exceedingly poor, her relationship with her son conflictual. Each time she refused offers of assistance and admission to residential care. Each social worker had approached the referral as a straight information-giving task. None had thought to explore the meaning of the many referrals or, apparently, the fears which the widow may have been experiencing about her son, growing older, admission to institutional care, and the defences which she used against them. They had not positively reframed her requests for, and then refusals of, services. Rather, social workers were becoming dismissive of her referrals, regarding them as 'more of the same'. Where problems are especially intransigent, a paradoxical approach may be indicated. A no-change prescription may be suggested or the problem may be prescribed (i.e. more of the same requested). Alternatively, a paradoxical injunction may be offered not to behave in a certain way: for example, not to try to sleep, or only to behave in a particular way at particular times, such as only having temper tantrums at teatime (Leicester Family Service Unit, 1981). These are examples of going with the system's momentum, avoiding becoming part of the problem and enmeshed in resistance and a system's investment in maintaining the behaviour of its members for fear of the consequences of change. It is vital to follow a paradox through once set: that is, to express doubt or concern should tasks be achieved or problems resolved (Cade and Southgate, 1979; Jenkins, 1980; Papp, 1980).

One intervention technique is circular questioning. Traditionally we are used to asking direct questions. However, in situations where participants have a fixed definition of the problem, a rigid idea about what is wrong, this traditional method can merely perpetuate more of the same. Circular questioning is one means of challenging this solid front, and enabling the system to examine the problems from the position and perspective of all those involved and to question why it might need the problem. For instance, social workers are sometimes confronted with an older person or a child who is defined as the problem and whose removal 'into care' is demanded with an urgency that can make practitioners feel they are being bulldozed. One response is to ask ranking questions: who is most concerned about it, who the next most, and so on; before and after questions: what is happening before, what happens after; future oriented questions: what would happen if A was removed into care, or, if B was not living here, who would be most affected by this, how would things be different, who would be most likely to misbehave or have a problem; commenting on relationships: asking one person to comment on their experience of the relationship between two others (for instance, asking a child to comment on the parents' relationship, or asking two people to look at how a third person may experience them). Such questions introduce more information into the system and therefore open up the possibility of changes in relationships and attitudes.

Tasks may be used to alter or challenge the current solution and structures used by members of the system. The variety of possible purposes includes: promoting skills, differentiating roles between members of a system, enhancing communication, promoting boundary setting or proximity, changing behaviour or maintaining the momentum of change (Sutcliffe *et al.*, 1985). Tasks shift responsibility for change to the system's members. Non-completed tasks can be reframed from failure to important information about the system since, through circular questioning, blocks and relationship patterns will be revealed: who found it most/least difficult; who tried to initiate performance of the task; what happened. The same analysis, who found tasks easy or difficult, what changed, where next, should be used for successfully negotiated tasks. Again, tasks should include everyone in the system and focus on what people do and believe rather than what they are. They must be precise and achievable. Everyone should be clear about what is expected.

Also available are action techniques such as role reversal, where users role-play workers and workers the members of the system in focus; enactment, where users demonstrate a scenario they are concerned about; rehearsal, where users are asked to practise desired behaviour; sculpting, to give visual evidence of relationship patterns such as distance, proximity, levels of (dis)comfort, and boundaries, and to change these arrangements physically. These are all designed to challenge structures, be they boundaries, belief systems or defences, by introducing difference.

Interpretations, such as 'I was wondering if...', enable the introduction of new information in to the system. For example, pointing out patterns and significant changes in the ways in which members of a system relate to each other, or commenting on people's non-verbal behaviour and contrasting this with what they are saying, may enable them to make connections and reflect on how they are interacting. Once again, exploring the not so obvious may be important since users may seek to disclose their fears covertly and in a disguised form, rather than openly. Thus an adolescent who had been anorexic and was expecting her first child remarked that she was worried about her increase in weight. The social worker sought to reassure her, perhaps thereby mirroring the young woman's own need to believe, and to have others believe, that she would be a successful mother. However, the comment could have 'hidden' but 'offered' ambivalence about the pregnancy, anxieties about the strength and permanence of her relationship with the baby's father, and continuing problems relating to her self-image. These areas might have been opened up by the social worker wondering if the young woman was concerned about one or more of them, either asking her directly or indicating first that such fears and ambivalences are not uncommon in general experience. The objective of any intervention is to enable reappraisal and change in the system as a result of reflection on how other people may see or experience particular individuals or behaviour (Hoffman, 1981). Interventions, then, are most effective when they cut across 'traditional' perspectives, stereotyped responses and escalations, and require individuals to stop and think about relationships, assumptions and perceptions within the system.

On-going work

Perhaps because each situation is unique, social work literature often neglects how to implement and maintain change programmes: that is, how to keep the system open and avoid closure and 'stuckness' (Corby, 1982). However, some general principles can be discerned and some potential blocks identified. The overriding message is that the worker–user system can both create and maintain problems and that focusing on task and neglecting the emotional content of the process is therefore liable to promote 'stuckness' and closure.

The professional task should continue to display care in securing the setting in which work is to take place. Since transference dynamics based on attachment and life experiences are rarely static, and since interactions with significant others are influenced and often distorted by past events, continued attention must be paid to limit-setting, accessibility, reliability, holding and negotiating the pace of work and psychological/physical distance between worker and user (Skidmore, 1988). This involves monitoring the level of rapport and strength of the therapeutic alliance, the direct and covert messages about the worker from users, and the roles which members of the system in focus invite the worker to play. It involves a readiness to be the transference figure with whom users may venture new, different behaviour. Work which neglects a user's experience of previous attachments and figures with power and authority is unlikely to create conditions where the user can shed anxious or dysfunctional behaviour patterns (Skidmore, 1988). Thus, silence may be a communication of difficulties in the transference and be a defence against anxiety. One user avoided communication with a new social worker, anxious that this worker would abandon her as she perceived the previous practitioner to have done on leaving the agency. Naming this observation and the anxieties underpinning the behaviour, and staying with it rather than reacting angrily against it, enabled a working relationship to form.

Social workers can be seen in many different ways: the good person felt to have been missing, with enormous expectations held of them, but with needs which perhaps have to be denied for fear of the feelings which would be released if these needs were met; and/or a feared repetition of experiences felt to have been abusive or disconfirming. An essential component in the work may have to be how users inappropriately construe the worker's feelings and behaviour and act as a result. This analysis can be extended to typical reactions towards other significant people, how these may be understood in terms of previous relationship experiences, and how they result in the user being a closed system (Bowlby, 1979). This reflective interchange, where the worker accepts and interprets the transference dynamics, can release what has remained hidden or has been felt to be unattainable, thereby enabling new behaviours and experiences (Gammack, 1982). For example, a mother, on being left by her violent husband, sought to deny her many feelings because she thought the social worker would disapprove and condemn her. This linked with the disapproval and condemnation she felt she had received from her husband and parents. Her response had been to deny her pain and herself. By commenting first on the absence of any apparent feeling about the separation and then on her rigid posture as a defence against feelings she anticipated would be overwhelming and labelled 'bad', the mother was able to cry and express her anger and relief. She experienced difference in the relationship and began a process of self-actualisation.

Whether working with abused and troubled children or adults, or with individuals entering care, the professional task involves recognising their feelings and finding a shared understanding of them. This may mean helping people locate and express their uncertainty, conflict, pain, fear, emptiness, self-reproach and ambivalence. It may require the sensitive exploration of defences against these feelings, perhaps rationalisation, denial, the use of symptoms to mask feelings or retain secrets about relationships, or compulsive self-reliance. The task involves finding the hurt, troubled part of the individual, since this holds the potential for difference and change. Such work will require considerable patience. Since people often feel that they walk a tightrope between 'loyalty' to their family and being 'authentic' or 'true' to themselves, workers must be experienced at constructing a safety net which users perceive will hold them when they confront their 'hidden feelings' or strive for different relationships.

This requirement of patience illustrates another part of the maintenance process within on-going work, namely analysis of the worker's countertransference, feelings or behaviour arising from the user's material; and the worker's own transference, emanating from previous individual and/or family experiences. These dynamics can have one or more outcomes: hate or hostility towards users, a reaction perhaps to clients who are defiant or who perpetrate abuse; overinvolvement, perhaps compulsive caregiving to mask the need for love which was missed; withdrawal, where workers feel rejected or vulnerable in the face of angry, aggressive clients, or where they 'abandon' clients because of the pain of their material; intellectualisation and rationality, as a defence against pain, reflected in comments like 'Don't cry' or 'Pull yourself together'; overactivity or passivity and helplessness, as a response to felt impotence; anger, from not appreciating the defences and attachment dynamics which influence a user's response to the worker; feeling to blame, where the worker may have taken in a user's projection; avoidance of authority, often a response to the pressure exerted by users who, through their behaviour, seek to recruit workers into a collusive denial of what is happening. These dynamics provide information about the work. Analysis of the countertransference will reveal data on how users see themselves and relationships, and will assist workers both in staying open rather than becoming part of the problem and also in understanding behaviour and presented material. Neglecting these powerful emotions can result in ineffective and dangerous work since, if unresolved, they create a closed or defensive system where one view is held to the neglect of all others: for example, a worker may 'need' to see abusive parents as caring in order to accommodate to their aggression and to the worker's fear of it (Trowell, 1986).

To maintain direction, what is required is a supervisory viewpoint (Casement, 1985), a meta position to the role which focuses on key questions.

1.　What is happening?
2.　What is obstructing the work: fear of catastrophe; unresolved issues or feelings about the relationship creating anxiety and defences; problems or methods not agreed; goals or tasks unrealistic or unclear; tasks frustrated by others; stuck in one approach (Corden and Preston-Shoot, 1987)?
3.　What role is the worker playing and being asked to play, by whom and for what purpose? Has the worker become trapped, enmeshed, sucked-in?

4. Is a review necessary to assess work done, revise initial hypotheses and determine what further work, if any, is required?
5. What is the purpose of the work? Will the purpose of the work be achieved by the action planned or being implemented?

Terminating work

Unresolved feelings about closure are a potent source of subsequent relapse (Malan, 1979). Terminating work is a difficult phase to negotiate, especially when the relationship has been strong, and is likely to reactivate feelings about previous attachments. Workers should not assume that, just because these feelings have been discussed before, they do not need to be worked through afresh, and neither should fantasies about why social workers may be closing the case be reassured away. Feelings about closure, together with any acting-out behaviour – such as premature withdrawal, relapse or presentation of new problems – must be discussed, the loss acknowledged and feelings worked through. Equally, it may be necessary to build in time to consolidate work done and changes achieved, a factor which can be incorporated into working agreements by means of disengagement contracts which allow the contact between worker and user to be reduced gradually before final closure (Corden and Preston-Shoot, 1987).

7

Supervision, consultation and individual and organisational tangles

There is a 'surprising paucity' of research and theorising about the ingredients necessary for effective supervision, coupled with widespread criticism from practitioners about the quality and reliability of supervision sessions, and confusion expressed by supervisors and line-managers as to what supervision should comprise (Clare, 1988). If social workers are to survive and be effective they require adequate preparatory training and good ongoing supervision. Without it their exposure to anxiety, anger and the dependency feelings of clients, to emotional and physical overload, is likely to erode their intellectual and emotional resources, their morale and their confidence (Clare, 1988). They are less likely to be able to retain hold of their skills and strengths, or to develop their practice competence. They are more likely to experience difficulties in keeping to their tasks and roles and retaining direction, and may succumb to collusive participation with service users: that is, to form a closed system as a result of the emotional pressures and dynamics contained within the work (Temperley and Himmel, 1986). Without supervision practitioners will experience difficulty retaining a meta position to monitor their interventions and their effectiveness, to check whether they are seeing what they want to see and not seeing what they want to miss, to analyse the process, to appraise their decisions critically, and to challenge their own blind spots. In the face of stressful work and demoralisation, arising from the slowness of change, and the volume and intractability of problems, practitioners are prone to regard work as persecutory.

In this chapter we apply our psychodynamic and systemic perspective to the crucial subject of supervision. What is it for?

What processes are at work in it? What should it be aiming to achieve? How can it best be structured? The differences between 'administrative' and 'consultative' supervision, as well as the pros and cons of different models of supervision will be explored. Our emphasis is two-fold. What sort of supervision equips practitioners to give the best service to clients *and* looks after the best interests of the social workers? It will be obvious that these emphases are, or at least should be, inextricably linked.

Supervision: administrative or consultative?

Everyone knows that social work training, in common with most forms of professional training, just about equips practitioners to 'get started' in the job, and that it then takes much time and experience to become a good social worker. It is also widely acknowledged that supervision plays a vital part in this process. Without regular and effective supervision, it is difficult for anyone to develop their potential as social workers and to learn to monitor the quality of their work. Given this fact, it is surely surprising that supervision is not taken more seriously. It has become the traditional focus of disgruntlement among practitioners: there is too little of it, it is of the wrong kind, it is never available when needed most. Among supervisors there appears a lack of clarity about the nature and aims of supervision: is it primarily about checking up on the worker's performance and 'covering' the department, or is it about giving personal support? How far should it be tailored to individual requirements? What happens when the type of supervision required is beyond the supervisor's experience or competence? Should it always avoid shading into a counselling relationship?

Clearly there ought to be no dispute about the need for social work supervision, but the precise nature of that need is itself in need of clarification. If supervision is seen as a two-way recursive process between supervisors or line-managers and practitioners, then there are needs to be met in both directions. Hierarchically speaking, the 'downward' requirement, from supervisor to supervisee, could be called 'administrative' in that one of the main organisational functions of supervision is to ensure that administrative requirements are being met. The 'upward' requirement, from practitioner to supervisor, could then be seen as predominantly 'consultative', a request for help of a more professional or personal nature in dealing with the demands of casework. Of course, this is a drastic oversimplification: most social workers also need to know that they are doing a good job and getting the administrative and legal procedures right. Similarly, many line-managers are not simply interested in bureaucratic rules and 'quality control'. They are also concerned to support their staff and to help them develop themselves professionally. Nevertheless, there is a certain inevitable tendency within large welfare bureaucracies, particularly when they are hard-pressed, for the 'downward' administrative force to predominate, with the result that social work supervision becomes more and more business-like, and the 'upward' consultative need becomes increasingly frustrated. As we have argued in previous chapters, there is a tendency for administrative factors, such as the availability and cost of certain resources, to dictate the nature of the work being done. Naturally, this affects practitioners as well as clients.

There are several issues here which merit further consideration. First, there is an inherent tension within the social work role. Most front-line social workers are in fact expected to be competent 'self-managers' with a good deal of professional autonomy (Glastonbury *et al.*, 1987). This creates a difficult balancing act for social work managers who are sometimes caught between encouraging their workers to take the initiative and reining them in so that overall bureaucratic control can be maintained. From a different perspective, England (1986) makes a similar point. In his view the essence of social work lies in the worker's intuitive and creative use of 'self'. On the other hand, agencies are obliged to work by rules and procedures. The result is a sort of double-bind: the necessarily bureaucratic management of social workers can only cramp their creativity and dilute the quality of their work. This internal conflict about the very nature of social work activity is reflected in what we are calling the 'administrative' and 'consultative' aspects of supervision.

Second, the role of line-managers or team leaders is a complex one fraught with many conflicts. It embraces more than a dozen different functions, one of which is supervision of team members (P. Smith, 1984). Very often it is in the person of the team leader that the 'downward' administrative needs of the organisation and the 'upward' consultative needs of the workers meet and clash. Much of the team's stress is deposited with the team leader who may then find it very difficult to unload anywhere else, particularly if his or her own managers are more concerned with bureaucratic obligations than with the emotional stresses of the work. The fact that there is no widespread acknowledgement that managers may themselves require supervision, let alone support, is surely indicative of the defensiveness which has been built into social work organisations in response to the anxieties aroused by the task.

As far as the team leader's supervision of the team is concerned, it is asking a lot of one person to combine the roles of case supervisor and manager. Some individuals manage this very successfully but there is surely a strong argument for 'opening up' the whole area of casework supervision so that workers are free to consult with other colleagues or other supervisors who have particular areas of experience or expertise. A. Brown (1984) puts the case for this approach to 'consultation'. If we accept that the consultative and administrative components of supervision can be fruitfully separated, then there is surely an overwhelming case for the establishment of many more specialist practitioner posts which would involve a worker keeping a caseload in addition to offering consultation or training to colleagues. It seems absurd that the best practitioners frequently have to leave direct practice behind in order to advance their careers by becoming 'managers'.

We shall now concentrate on the consultative rather than the administrative components of supervision. What is required of social workers, both personally and professionally, in their day-to-day contact with clients, and what in turn do social workers require from their supervisors?

What social work does to social workers

Although it is commonly recognised that social work clients are among the most disturbed people in the community, it is often overlooked that they are also among the most disturbing (Temperley and Himmel, 1986). The reason clients can be so disturbing is that they generally lack the capacity or opportunity to articulate and 'work through' their distress and are driven instead to act it out. Internal conflicts are expressed as interpersonal ones, or they use their external world to 'dramatise' (Hinshelwood, 1987) their internal world in an attempt to escape their psychic pain. This means that social workers are daily exposed to intense emotional pressure. This pressure operates on two levels. First, there is the very obvious level of actual events and real situations. Social workers encounter raw hardship, pain and loss. Cases involving the physical or sexual abuse of children are certainly among the most extreme examples here and, of course, the nature of this work is such that even the most experienced and competent workers may be severely tested. Second, there is the less obvious but no less powerful level of interpersonal dynamics Our discussion of transference, counter-transference and projective identification has already alerted us to the fact that anyone who works closely with damaged or distressed people is bound to be on the receiving end of powerful projections, and that such projections are likely to produce powerful reactions in the worker.

In many ways this second level of interpersonal pressure is harder to deal with than the first because much of it occurs unconsciously, or at least in ways which are disguised and hard to detect. Social workers are frequently left feeling angry, drained, exhausted, unappreciated or useless, without really understanding why. This is one of the hallmarks of the process known as projective identification (Steiner, 1976). Even if social workers and their supervisors are aware of the first and more obvious level of emotional pressure, and can use supervision constructively to deal with it, it may well be that this second, deeper level of interpersonal disturbance eludes them. That is to say, it may elude them consciously whilst at the same time finding its way into the supervision sessions at a less conscious level. At any event, it is this complex and elusive level of interpersonal stress that we wish to draw particular attention to here.

We can examine this second level of emotional pressure more closely by looking at the impressively honest account given by an experienced social worker of his early experience of working with disturbed families. Reflecting on this, Jordan (1974) distinguishes between 'primary collusion', where the worker accepts the family's own definition of its problem (for example blaming everything on the child's behaviour), and 'secondary collusion', where the worker somehow gets saddled with 'all the painful feelings arising from the family's situation'. Concentrating on secondary collusion as the more complex phenomenon, and the one from which the worker finds it more difficult to extricate him- or herself, Jordan confesses that he sometimes allowed his own emotional investment in a case to reach the point where it was actually preventing the clients from finding their own resolution to the problem. In one instance, after a couple had separated, the husband remarked that Jordan had seemed more concerned to keep them together than they were themselves. Thus Jordan writes (1974):

> For what is this secondary collusion I have described? Why was it that the compulsion I felt to rush about even more desperately and absurdly to keep these families together was so insistent, so painful, so disturbing of sleep, so distracting from other tasks? It must be either the case that I am some kind of nut, hung up on my own early traumas, and constantly re-enacting them with certain of my clients; or else that my own immensely strong feelings about these people were in part at least a reflection of their desperate, but denied needs for each other. The more they tried to escape from these feelings, the more of these I felt, and the more deeply I became involved in the family drama.

Jordan then poses the question whether social workers should always resist being drawn into their clients' emotional turmoils, or whether with certain clients practitioners cannot avoid working with some of these feelings in themselves, using them for better or worse.

Commenting on this contribution in the same volume, Casement (1974) points to the different types of countertransference response at work here. On the one hand there is Jordan's *personal* countertransference response to the client's situation based on his own painful childhood experience of separation from his family. This impelled him to make heroic but ultimately unhelpful efforts to keep couples and families together. Every practitioner has similar areas of personal experience which determine their 'gut reaction' to particular people or situations. This is countertransference in the traditional Freudian sense. On the other hand there is what Casement terms a *diagnostic* countertransference response which has much more to do with what is being disowned by the particular individual, couple or family, and projected on to the worker. This is the more recent understanding of countertransference. By stopping to examine what a particular family was doing to him, Jordan was able to separate out his different levels of personal response and to realise that he had become the repository for his clients' split-off and projected feelings.

What makes this situation even more complex is the fact that whatever it is that 'gets under our skin' in this way is bound to depend on how receptive we are to particular feelings and particular situations. This in turn depends on our own personal experience. In other words, 'personal' and 'diagnostic' levels of countertransference response may be very closely intertwined. The overall effect is that social workers may be very profoundly stirred up by their clients in ways which are determined by the particular 'system' they co-create with them. In object-relations terms such a system can be viewed as a product of the two-way projection–introjection process between worker and client in which existing internal object-relationships are externalised and imposed on the 'real' situation: hence, in this example, Jordan's strong identification with clients whom he perceived as being in danger of losing a loved and needed object. Some of our personal reactions will be very clear to us if we can face a bit of self-examination but, however hard we look, there is likely to be a whole area of unconscious emotional response which remains submerged, and which is only visible through its effects. It is this area that supervision or consultation, if it is to be truly effective, needs to be able to address.

It is perhaps easier for social workers to acknowledge that other professionals, such as doctors or psychotherapists, have this problem than that they themselves have to contend with it. Indeed, there is a body of thinking within social work which prides itself on being able to get on with the job like a sort of 'maintenance mechanic', untroubled by self-indulgent introspection (Davies, 1985). In our view, regardless of whether or not social workers see themselves as 'therapists', they cannot escape the profound emotional or psychological impact that their clients are bound to have on them. Each social worker may be most strongly affected by particular people or situations: different things get under different skins. However, practitioners are certainly kidding themselves if they think they can remain detached and professionally 'in control' at all times. Social work training and supervision have to take on board this simple truth.

The widening circle: from individual to team to organisation

Such is the power of these interpersonal forces that it may not simply be the individual worker who is affected. By a curious contagion, transactions between colleagues may come to 'mirror' a particular aspect of the client's or family's dynamics, or of the client–worker relationship. Relationships within teams, between teams, or even between different agencies and organisations, may mysteriously take on the dysfunctional properties of the particular clients or families with whom they are dealing.

For example, Main's (1957) classic article 'The ailment' is a study of the powerful effects that a particular group of highly disturbed psychiatric patients had upon the nurses. The 'ailment' in question is not so much the condition of the patients but rather the distress, amounting at times to almost a sickness, which was induced in members of the caring staff and which affected their working relationships. Main uses a Kleinian object-relations model to account for this phenomenon, seeing it as the product of primitive splitting and projective mechanisms on the part of the patients, which evoked powerful counteridentifications from the nurses. In similar vein, Lewis (1979) describes the effects of certain surgical patients and their families upon members of a clinical team. He shows how the professionals can sometimes be plunged into hopelessness and inactivity, or else feel spurred to 'do something' even when it may be more advisable to refrain. Countertransference pressures of this kind are not unknown to social workers. Berkowitz and Leff (1984) describe work with schizophrenic patients and their families in which the negative reaction of the team to the families appeared to mirror the interactions within the families. It was only when such reactions within the clinical team were viewed as countertransference information that a way could be found to break the deadlock in the treatment. How often do social workers look at what clients are doing to them personally and then use this as information about what is going on for the clients?

Mirroring and countertransference reactions provide clues to underlying family dynamics (Skynner, 1979) and illustrate how workers may affect clients, and clients workers, without knowing it, and how this can be acted out in other settings. Thus clients acting out their 'disturbance' may find echoes in parallel 'acting out' among the professionals (Temperley and Himmel, 1986). Inter-agency dynamics and processes may reflect and mirror those in a couple or family. Family members may perhaps not discuss 'secrets' which everyone on some level knows about, this collusive silence being mirrored in the professional network which fails also to communicate about the difficulties experienced in the family.

One of the most compelling psychoanalytic accounts of this process is provided by Britton (1981). He uses a familiar theatrical metaphor to illustrate his main theme, namely that 'contact with some families may result in professional workers or their institutions becoming involved unknowingly in a drama which reflects a situation in the relationships of the family or within the minds of some of its individual members; and that this is not recognised but expressed in action'.

This 'acting out' by professionals of what is projected on to them by their clients fits squarely with our discussion of counter-transference and projective identification. We are on the same territory here as McDougall's 'psychic theatre' (1986), Sandler's 'role-responsiveness' (1976) and Byng-Hall's 'scripts' (1988) into which professionals can be 'recruited'. Referring to Sigmund Freud's (1914) notion of the 'compulsion to repeat' in action rather than to 'remember' and to 'work through' in conscious thought and word, Britton reflects on this process whereby 'new participants become the vehicles for the reiterated expression of the underlying dynamic'. This, of course, perfectly describes a closed interpersonal system, though one which may offer the illusion of a great deal of activity and change, as new 'actors' are recruited into the on-going drama. Other colleagues as well as other agencies are frequently drawn into the action, all of them unknowingly 're-enacting' the same basic themes.

Family therapists have generally developed a different approach to these problems. In keeping with a systems approach they have been less concerned with the particular intrapsychic or interpersonal mechanisms by which such processes are deemed to occur, and more concerned with finding ways to disentangle both workers and clients from their systemic enmeshment. A nice bridging concept to this approach is the term 'system countertransference' (Reder and Kraemer, 1980) which accounts for the fact that client pathology can so easily spread right through the professional ranks so that everyone ends up driven by the same dynamic. Generally, though, systemic workers have preferred to talk in more circular terms of social workers becoming 'part of the problem', getting caught up with their clients in the same 'repetitive cycles' and becoming 'part of the homeostatic process' which prevents change (Dungworth and Reimers, 1984; Dimmock and Dungworth, 1985). 'Stuckness' is a familiar feature of working with families and it can engulf not only the family therapist but also the supervisory team and, perhaps, other members of the agency or agencies involved (Treacher and Carpenter, 1982; Carpenter *et al.*, 1983). As we have seen, a major development here has been the adoption of a broad 'systems approach' (cf. Bateson, 1970) which goes beyond a narrow focus on family therapy and which examines the total system (Treacher and Carpenter, 1984). This means that professionals have to include themselves in the system to be treated, and that often the most effective interventions will be those aimed at one's own agency or at the 'interfaces' between clients and professionals or between different professional groups. This is particularly evident in those long-term or 'multi-problem' cases where a number of different agencies become involved. Thus, when the relationship between a particular agency and family becomes stressed, the agency may 'triangle in' another agency in order to reduce the tension, just as parents who are in conflict will often 'triangulate' a particular child in order to ease their own relationship problems (Carl and Jurkovic, 1983). Particular attention should, therefore, be paid to ways in which the 'referring person' might have become part of the problem which is being referred (Selvini Palazzoli *et al.*, 1980b). In all such cases a new worker may be required who can act as a 'consultant', treating as their 'unit of attention' both the family and the professional network: that is, the multi-agency family system (Reder, 1986). In this way the use of network meetings may help to unscramble the systemic entanglement of the various dramatis personae: for example, in statutory child care cases (Dimmock and Dungworth, 1983, 1985).

Closed systems in social work practice

It will be clear that what we are drawing attention to here is a phenomenon which can occur at many different levels. Individual social workers may themselves be hooked into particular clients or situations. Colleagues and supervisors may then be recruited into the same process. On a larger scale, teams and agencies may unwittingly become involved in a dramatisation of the dynamics operating in a given case. All professional relationships may be similarly affected, including those which are expressly designed to monitor such processes. In residential and day-care establishments the problems will naturally tend to be even more intense owing to the 'hot-house' factor of close living and working proximity. In their study of staff relationships in a psychiatric day hospital, for example, Bennett *et al.* (1976) found considerable evidence to confirm their hypothesis that 'any unresolved conflict in the patient group will be reflected automatically in a similar pattern in the staff interactions, and vice versa'. Field social workers must be aware of what can be projected on to them by residents (children, older people, ex-psychiatric hospital patients) as well as by staff groups who care for them.

Whatever the differences here between psychodynamic and systemic approaches, we can again sum up the central issue for social workers in terms of 'open' and 'closed' systems. Social workers are constantly working with a whole variety of people whose lives are becoming, or have already become, closed down, whether through old age, illness, material hardship, emotional or physical deprivation, or abuse. Social workers are regularly faced with situations which require an input of fresh energy or fresh resources in order to break the deadlock. Sometimes the only solution is physically to rearrange the system by removing one or more of its members to care. Much social work may, therefore, be described as an attempt to open or keep open a closed or closing system. Clearly, by the very nature of things, practitioners are not always successful, often for reasons beyond their control. This much is common knowledge. What we are also arguing here is that sometimes they unwittingly become part of the closed circuit themselves, thus contributing to the persistent failure of attempted solutions. This may happen when their own emotional reactions, at whatever level, get the better of them, or when clients succeed in getting them to 'act out'. Institutions may also find themselves unwittingly perpetuating problems rather than solving them (Bruggen and O'Brian, 1987). There are obviously many ways in which social workers can create or perpetuate a closed system with their clients. Figure 7.1 offers a summary of some of the commonest pitfalls in worker–client interactions. These are things practitioners *can* do something about if they are helped to be aware of them through effective supervision or consultation.

Figure 7.1(a) represents a worker who has allowed him- or herself to be recruited into the client's inner world in order to play some role therein, presumably a role which is in some way gratifying to

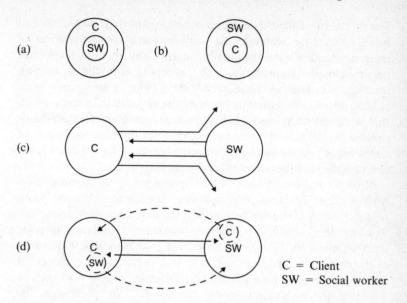

Figure 7.1 *Pitfalls in client–social worker interactions*

both parties. In family work it could also represent a therapist or team which has been sucked into the family system. This is the kind of closed system we have just been discussing, with the worker(s) clearly installed as 'part of the problem' so that nothing can change. This is also the picture presented by Jordan (1974) in his discussion of primary and secondary collusion. Figure 7.1(b) is perhaps even more disturbing, and thankfully quite rare. It represents the converse of 7.1(a), in which the client has been incorporated into the worker's inner world in order to satisfy some personal need. In such a case the worker would not be working with a 'real' client at all but with some sort of figment of internal fantasy.

Figure 7.1(c) represents another type of closed professional–client system in which the individual worker or team is defending so strongly against being absorbed or overwhelmed that very little new information penetrates in either direction. Casement (1985) eloquently describes the sort of individual work which becomes so submerged in its own pet theories and prejudices that communications from the client 'bounce off' or are met with clichéd comments or interpretations. Byng-Hall (1988) makes the same point for family therapists: namely, that there is a strong tendency for therapy teams to protect their own group cohesion and their own cherished belief systems by 'screening out' any feedback about the effect of their interventions on the family. In this way therapy teams can become closed systems in much the same way as myths close down individuals or families. Here, too, nothing can change because there is little informational traffic between the two sides. In social work this situation may arise when the worker or team feels so hard-pressed that it protects itself by blocking out the 'bombardment' of client needs and demands, and by concentrating fixedly on what it can provide, whether or not this is appropriate.

Needless to say, Figure 7.1(d) represents a more productive worker–client system, with two-way communications and their feedback being processed in a more open way. Each participant has, among other internal models, a constantly evolving internal representation of the other. The worker is able to accept that part of the client which is projected on to him or her, and to 'process' it and re-project it without getting taken over by it. This may then be available for reintrojection by the client. This process is the paradigm for all psychoanalytic therapy. In this way the client may be able to 'take in' some of the worker's healthy functioning (what therapists sometimes call introjecting the therapist as a good object) and to replace 'a relationship based on transference' with 'a realistic relationship in the outer world' (Fairbairn, 1958).

What are the implications of all this for social work supervision? First, social workers need to recognise and to accept what social work does to their feelings. It is no use trying to pretend that they can remain unaffected by their work. It stirs them in the most painful and confusing ways, as well as having effects on them of which they frequently remain unaware. Supervision has to address this personal dimension, whatever else it may seek to address in terms of administrative requirements. Good supervision should enable practitioners to cope with this personal dimension and survive it. Supervision should not be confused with counselling or therapy, but it certainly should help practitioners to identify those areas of their personal lives which might need 'sorting out' in relation to their work.

Second, as well as surviving such a process, social workers need to be able to use their own emotional responses in order to work more effectively. Social workers cannot avoid working with some of these feelings in themselves (Jordan, 1974). This constitutes the 'art' of social work: social workers' creative use of their most valuable resource, themselves (cf. England, 1986). Social work supervision should nurture this art: it should foster the practitioner's self awareness and expand his or her personal repertoire. This can only be done by encouraging social workers to enter their clients' world and to experience it from the inside, but without becoming part of a closed system. It is the role of supervision to ensure that the worker– client system remains as open as possible.

The supervision process: keeping the system open

Unfortunately, like any other interpersonal activity, social work supervision can itself become a closed system: for example, through collusive avoidance by both parties of areas in which the worker is acutely distressed or failing to make headway. Constraints of time and energy in a busy team can also be used defensively to ensure that supervision sessions have to be trimmed down to the bare administrative essentials. One of the most subtle ways in which supervision can become a closed circuit is through what Mattinson (1975) has called 'The Reflection Process'. Broadly speaking, this describes the phenomenon where the worker's countertransference is carried over into an adjacent situation, perhaps a supervision session or a case conference, or interactions with other workers (Mattinson and Sinclair, 1979). This process, as it occurs in supervision, has been variously described as 'parallel process' (Gross Doehrman, 1976), 're-enactment' (Pedder, 1986), 'second-order transference' (Holmes, 1986), or 'mirroring' (see A. Brown, 1984, pp 46–7). Put simply, whatever is going on between worker and client may also get played out between worker and supervisor, without either of them realising it. Frequently the nub of this process will be some unresolved difficulty in the worker. Pedder (1986) sums this up by remarking that, in supervision, the problem workers choose to talk about may very much represent an aspect of themselves and be repeated in the supervisory session. If this goes undetected then supervision sessions may quickly settle into an uncomfortable groove and stay there, despite the supervisor's best efforts to offer appropriate help or advice. Both parties remain unaware of the underlying dynamic, and the result is likely to be increasing frustration, followed by grateful retreat into a more administrative mode of supervision. We shall illustrate some of these points, and draw together some of the other themes we have been addressing, with an example from recent practice.

A male social worker was working jointly on a case with a female psychiatric nurse. They were offering marital counselling to the parents of a young female in-patient, and were weighing up whether or not to include the daughter in the sessions. The social worker was encouraged by his team leader to have a series of consultations with a colleague in a neighbouring team who had a special interest in this sort of family work.

Briefly, the circumstances were as follows. The daughter had been hospitalised for supposedly 'psychotic' ideas, some of which seemed to focus upon 'funny things' being done to her body. She was described as immature and attention-seeking, sometimes in an overtly sexual manner. Her parents, particularly her father, were felt to be overinvolved and overindulgent, and there were constant 'scenes' between daughter and parents which followed the same pattern of excessive attention-seeking on the part of the daughter, which evoked overdramatised caregiving from the parents.

The social worker had two main anxieties. First, he was having problems in his working relationship with the nurse, who reportedly favoured a behavioural approach and who tended to be quite directive with both daughter and parents. The two workers had so far had difficulty arranging a time to discuss their different approaches and work out an agreed strategy. Second, he was worried about what might happen if they included the daughter in the interviews. Whenever she had previously appeared, uninvited, there had been a 'scene' which had proved difficult to control for the therapists.

At a consultation following the first family session in which the young woman had been included, the social worker found to his surprise that he had completely 'forgotten' what had happened in that session. He thought he remembered writing something down, but could find no trace of his recording. He could still clearly recall previous sessions, a fact which made his blank memory of this one all the more striking. All he remembered was that the session had gone surprisingly well: there were no 'scenes' or disturbances, and the atmosphere had remained happy and relaxed, a big relief all round. He had even come away from the session without his customary headache!

What was happening here? The consulting colleague was able to help the social worker reflect on a number of points. First, the blank memory. Completely 'forgetting' something may mean that it is so painful that it needs to be pushed out of consciousness (see Chapter 1). In this case, however, it has a different flavour. There is a striking atmosphere of relief that the session was much 'better' than expected. It seems to have suited all parties to keep everything friendly: more like a social encounter than a therapy session. In other words, there are clear signs of a cosy *collusion* between workers and clients to keep away from anything too disturbing or threatening. By asking the social worker, 'What do you think the family might have been *doing* to you to make your mind go blank?', the supervisor helped his colleague to understand that a very *active* process was almost certainly at work beneath the family's low-key affability. They were actively neutralising the therapists and steering them away from any areas of potential conflict. For their part, the therapists were evidently quite happy to be neutralised in this way. For one thing, it prevented them from having to confront the conflicts within their own working relationship, something about which the social worker showed particular anxiety. The family had perhaps unconsciously tuned in to the workers' own predilection for *avoidance* as a defence (they had successfully avoided meeting to resolve their working difficulties, and perhaps their style of working was detectably hesitant and unchallenging). A neat 'closed system' was thus created in which a combined defensive strategy of avoidance ensured that the covert needs of all parties were met. Furthermore, everyone was able to come away thinking that it had been a 'good' session, happy and relaxed. In reality, of course, no real work had been done at all, hence none was remembered or recorded.

Second, having focused on what the worker might have been avoiding, the supervisor turned to what the family might have been keen to avoid in this session. Why was a session which included their daughter so different from previous sessions with parents on their own? Readers will no doubt frame their own hypotheses on the basis of information already given. If we add that the young woman also shouted 'Help me, help me!' on the ward for no apparent reason, then it is not too difficult to speculate about possible 'family secrets'. Whatever might have been going on, the family system was obviously keeping itself closely guarded whilst giving the outward appearance of being relaxed and 'open'.

Third, from this point supervision was able to explore the possibility that some degree of 'mirroring' or 'reflection' of the family dynamics might be occurring in the therapy partnership. Again the submerged and undiscussed conflict between the social worker and the nurse is the key factor here, providing a sort of nucleus around which other things might cluster. By allowing this conflict to persist, the workers were perhaps reproducing a professional version of the marital dynamic. If one hypothesised that the daughter's 'psychotic' symptoms were the expression of a disowned and projected marital disturbance, then the workers, by focusing all their own anxiety and attention on the young woman's behaviour, might well have been reproducing the same pattern. If the young woman behaved 'badly' in the session it would have exposed their own divergent approaches to dealing with such behaviour, and this might have brought their strained relationship into the open. Thus the combined worker–client system looked after itself by keeping the session well ordered and totally 'safe'. The daughter remained calm and well behaved, and everyone was happy: the parents because they could play 'happy families' and keep their own conflicts and secrets out of sight, and the workers because there was no testing behaviour to bring out their own secret rift. Presumably the daughter was happy because she had at last been allowed into a family session after being kept out for so long, and was no doubt being rewarded with a great deal of attention.

As far as the consultation sessions themselves are concerned, it is possible to see one or two signs of 'reflection' or 're-enactment' creeping in there, too. It was striking that the social worker and the 'consultant' also experienced difficulty arranging their meetings, which tended to get rearranged and disrupted quite a lot. In the 'blank memory' session the consultant also found himself struggling with a feeling that his time was somehow being wasted; the social worker could not even remember the session they were supposed to be discussing. It took some effort to resist this feeling and to investigate the underlying process. If he had simply taken the situation at face value he would probably have lost interest in the consultations, and thus the 'avoidance' strategy would have triumphed in the consultative relationship as well as in the therapeutic one.

On a broader view this consultation example raises further important issues to do with professions and institutions. The consultation was perhaps helpful as far as it went, but it would undoubtedly have been more productive if the co-therapist could have been included as well. Though many of us would find this entirely natural in a multi-disciplinary setting, it is not an idea which commands universal approval. Often practitioners stay within their professional boundaries because they provide them with a sense of identity and with a certain corporate comfort. Other professions may be viewed with attitudes ranging from suspicion to outright hostility or contempt. Practitioners develop stereotyped views of these other professions, sometimes needing to maintain these perspectives in the face of contrary evidence in order to preserve their own self-image. There is also the recurrent fear that if workers do not defend their professional identity, they run the risk of being 'taken over' or of having their power and status eroded.

All this, of course, is depressingly similar to people's ingrained attitudes towards anyone who is markedly 'different' (of different race, creed or sexual orientation, for instance). In the above consultation example, no attempt was made by the supervisor to examine the social worker's beliefs about the approach and attitudes of his nursing colleague, which may have owed more to stereotyped thinking (perhaps along the lines of 'Nurses adhere to the medical model, are directive and favour behavioural approaches') than to reality. Neither was there any analysis of the gender configuration, or of attitudes to people of the opposite sex, in the therapist–family–supervisor system. In a joint consultation session such beliefs (or fantasies or projections) could be examined; genuine differences of personal or professional approach could be identified and dealt with, thus releasing the concerted energy of two skilled professionals for more effective use with the family. It is quite possible that the nurse also entertained stereotyped ideas about the social worker (for example, that he was a woolly, non-directive, 'see what happens' sort of therapist), and this belief might well have encouraged her to be more 'directive' than she would otherwise have chosen to be. If this were so, the therapy partnership itself would be a sort of closed sub-system, buttressed by what Obholzer (1987) calls 'institutional projections'.

The omissions from the consultation and the possible reflections which had leaked into the supervisor–worker system raise the essential but often neglected priority of supervision for supervisors. Supervisors are just as likely as workers to bring personal and/or professional issues, triggers and blind spots into their work, or to succumb to dynamics within a case. Supervisors have their own punctuation, their own view of reality and of the systems in focus. Since this can make for closure, someone taking a meta-view of the supervisor-plus-system can potentially be helpful. In a worker–supervisor system both participants can foul up the process. Unresolved difficulties in the supervisor and/or structural features such as gender are just as influential in the process as factors internal to the case or to the worker.

Models of supervision and consultation

Individual supervision

The above account was, of course, an example of traditional one-to-one supervision, which is still perhaps the main form of supervision or consultation available to most practitioners. It derives from a tutorial or apprenticeship model and is based on the notion that, as the name suggests, the supervisor 'oversees' the work of the supervisee from a loftier position. Much traditional social work supervision is taken up with practical and administrative matters. This is a vital supervising task, highlighted recently by the enquiry into a child care tragedy in Southwark where it was discovered that inexperienced social workers were being supervised on high-risk cases by inexperienced supervisors (*Community Care*, 20 July 1989). The desperate staffing situation in some authorities makes it understandable that the bulk of available supervisory resources should be devoted to ensuring that basic standards are being met. In such circumstances it may be felt that anything further in the way of looking at 'casework process' would be a luxury. Ironically it becomes, in our view, even more vital to attend to process issues when practitioners are too busy or too overwhelmed with anxiety to reflect clearly about what they are doing. It is precisely these circumstances which intensify practitioner disturbance and which may produce all manner of 'acting out'.

Co-supervision

This refers to a more 'self-help' variety of supervision (or consultation) in which two workers make an agreement to discuss particular cases or particular issues to do with their work. The attractive feature for many practitioners is that it is done on an 'equal' footing, each helping the other and neither being viewed as the 'expert', although of course there is nothing to stop the pair seeking the help of another supervisor on particular matters.

Team or group supervision

This refers to any sort of social work supervision in which a group of workers (from the same team or from different teams or agencies) meet together on an occasional or regular basis in order to discuss their cases and to explore related issues. Usually the group will be convened by a team leader or specialist worker, but another viable model is that of a peer group, colleagues on an equal footing who are perhaps drawn together by a special interest, such as family therapy, or who simply wish to provide for themselves an experience of supervision which is not being catered for in their work setting.

Groups are very powerful entities. They can provide a rich and rewarding experience when they work well, or a dismal one when they work badly. It is particularly important for a supervision group to hold on to its *task*, the co-supervision of cases, in the face of inevitable pressures from within the group to steer it in other directions. For this reason it is usually helpful to have a designated convener, perhaps someone from outside the immediate 'system' if this is possible, or at least someone from within the system who is prepared to keep the group on a productive track.

It is a mistake to think that supervision groups have to spend all their time talking. It can be very illuminating, besides being very good for group cohesion and productivity, to use occasional techniques such as 'sculpting' or role-play to explore the material being presented.

Live supervision

This is a mode of supervision which has come strongly into vogue from the world of family therapy. Its big advantage is that the supervisor (or supervising team) is in immediate touch with anything that is occurring in the interview or therapy session, including the part being played by the interviewers. In traditional supervision a verbal account is presented some time 'after the event' to a supervisor who has to try and get at the material through several layers of 'editing'. Even if the worker brings audio or video tapes, the whole thing is still being viewed 'after the event'. Live supervision short-circuits this whole process. At its best it can give the supervisor an unparalleled 'feel' of what is going on between client and worker. It may also prompt interventions from the supervisor which can be put to immediate use, rather than being carried back to the following session some time later, by which time they have usually lost a good deal of their relevance and force. Although use of a one-way screen is preferable, live supervision does not depend on the availability of such a resource for its effectiveness. It is interesting to consider what extra impact live supervision might have made in the above example of casework consultation.

The merits of live supervision in the training of social work practitioners are well presented by Hayles (1988), who points out that the traditional model of seeing clients alone and then reporting back, selectively, to a supervisor, fails to stimulate new learning or the putting into practice of new skills and techniques. Although it can be very uncomfortable for the supervisee, live supervision creates a much more open system of experiential learning, making it virtually impossible simply to stick with old habits. Despite its practical difficulties in terms of staff time and observation facilities, live supervision is, in our view, immensely productive and will undoubtedly play an increasing part in social work training and practice.

Organised chaos: consultation to teams, agencies and institutions

Another trend which has been firmly consolidated by the family therapy movement, although it already had a long psychodynamic pedigree, is the practice of teams, agencies or institutions calling in a 'consultant' to look at how they operate. This may apply to the work they are doing with particular clients (for example, live consultation to the therapist-plus-family system, as described above) or to relationships within the working team. The format may be a 'one-off' consultation with a visiting guru or a series of regular sessions. Social workers are often suspicious of such practices, perhaps because so many group-process techniques have become more closely associated with the world of business management training than with that of the personal social services. In our experience, however, consultations of this kind have a great deal to offer to social workers, whose organisations have a strong tendency to become defensively entangled in their own internal processes to the detriment of the task (see Chapter 5).

It is well known that working groups tend to develop some of the characteristics of family systems. This is hardly surprising, given the percentage of our lives which is devoted to work, and the intimacies and animosities which frequently develop between colleagues. Organisational psychologists use terms like 'informal organisation' and 'psychological contract' to describe the hidden personal agendas which frequently lurk beneath the more formal terms of employment (see Blackler and Shimmin, 1984). In professions like social work this personal dimension of the job is all the more intense because the work itself is so intensely personal. Another way of putting this is that the sort of people who go into social work are perhaps more inclined than most to look for strongly personal gratification in their work. Given these considerations it is not surprising that social workers inhabit a highly-charged working environment in which, for all sorts of reasons, interpersonal dynamics may drastically affect both the perception and the performance of the task. One way of sorting out these processes is to call in a consultant from outside the system.

An example from recent experience may illustrate some of the issues commonly encountered. A multi-disciplinary mental health team invited a social worker to act as facilitator at their weekly staff sensitivity group. They felt they had done as much self-examining as they could on their own, and that they needed someone from outside to help them look more deeply at what was happening, or not happening, in the team. They felt they were generally 'too nice' to each other and that they needed to confront some of their less friendly feelings for each other. As work progressed it became clear that almost every one of the workers had enormous *personal* investment in the team and a great desire for it to 'succeed' (although obviously 'success' meant different things to different people). For various personal reasons they each needed the team to meet needs and match expectations which were clearly being imported from their personal lives and from their experience of previous professional settings. For example, several team members were greatly affected whenever anyone was absent, feeling that this threatened the team's cohesion and hampered its work. Another worker was going through a major personal crisis which raised enormous anxieties in everyone else in the team. As the team began to focus on interprofessional tensions it became more and more obvious that professional and personal matters were inextricably entwined. The professional issues could not be tackled without addressing the interpersonal needs and anxieties.

This picture would not be untypical of many social work teams. Far from being a self-indulgent distraction, consultation sessions with an outside facilitator may offer the only hope of freeing the team, agency or institution to do its job more effectively.

Similar tangles can affect and render less effective interdisciplinary encounters, as has been shown in several child abuse enquiries where the interconnectedness of systems has clearly been marked by forces making for closure. The types of intra- and interagency dynamics in which practitioners can become embroiled are varied.

First, let us consider splitting. Different professional groups have different emphases and timescales within any task, different models of understanding the phenomena which give rise to the task, as well as individual preferences, attitudes and sensitivities. In addition, they may have different levels of contact with service-users which may produce overpessimistic or overoptimistic attitudes. Finally, stereotypes (images of the roles various professional groups are seen to occupy) and beliefs about status may creep into interrelationships. Child abuse case conferences, child care reviews and planning meetings may be sabotaged by such 'splits' which, in themselves, may mirror similar splits within user–family systems.

Second, there is group collusive cohesion. Here the dynamic is conformity and denial of difference as a defence against the anxiety aroused by the nature of the task. This phenomenon of 'groupthink' (Blackler and Shimmin, 1984) may have at least two outcomes. In one, the feelings are discharged against the clients, as in conferences where hostility or helplessness about a family strongly influences decisions taken. In another, professionals agree on what can be agreed upon, losing a sense of the wholeness of the task. For example, a case conference agreed on place of safety orders for two girls, one of whom had been sexually abused by her step-father, but failed to even consider the five boys in the family on whom no medical evidence had been found. To have considered them would have required the meeting to face disagreements between its members on grounds for removal, or how removal should be effected, or even on whether boys were likely to be sexually abused by a male parent.

Third, there is also neglect and abuse. The fear of failure, the volume of work and the absence of consensus on acceptable risk-decisions based on thorough assessments by professionals, culminates in an almost obsessive emphasis on task. In the course of this, workers are neglected, if not abused. Team leaders insist on allocating cases beyond the limits of worker endurance or safety. Inexperienced workers carry high-risk cases. The system effectively sacrifices its workers (workers' skills are not matched to case needs, caseloads are too high for effective work, resources and training are limited), and denies their practice realities and needs in order to maintain some semblance of accomplishing its task. Social workers are, effectively, recruited to diffuse stress within the welfare system and wider society.

To promote openness, a four phase approach to intra- and interagency contact is desirable, however well established a group may be.

Overview

One should recognise factors making for non-rational decision-making, such as a family where no progress has been made and high levels of anxiety have been aroused after considerable agency inputs, or a situation where professionals from different organisations may be acting out roles taken by family members. Taking an overview means analysing the interactions and interrelationships within the system, communicating about them and answering a basic question: in which part of the system does the problem lie?

Preliminaries

Group members must share their beliefs, anxieties, level of morale, values and attitudes about the task, together with any relevant history as it affects the system (Coulshed and Abdullah-Zadeh,

1985) if these are not to create suspicion and resistance, infiltrate covertly and sabotage task performance. This must inevitably be linked with a focus on any pressures from outside the group meeting which might influence it in a particular direction. Thus: what pressures exist? In what direction are they pulling and press-ganging the group? What response can be devised? Are the pressures legitimate? Can the task be performed effectively?

Initial statements

These are two-fold. First, what each member wants from a particular contact, the key questions being: why am I here? What do I want? What will I settle for? Second, role negotiation, characterised by answers to: what is my role? What do I feel about this? Who needs to be included in the decision making system and why? Are all the required roles covered? What skills and responsibilities does the system possess and need?

Discussion in process

An open discussion must consider alternatives, especially those people may be keen to avoid; share information, especially that which members may not want others to know about; share assumptions about roles and tasks; articulate differences, uncertainties and conflicts of view (Holdaway, 1986); clarify limitations on each person, what they can and cannot do, and why; communicate about what is not being said and what the feared consequences are of things being said. Key systemic, circular questions will help to utilise resources and knowledge available to the system by introducing information about process and drawing participants' attention to interconnections and patterns: what do I/ others think I/they have done well? What might I/we/they have done differently? Whose help could be enlisted? What might *A* suggest? What might I/we do about *B*? How might *C* perceive what I/we are doing? How do I perceive what *A* and *B* are doing/saying? What am I/we/they finding difficult? Why might this be? How might I/we/they address this? These processes may be more easily accomplished where one person holds a 'consultant' position, present but outside the system.

Supervising child abuse work: a post-Cleveland view

All social work tasks present their own unique difficulties and demands, but perhaps no area of the work is more challenging to the worker – personally, technically and legally – than that of child protection. The physical and sexual abuse of children has come to occupy a special place within social work for a number of obvious reasons. The enormity of offences committed against vulnerable children, the sheer volume and complexity of such cases, the risks they involve and the social and legal requirements which attend them, all ensure that social workers have to give priority to this area of their work. Successive child care 'scandals' have sharply rattled the public conscience and have focused public concern. Society requires that social work protects its children and on no account 'allows' a child for whom it has assumed any statutory responsibility to be cruelly treated or abused, let alone killed. Social workers who fail to prevent such tragedies are blitzed by public outrage and pilloried by the media. On the other hand, if social workers are perceived as being too keen to remove children to the relative safety of care, they are equally open to criticism or abuse.

This conflict about how social workers should protect society's children can be pictured, psychodynamically, as child protection workers fulfilling a sort of 'ego' role, struggling to control the unruly impulses of the 'id' (the outbreak of raw sex and aggression within abusing families), whilst at the same time coming under pressure from the 'superego' demands of society's moral and legal imperatives (Trowell, 1986). This neat division of functions and feelings is, of course, an oversimplification. The complicating factor here is that all three functions are at work in everyone; 'Unconsciously we are all abusers' (Mollon, 1988). This is the complex, unpalatable truth of child abuse work which has profound implications for both abusers and abused, for social workers and their supervisors and for society as a whole.

Let us consider some of the effects of child abuse on the workers who are most intimately involved with it, and then explore some of the implications for social work supervision and training.

It is well known that child abuse produces strong reactions in those professionals who come into close contact with it. Bacon (1988) describes an abuse case conference which found itself collectively impelled to reject the family and the child. Carr (1989) identifies five different types of reactions within teams of workers dealing with abuse cases, and uses the term 'countertransference' in something like its original sense to describe them. In other words he is pointing to the sort of unconscious reaction which social workers are subject to, and which is shaped by their own particular personality and life experience. Hence professionals may have a powerful impulse to 'rescue the child' or to 'rescue mother and child while persecuting the father', impulses which may easily determine the direction of the work and blind workers to other possible viewpoints. Such impulses might then bring workers into conflict with colleagues who adopt a different stance. As a number of recent writers have pointed out, particularly in the wake of the Cleveland affair, child abuse commonly has a powerful and pervasive *splitting* effect; on individuals, families, on professional teams and on society as a whole.

Two recent newspaper articles make this point with particular clarity. Timmins (1989) comments on the two 'sides' of the Cleveland controversy as reflected in both the professional and the public debate. He notes that many people, including the key protagonists in the drama, could see only what they already believed. Such a sharp polarisation of views is a sure sign that powerful unconscious reactions have been mobilised which are not amenable to rational persuasion. Indeed, paraphrasing Carr (1989) we could perhaps describe these fixed positions as, on the one side, 'Rescue the wronged families and persecute the professionals'; and, on the other, 'Rescue the professionals and persecute (or perhaps prosecute) the abusers.' In a similar article Watts (1989) notes that 'to cleave' means to split, and comments that 'Cleveland' has split Britain in two. For many people, she says, the existence of child sexual abuse on such a large scale is so unthinkable that they simply reject the idea out of hand. 'An offence against a belief system', she goes on, 'does not require reference to primary sources of information.' Here again we can spot the same 'counter-transference' phenomenon; a powerful, gut-level reaction which is not open to rational debate. The point to note here is that professional workers are just as susceptible to the process as other members of the public.

Kraemer (1988) offers a sophisticated and profoundly disturbing analysis of this 'splitting' phenomenon as it affects professional workers in cases of child sexual abuse. His main point is that working with abuse cases can divide colleagues against each other in ways which turn out to be 'unexpectedly personal'. Examining this phenomenon he argues that child sexual abuse is inherently divisive; it splits children from parents, mothers from fathers, families from their natural support networks, and professional workers from each other. It also splits the victim from him- or herself. We are all familiar with the partitioning that goes on within the child's own mind (formation of multiple personalities, 'forgetting'), as an attempt to cope with the fact that a trusted (and often loved) parent can also be the perpetrator of something incomprehensibly hurtful and frightening. The child is often in an impossible dilemma and may actually be threatened with the break up of the family if he or she 'tells'. It is common for abused children to feel that what has happened must be their own fault. An appalling personal legacy of division and disharmony is frequently carried into adult life. As far as a male abuser is concerned, he may lead a sort of 'double life', fronted by the image of the loving father, uncle or brother. Similarly the mother may 'know' what is happening but shuts it out of full awareness. Such splitting, says Kraemer, produces a sort of 'stupidity' in which the mind is divided against itself. He argues that the same thing happens to the professional workers, adding that sexual abuse is different in kind from any other problems they encounter and 'cannot be contained by our usual professional attitudes'. This is because it stirs impulses and fantasies in all of us which we may find profoundly disturbing. The thought of child sexual abuse and incest arouses the most primitive anxieties, leading to the mobilisation of primitive splitting and projective defences.

It is clear that child abuse work confronts practitioners with the same personal and professional challenges as any other area of the work, but in a more intense and concentrated form. For this reason it makes special demands on social work training and supervision. Those who train others to tackle such work or who supervise others in its day-to-day handling should not only be thoroughly conversant with the law relating to child protection and with their own departmental procedures, but should also be aware from first-hand experience of the direct *personal* impact such work invariably has upon the worker. Both supervision and on-going training should be equipping practitioners to *think* and to *act* in ways which take account of the splitting and stupefying effects on professionals of exposure to cases of abuse. Otherwise workers will continue to be worn down very quickly by such work and departments will continue to fail to meet the rising tide of referrals.

This means that those with supervising or training responsibility should be relatively at ease with their own sexuality and their own aggression. We would also argue that a working knowledge of psychodynamics (alongside their existing knowledge of 'human growth and development') is a basic requirement for all practitioners and absolutely essential for supervisors and trainers. Social workers with a specialised knowledge of psychodynamic processes should be more widely used as consultants by social services departments (Temperley and Himmel, 1986). If ever there was an area of work in which this was needed it is the area of child abuse. Otherwise it is difficult to see how social workers can find ways of counteracting the defensive splits which inevitably occur, not only within themselves but between themselves, as well as between themselves and their colleagues in other professions.

Postscript: openings into closed systems

Several themes have run through this book. Social work is a stressful and difficult, if not impossible, profession. Practitioners are required to work within disturbing, sometimes violent situations, with people who are severely disadvantaged and deprived materially and emotionally. Social workers regularly confront practice dilemmas; the necessity of having to take difficult decisions, in which there are no right answers, based on a delicate assessment of risks, needs and competing (if not conflicting) rights; and a myriad of pressures, including from within. The result is a complex maze and interaction of personal, professional, interagency and societal dynamics and pressures, and potential tangles between service-users, social workers, agencies and society. Figure P.1 attempts to represent diagrammatically how this complexity can lock all the participants into a closed system, individually and interpersonally, within and between. Workers bring to the task their personal and professional experience which may, via transference and projection, disrupt the helping encounter. What clients bring may trigger and provoke reactions in the workers (countertransference). Finally, societal attitudes – for example, ageism, intolerance of difference, conflicts in explanations for child abuse or heterosexism – are avoided or deflected through social work. These 'realities' may provoke dissonance, commonly reflected in comments that compare the training received and initial motivations for entering social work with the job encountered. Individually or in combination, they can produce a system prone to such dysfunctional defence mechanisms as mirroring, omnipotent acting-out, collusion, and avoidance or denial of authority.

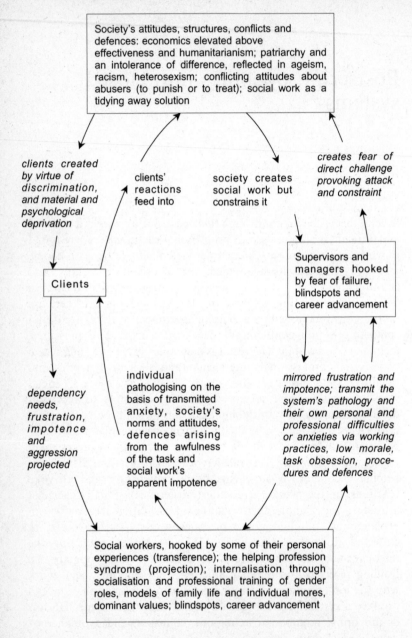

Society's attitudes, structures, conflicts and defences: economics elevated above effectiveness and humanitarianism; patriarchy and an intolerance of difference, reflected in ageism, racism, heterosexism; conflicting attitudes about abusers (to punish or to treat); social work as a tidying away solution

clients created by virtue of discrimination, and material and psychological deprivation

clients' reactions feed into

society creates social work but constrains it

creates fear of direct challenge provoking attack and constraint

Clients

Supervisors and managers hooked by fear of failure, blindspots and career advancement

dependency needs, frustration, impotence and aggression projected

individual pathologising on the basis of transmitted anxiety, society's norms and attitudes, defences arising from the awfulness of the task and social work's apparent impotence

mirrored frustration and impotence; transmit the system's pathology and their own personal and professional difficulties or anxieties via working practices, low morale, task obsession, procedures and defences

Social workers, hooked by some of their personal experiences (transference); the helping profession syndrome (projection); internalisation through socialisation and professional training of gender roles, models of family life and individual mores, dominant values; blindspots, career advancement

Figure P.1 *A closed system*

Social workers, therefore, need theories to shape and inform their work, to understand and intervene in this complexity. They also need to understand themselves, service-users, organisational systems, the wider context in which workers and clients meet, and the effect each of these may have on the others. If practitioners are to survive and to practise creatively and effectively, they must make sense of their practice and of the context in which it takes place. Theory, then, is essential for contemporary social work practice. A combined psychodynamic and systems approach is highly relevant since both are concerned with interactions, with what goes on between people, with processes of openness, closure, double-binds and patterns which influence thoughts, feelings and behaviour.

Nonetheless, however useful theories may be in understanding and describing what is going on in and around social work, practitioners may still feel impotent and paralysed, overburdened by the seemingly endless flow of pressing demands and the compromises, apparently necessary in practice, which pull them away from research findings and the theory of good practice. Some encouragements, openings into closed systems, may be discerned from the two theories which have provided the foundation building blocks for this book.

1. *Overview.* Both theories illuminate the connectedness of parts within systems and the circular nature of interactions within and between. Thus, wherever social workers intervene, they will make a difference. Both theories provide a 'pulling back' in order to view practice from outside. The debates about the superiority of casework as against community work are debates about false polarities. The social and the individual are dynamically and systemically connected. Social work must intervene in both and at the interface between the two.

2. *Preliminaries.* Theory provides a tool with which to analyse and describe. It provides a framework for understanding what is going on. Social workers can therefore describe the practice realities and dilemmas which they face, the pressures which they encounter, and offer their critical analysis of these. Theory provides a voice.

3. *Role negotiation.* Open systems are characterised by, *inter alia*, channels of communication which enable information to be

exchanged. Social workers must speak about the task, its difficulties and, at times, its sheer awfulness. To remain silent about the compromises often demanded of practitioners by inadequately funded, supervised and trained services, and to struggle alone with role conflicts (for instance, between empowerment and social control, treatment and punishment, needs and resources), is to collude with the status quo. Thus there must be open communication, with service-users and managers, centred on why we are here, what we see as our role, and how we might enable change.

4. *Discussion in process*. The key question is always 'What is happening here?' The challenge and opportunity for social workers is to hold up a mirror and reflect back what may be seen. Thus workers with supervisors and managers must communicate about practice realities, about what can and cannot be done, and about the feared consequences of not being able to do what is demanded. Rather than absorb projections from society, social workers and their managers must describe what is happening. With service-users social workers must equally not absorb projections but rather share what they see and introduce different possibilities about a situation. These actions may break the grip of intrapsychic, interpersonal and social systems and allow a different version of reality to be installed.

Theories provide an understanding of what is and a vision of what may be. Psychodynamic and systems theories provide an understanding of what social workers, service-users and supervisors may experience and how they may become locked in particular positions. Equally, they provide some keys for opening the systems, keys which we hope this book has gone some way towards clarifying.

References

Addison, C. (1982) 'A defence against the public? Aspects of intake in a social services department', *British Journal of Social Work*, 12 (6), 605–18.

Alexander, P (1985) 'A systems theory conceptualisation of incest', *Family Process*, 24, 79–88.

Allen, M. (1988) 'Stemming the flood', *Social Work Today*, 20 (10), 14–15.

Allen, R. (1989) 'The rapid erosion of a heady ideal', *Social Services Insight*, 4 (7), 20–1.

Arden, M. (1984) 'Infinite sets and double–binds', *International Journal of Psychoanalysis*, 65, 443–52.

Arden, M. (1986) 'On not knowing all the answers', *Free Associations*, 4, 139–49.

Ausloos, G. (1986) 'The march of time: rigid or chaotic transactions, two different ways of living time', *Family Process*, 25, 549–57.

Bacon, R. (1988) 'Counter-transference in a case conference: resistance and rejection in work with abusing families and their children', in G. Pearson, J. Treseder and M. Yelloly (eds), *Social Work and the Legacy of Freud. Psychoanalysis And Its Uses* (London: Macmillan).

Bailey, R. and Brake, M. (eds) (1975) *Radical Social Work* (London: Edward Arnold).

Baird, P. (1989) 'Lives devoted to the pursuit of bogus wisdom', *Social Work Today*, 20 (23), 32.

Bandler, L. (1987) 'Three British–American conferences: a psychodynamic bridge', *Journal of Social Work Practice*, May, 2–8.

Barclay, P. (ed.) (1982) *Social Workers, Their Role and Tasks*, (London: Bedford Square Press).

Bateson, G. (1970) 'A systems approach', *International Journal of Psychiatry*, 9 (2), 242–4.

Bateson, G. (1973) *Steps to an Ecology of Mind* (St Albans: Paladin).

Bateson, G. (1979) *Mind and Nature: A Necessary Unity* (London: Fontana).

Beckford Report (1985) *A Child In Trust* (London: London Borough of Brent).

Bennett, D., Fox, C., Jowell, T. and Skynner, A. (1976) 'Towards a family approach in a psychiatric day hospital', *British Journal of Psychiatry*, 129, 73–81.

Berkowitz, R. and Leff, J. (1984) 'Clinical teams reflect family dysfunction', *Journal of Family Therapy*, 6 (2), 79–89.

Bion, W. (1955) 'Group dynamics – a review', in M. Klein, P. Heimann, and R. Money-Kyrle (eds), *New Directions In Psychoanalysis* (London: Tavistock).

Bion, W. (1959) 'Attacks on linking', *International Journal of Psychoanalysis*, 40, 308–15.

Bion, W. (1961) *Experiences in Groups* (London: Tavistock).

Bion, W. (1962) *Learning from Experience* (London: Heinemann).

Blackler, F. and Shimmin, S. (1984) *Applying Psychology in Organisations* (London: Methuen).

Blackwell, R. and Wilkins, M. (1981) 'Beyond the family system', *Journal of Family Therapy*, 3 (2), 79–90.

Blech, G. (1981) 'How to prevent 'burn out' of social workers', in S. Martel, (ed.) *Supervision and Team Support* (London: Bedford Square Press).

Bloch, S. (1982) *What is Psychotherapy* (Oxford University Press).

Blom-Cooper, L. (1988) 'A patch for a punctured ideal', *Social Services Insight*, 3 (18), 12–14.

Bowlby, J. (1973) *Attachment and Loss, Volume 2: Separation: Anxiety and Anger* (London: Hogarth).

Bowlby, J. (1979) *The Making and Breaking of Affectional Bonds* (London: Tavistock).

Bowlby, J. (1988) *A Secure Base* (London: Routledge & Kegan Paul).

Box, S., Copley, B., Magagna, J. and Moustaki, E. (eds) (1981) *Psychotherapy with Families: An Analytic Approach* (London: Routledge & Kegan Paul).

Brandon, D. (1987) 'Social casework – rest in peace', *Social Work Today*, 18 (38), 8.

Braye, S. (1978) 'Anxiety and Defence in Social Work'. Unpublished thesis, Exeter University.

Braye, S. and Preston-Shoot, M. (1990) 'On teaching and applying the law in social work: it is not that simple', *British Journal of Social Work*, 20 (4), 333–53.

Brewer, C. and Lait, J. (1980) *Can Social Work Survive?* (London: Temple Smith).

Britton, R. (1981) 'Re–enactment as an unwitting professional response to family dynamics', in S. Box *et al.* (1981).

Brown, A. (1984) *Consultation – An Aid to Successful Social Work* (London: Heinemann).

Brown, J. (1964) *Freud and the Post Freudians* (Harmondsworth: Penguin).

Brown, D. and Pedder, J. (1979) *Introduction to Psychotherapy. An Outline of Psychodynamic Principles and Practice* (London: Tavistock).

Bruggen, P. and O'Brian, C. (1987) *Helping Families. Systems, Residential and Agency Responsibility* (London: Faber and Faber).

Buckley, P. (ed) (1986) *Essential Papers on Object Relations* (New York University Press).

Burnham, J. (1986) *Family Therapy* (London: Tavistock).

Burnham, J. and Harris, Q. (1988) 'Systemic family therapy: the Milan approach', in E. Street and W. Dryden (eds), *Family Therapy In Britain* (Milton Keynes: Open University Press).

Butcher, H. (1984) 'Conceptualising community social work – a response to Alan York', *British Journal of Social Work*, 14 (6), 625–33.

Butler, A. and Pritchard, C. (1984) *Social Work and Mental Illness* (London: Macmillan).

Byng-Hall, J. (1973) 'Family myths used as a defence in conjoint family therapy', *British Journal of Medical Psychology*, 46, 239–50.

Byng-Hall, J. (1979) 'Re-editing family mythology during family therapy', *Journal of Family Therapy*, 1 (2), 103–16.

Byng-Hall, J. (1985) 'The family script: a useful bridge between theory and practice', *Journal of Family Therapy*, 7 (3), 301–5.

Byng-Hall, J. (1988) 'Scripts and legends in families and family therapy', *Family Process*, 27, 167–79.

Cade, B. (1979) 'The use of paradox in therapy', in S. Walrond-Skinner (ed.), *Family and Marital Psychotherapy* (London: Routledge & Kegan Paul).

Cade, B. and Southgate, P. (1979) 'Honesty is the best policy', *Journal of Family Therapy*, 1 (1), 23–31.

Carew, R. (1979) 'The place of knowledge in social work activity', *British Journal of Social Work*, 9 (3), 349–64.

Carl, D. and Jurkovic, G. (1983) 'Agency triangles: problems in agency–family relationships', *Family Process*, 22, 441–51.

Carpenter, J. and Treacher, A. (1984) 'Introduction: Using Family Therapy', in A. Treacher and J. Carpenter (eds), *Using Family Therapy* (Oxford: Basil Blackwell).

Carpenter, J., Treacher, A., Jenkins, H. and O'Reilly, P. (1983) 'Oh no! Not the Smiths again! An exploration of how to identify and overcome "stuckness" in family therapy', *Journal of Family Therapy*, 5 (1), 81–96.

Carpy, D. (1989) 'Tolerating the countertransference: a mutative process', *International Journal of Psychoanalysis*, 70, 287–94.

Carr, A. (1989) 'Countertransference reactions to families where child abuse has occurred', *Journal of Family Therapy*, 11 (1) 87–97.

Casement, P. (1974) 'The supervisory viewpoint', in W. Finn (ed.), *Family Therapy In Social Work* (London: Family Welfare Association Conference Papers).

Casement, P. (1985) *On Learning from the Patient* (London: Tavistock).

Cecchin, G. (1987) 'Hypothesising, circularity and neutrality revisited: an invitation to curiosity', *Family Process*, 26 (4) ,405–13.

Christophas, C., Goldsmith, A. and Ellenbogen, J. (1983) 'Family therapy and the position of women. Collusion or challenge? *FSU Quarterly*, 30, 24–6.

Clare, M. (1988) 'Supervision, role strain and social services departments', *British Journal of Social Work*, 18 (5), 489–507.

Cooklin, A. (1979) 'A psychoanalytic framework for a systemic approach to family therapy', *Journal of Family Therapy*, 1 (1), 153–65.

Corby, B. (1982) 'Theory and practice in long-term social work: a case study of practice with social services department clients', *British Journal of Social Work*, 12 (6), 619–38.

Corden, J. and Preston-Shoot, M. (1987) *Contracts in Social Work* (Aldershot: Gower).

Coulshed, V. and Abdullah–Zadeh, J. (1983) 'The family as a unit of treatment: a case record', *British Journal of Social Work*, 13 (1), 39–55.

Coulshed, V. and Abdullah–Zadeh, J. (1985) 'The side effects of intervention?' *British Journal of Social Work*, 15 (5), 479–86.

Crowther, C. (1988) 'A psychoanalytic perspective on family therapy', in G. Pearson *et al.* (1988).

Curnock, K. and Hardiker, P. (1979) *Towards Practice Theory* (London: Routledge & Kegan Paul).

Cypher, J. (1973) 'Sections and strife', *Social Work Today*, 4 (4), 104–8.

Dana, M. and Lawrence, M. (1988) 'Understanding bulimia: a feminist psychoanalytic account of women's eating problems', in G. Pearson *et al.* (1988).

Dare, C. (1979) 'Psychoanalysis and systems in family therapy', *Journal of Family Therapy*, 1 (1), 137–51.

Dare, C. (1981) 'Psychoanalysis and family therapy', in S. Walrond-Skinner (ed.) *Developments in Family Therapy* (London: Routledge & Kegan Paul).

Dare, C. (1988) 'Psychoanalytic family therapy', in E. Street and W. Dryden (eds) *Family Therapy in Britain* (Milton Keynes: Open University Press).

Davies, M. (1984) 'Training: what we think of it now', *Social Work Today*, 15 (20), 12–17.

Davies, M. (1985) *The Essential Social Worker* (London: Heinemann).

Davies, M. and Brandon, M. (1988) 'The Summer of '88', *Community Care*, 733, 16–18.

Day, P. (1985) 'An interview: constructing reality', *British Journal of Social Work*, 15 (5), 487–99.

Dell, P. (1982) 'Beyond homeostasis: toward a concept of coherence', *Family Process*, 21, 21–41.

Dicks, H. (1963) 'Object relations theory and marital studies', *British Journal of Medical Psychology*, 36, 125–29.

Dimmock, B. and Dungworth, D. (1983) 'Creating manoeuvrability for family/systems therapists in social services departments', *Journal of Family Therapy*, 5 (1), 53–69.

Dimmock, B. and Dungworth, D. (1985) 'Beyond the family: using network meetings with statutory child care cases', *Journal of Family Therapy*, 7 (1), 45–68.

Douglas, R., Ettridge, D., Fearnheard, D., Payne, C., Pugh, D. and Sowter, D. (1988) *Helping People Work Together: A Guide To Participative Working Practices* (London: National Institute for Social Work).

Dowling, E. and Osborne, E. (eds) (1985) *The Family and The School. A Joint Systems Approach to Problems with Children* (London: Routledge & Kegan Paul)

Dowrick, C. (1983) 'Strange meeting: Marxism, psychoanalysis and social work', *British Journal of Social Work*, 13 (1), 1–18.

Dungworth, D. and Reimers, S. (1984) 'Family therapy in social services departments', in A. Treacher and J. Carpenter (eds), *Using Family Therapy* (Oxford: Basil Blackwell).

Dunham, J. (1978) 'Staff stress in residential work', *Social Work Today*, 9 (45), 18–20.

Eichenbaum, L. and Orbach, S. (1982) *Outside In...Inside Out* (Harmondsworth: Penguin).

Elkaim, M. (1986) 'A systemic approach to couple therapy', *Family Process*, 25, 35–42.

Ellis, J. (1978) 'Psychology and the unitary approach to social work: some issues for the curriculum', in M. Olsen (ed.), *The Unitary Model: Its Implications for Social Work Theory and Practice* (Birmingham: Birmingham University/British Association of Social Workers).

England, H. (1986) *Social Work As Art* (London: Allen and Unwin).

Evans, R. (1976) 'Some implications of an integrated model of social work for theory and practice', *British Journal of Social Work*, 6 (2), 177–200.

Eysenck, H. (1952) 'The effects of psychotherapy, an evaluation', *Journal of Consulting Psychology*, 16, 319–24.

Eysenck, H. (1965) 'The effects of psychotherapy', *International Journal of Psychiatry*, 1, 99–144.

Fahlberg, V. (1981a) *Attachment and Separation* (London: British Agencies for Adoption and Fostering).

Fahlberg, V. (1981b) *Helping Children When They Must Move* (London: British Agencies for Adoption and Fostering).

Fairbairn, W. (1943) 'The repression and the return of bad objects (with special reference to the war neuroses)', in Fairbairn, (1952).

Fairbairn, W. (1952) *Psychoanalytic Studies of The Personality* (London: Tavistock).

Fairbairn,W (1958) 'On the nature and aims of psycho-analytical treatment', *International Journal of Psychoanalysis*, 39, 374–85.

Feldman, L. (1982) 'Dysfunctional marital conflict: an integrative interpersonal–intrapsychic model', *Journal of Marital and Family Therapy*, 8, 417–28.

Ferreira, A. (1963) 'Family myth and homeostasis', *Archives of General Psychiatry*, 9, 457–63.

Fordham, M. (1969) *Children as Individuals* (London: Hodder and Stoughton).

Freud, A. (1968) *The Ego and the Mechanisms of Defence* (London: Hogarth).

Freud, A. (ed) (1986) *Sigmund Freud: The Essentials of Psychoanalysis* (Harmondsworth: Penguin).

Freud, S. (1900) *The Interpretation of Dreams* (*SE*, vols 4–5; London: Hogarth; *PFL* 4).

Freud, S. (1901) The Psychopathology of Everyday Life (*SE* 6; *PFL* 5).

Freud, S. (1905a) Fragment of an Analysis of a Case of Hysteria (Dora) (*SE* 7, *PFL* 8).

Freud, S. (1905b) Three Essays on the Theory of Sexuality (*SE* 7; *PFL* 7).

Freud, S. (1910) 'The future prospects of psycho-analytic therapy', *SE* 11, 139–51.

Freud, S. (1912) 'Recommendations for physicians on the psycho-analytic method of treatment', *SE* 12, 109–20.

Freud, S. (1914) 'Remembering, repeating and working through', *SE* 12.

Freud, S. (1925) 'Some psychical consequences of the anatomical distinction between the sexes'.,*SE* 19.

Freud, S. (1949) *An Outline of Psychoanalysis* (London: Hogarth).

Friedman, L. (1975) 'Current psychoanalytic object relations theory and its clinical implications', *International Journal of Psychoanalysis*, 56, 137–46.

Frosh, S. (1987) *The Politics of Psychoanalysis* (London: Macmillan).

Furniss, T., Bentovim, A. and Kinston, W. (1983) 'Clinical process recording in focal family therapy', *Journal of Marital and Family Therapy*, 9 (2), 147–70.

Gammack, G. (1982) 'Social work as uncommon sense', *British Journal of Social Work*, 12 (1), 3–22.

Gardener, D. (1988) 'A sharing approach to the management of stress', *Social Work Today*, 20 (7), 18–19.

Gill, A. (1988) 'In search of our holy grail', *Community Care*, 723, 22.

Glastonbury, B., Bradley, R. and Orme, J. (1987) *Managing People In The Personal Social Services* (Chichester: Wiley).

Goldner, V. (1985) 'Feminism and family therapy', *Family Process*, 24, 31–47.

Goldner, V. (1988) 'Generation and gender: normative and covert hierarchies', *Family Process*, 27, 17–31.

Goldstein, H. (1973) *Social Work Practice: A Unitary Approach* (Columbia: University of South Carolina Press).

Gorell-Barnes, G. (1979) 'Infant needs and angry responses – a look at violence in the family', in S. Walrond-Skinner (ed.), *Family and Marital Psychotherapy* (London: Routledge & Kegan Paul).

Gorell-Barnes, G. (1980) 'Family therapy in social work settings: a survey by questionnaire 1976 to 1978', *Journal of Family Therapy*, 2 (4), 357–78.

Gorell-Barnes, G. (1985) 'Systems theory and family therapy', in M. Rutter, and L. Hersov (eds), *Child and Adolescent Psychiatry: Modern Approaches*, 2nd ed (Oxford: Basil Blackwell).

Greenberg, J. and Mitchell, S. (1983) *Object Relations in Psychoanalytic Theory* (Harvard University Press).

Gross Doehrman, M. (1976) 'Parallel process in supervision and psychotherapy', *Bulletin of the Menninger Clinic*, 40 (1).

Hall, A. and Fagen, R. (1956) 'Definition of a system', *General Systems Yearbook*, 1, 18–28.

Hamilton,V. (1987) 'Some problems in the clinical application of attachment theory', *Psychoanalytic Psychotherapy*, 3 (1), 67–83.

Hare-Mustin, R. (1987) 'The problem of gender in family therapy theory', *Family Process*, 26, 15–27.

Harris, N. (1987) 'Defensive social work', *British Journal of Social Work*, 17 (1), 61–9.

Hartman, A. (1969) 'Anomie and social casework', *Social Casework*, 50 (3), 131–7.

Hayles, M. (1988) 'Becoming a social work practitioner: the use of live supervision in the practice placement', *Journal of Social Work Practice*, 3 (2), 74–84.

Heard, D. (1974) 'Crisis intervention guided by attachment concepts – a case study', *Journal of Child Psychology and Psychiatry*, 15, 111–22.

Heard, D. (1978) 'From object relations to attachment theory: a basis for family therapy', *British Journal of Medical Psychology*, 51, 67–76.

Heimann, P. (1950) 'On counter–transference', *International Journal of Psychoanalysis*, 31, 81–4.

Hinshelwood, R. (1983) 'Projective identification and Marx's concept of man', *International Review of Psychoanalysis*, 10, 221–6.

Hinshelwood, R. (1987) *What Happens in Groups: Psychoanalysis, The Individual and The Community* (London: Free Association Books).

Hoffman, L. (1981) *Foundations of Family Therapy* (New York: Basic Books).

Holdaway, S. (1986) 'Police and social work relations – problems and possibilities', *British Journal of Social Work*, 16 (2), 137–60.

Hollis, F. (1958) 'Personality diagnosis in casework' in H. Parad (ed.), *Ego Psychology and Dynamic Casework* (New York: Family Service Association of America).

Hollis, F. (1970) 'The psychosocial approach to the practice of casework', in R. Roberts and R. Nee (eds), *Theories Of Social Casework* (Chicago: University of Chicago Press).

Holmes, J. (1983) 'Psychoanalysis and family therapy: Freud's Dora case reconsidered', *Journal of Family Therapy*, 5 (3), 235–51.

Holmes, J. (1985a) 'Family and individual therapy: comparisons and contrasts', *British Journal of Psychiatry*, 147, 668–76.

Holmes, J. (1985b) 'The language of psychotherapy: metaphor, ambiguity, wholeness', *British Journal of Psychotherapy*, 1, 240–54.

Holmes, J. (1986) 'Teaching the psychotherapeutic method: some literary parallels', *British Journal of Medical Psychology*, 59, 113–21.

Home, H. (1966) 'The concept of mind', *International Journal of Psychoanalysis*, 47, 42–9.

Howe, D. (1980) 'Inflated states and empty theories in social work', *British Journal of Social Work*, 10 (3), 317–40.

Howe, D. (1987) *An Introduction to Social Work Theory* (Aldershot: Wildwood House).

Hyde, K. (1988) 'Analytic group psychotherapies', in M. Aveline and W. Dryden (eds) *Group Therapy In Britain* (Milton Keynes: Open University Press).

Irvine, E. (1956) 'Transference and reality in the casework relationship', in Irvine (1979).

Irvine, E. (1979) *Social Work and Human Problems* (Oxford: Pergamon Press).

Jaques, E. (1955) 'Social systems as defence against persecutory and depressive anxiety', in M. Klein, P. Heimann and R. Money-Kyrle (eds), *New Directions in Psychoanalysis* (London: Tavistock).

Jenkins, H. (1980) 'Paradox: a pivotal point in therapy', *Journal of Family Therapy*, 2 (4), 339–56.

Jenkins, H. (1985) 'Orthodoxy in family therapy practice as servant or tyrant', *Journal of Family Therapy*, 7 (1), 19–30.

Jordan, W. (1974) 'Primary and secondary collusion when working with families', in W. Finn (ed) *Family Therapy in Social Work* (London: Family Welfare Association Conference Papers).

Jordan, W. (1982) 'Social work, the state and the family', *FSU Quarterly*, 26, 24–36.

Joseph, B. (1985) 'Transference: the total situation', *International Journal of Psychoanalysis*, 66, 447–54.

Joseph, B. (1987) 'Projective identification – some clinical aspects', in J. Sandler (ed) *Projection, Identification, Projective Identification* (New York: International Universities Press). Reprinted in Spillius (1988).

Joseph, B. (1988) 'Object relations in clinical practice', *Psychoanalytic Quarterly*, 57, 626–42.

Kaffman, M. (1987) 'Failures in family therapy: and then what?', *Journal of Family Therapy*, 9 (4), 307–28.

Kantor, D. and Neal, J. (1985) 'Integrative shifts for the theory and practice of family systems therapy', *Family Process*, 24, 13–30.

Kaye, J. (1986) 'My mind is alive and well and fouling up the system: existential – phenomenological considerations in family therapy', *Journal of Family Therapy*, 8 (2), 183–204.

Keeney, B. (1979) 'Ecosystemic epistemology: an alternative paradigm for diagnosis', *Family Process*, 18 (2), 117–29.

Keeney, B. and Sprenkle, D. (1982) 'Ecosystemic epistemology: critical implications for the aesthetics and pragmatics of family therapy', *Family Process*, 21, 1–19.

Kingston, P. (1979) 'The social context of family therapy', in S. Walrond-Skinner (ed) *Family and Marital Psychotherapy* (London: Routledge & Kegan Paul).

Kingston, P. (1982) 'Power and influence in the environment of family therapy', *Journal of Family Therapy*, 4 (3), 211–27.

Kingston, P. and Smith, D. (1983) 'Preparation for live consultation and live supervision when working without a one–way screen', *Journal of Family Therapy*, 5 (3), 219–33.

Klein, M. (1928) 'Early stages of the Oedipus conflict', *International Journal of Psychoanalysis*, vol. 9. Reprinted in J. Mitchell (ed.) (1982) *The Selected Melanie Klein* (Harmondsworth: Penguin).

Klein, M. (1946) 'Notes on some schizoid mechanisms', in M. Klein (1975) *Envy and Gratitude and Other Works* (New York: Delta). Also in J. Mitchell (ed.), *The Selected Melanie Klein* (Harmondsworth: Penguin).

Kohon, G. (1986) 'Countertransference: an independent view' in G. Kohon (ed.), *The British School of Psychoanalysis: The Independent Tradition* (London: Free Association Books).

Kovel, J. (1976a) *A Complete Guide To Therapy* (New York: Pantheon; also published by Harmondsworth: Penguin, 1978).

Kovel, J. (1976b) 'The Marxist view of man and psychoanalysis', *Social Research*, 43 (2), 220–45.

Kraemer, S. (1988) 'Splitting and stupidity in child sexual abuse', *Psychoanalytic Psychotherapy*, 3 (3), 247–57.

Lask, B. (1980) 'Evaluation – why and how? (a guide for clinicians)', *Journal of Family Therapy*, 2 (2), 199–210.

Lask, B. (1987) 'Editorial – from honeymoon to reality, or how to survive a plague on our house', *Journal of Family Therapy*, 9 (4), 303–5.

Lawrence, M. (1984) *The Anorexic Experience* (London: Women's Press).

Leicester FSU (1981) *Solving Family Problems: A Statement of Theory and Practice* (Leicester: Family Service Units).

Leonard, P. (1975) 'Exploration and education in social work', *British Journal of Social Work*, 5 (3), 325–33.

Lewis, E. (1979) 'Counter–transference problems in hospital practice', *British Journal of Medical Psychology*, 52, 37–42.

Lomas, P. (1987) *The Limits Of Interpretation* (Harmondsworth: Penguin).

Lyon, C. (1989) 'Professional decision–making in child abuse cases: the social worker's dilemma – part 1', *Family Law*, 19, January, 6–10.

MacKinnon, L. and James, K. (1987) 'The Milan systemic approach: theory and practice', *Australia and New Zealand Journal of Family Therapy*, 8 (2), 89–98.

MacKinnon, L. and Miller, D. (1987) 'The new epistemology and the Milan approach: feminist and sociopolitical considerations', *Journal of Marital and Family Therapy*, 13 (2), 139–55.

Main, T. (1957) 'The ailment', *British Journal of Medical Psychology*, 30, 129–45.

Malan, D. (1963) *A Study of Brief Psychotherapy* (London: Tavistock).

Malan, D. (1973) 'The outcome problem in psychotherapy research', *Archives of General Psychiatry*, 29, 719–29.

Malan, D. (1979) *Individual Psychotherapy and the Science of Psychodynamics* (London: Butterworths).

Mason, B. (1983) 'The family, the social worker and the professional network', *FSU Quarterly*, 29, 23–30.

Mattinson, J. (1975) *The Reflection Process in Casework Supervision* (London: Institute of Marital Studies).

Mattinson, J. and Sinclair, I. (1979) *Mate and Stalemate* (Oxford: Basil Blackwell).

Mayer, J. and Timms, N. (1970) *The Client Speaks* (London: Routledge & Kegan Paul).

McDougall, J. (1986) *Theatres of the Mind. Illusion and Truth on the Psychoanalytic Stage* (London: Free Association Books).

Menzies, I. (1970) *The Functioning of Social Systems as a Defence against Anxiety* (London: Tavistock).

Menzies Lyth, I., Scott, A. and Young, R. (1988) 'Isabel Menzies Lyth in conversation with Ann Scott and Robert Young', *Free Associations*, 13, 17–47.

Mercer, M. (1981) *Aspects of professional development in social work: growth of the professional self* (London: Group for the advancement of psychodynamics and psychotherapy in social work (GAPS)).

Miller, J. (1965) 'Living systems: cross–level hypotheses', *Behavioural Science*, 10, 380–411.

Minuchin, S. (1974) *Families and Family Therapy* (London: Tavistock).

Mitchell, J. (1974) *Psychoanalysis and Feminism* (Harmondsworth: Penguin).

Mitchell, J. (1984) 'The question of femininity and the theory of psychoanalysis' in *Women: The Longest Revolution* (London: Virago). Reprinted in G. Kohon (ed.) (1986) *The British School of Psychoanalysis* (London: Free Association Books).

Mollon, P. (1988) 'Oedipus now: the psychoanalytic approach to trauma and child abuse', *Changes*, 6 (1), 17–19.

Mortell, P. (1981) 'The uses of paradox', *FSU Quarterly*, 23, 14–63.

Moyes, B. (1988) 'The psychodynamic method in social work: some indications and contra–indications', *Practice*, 2 (3), 236–42.

Mullender, A. and Ward, D. (1985) 'Towards an alternative model of social groupwork', *British Journal of Social Work*, 15 (2), 155–72.

Obholzer, A. (1987) 'Institutional dynamics and resistance to change', *Psychoanalytic Psychotherapy*, 2 (3), 201–6.

Ogden, T. (1979) 'On projective identification', *International Journal of Psychoanalysis*, 60, 357–73.

Ogden, T. (1983) 'The concept of internal object relations', *International Journal of Psychoanalysis*, 64, 227–41.

Osborne, J. (1988) 'Why do they stay?', *Community Care*, 724, 26–7.

Papp, P. (1980) 'The Greek chorus and other techniques of paradoxical therapy', *Family Process*, 19, 45–57.

Parsloe, P. (1986) 'What skills do social workers need?' in M. Marshall, M. Preston-Shoot and E. Wincott (eds), *Skills for Social Workers in the '80's* (Birmingham: British Association of Social Workers).

Parton, N. (1986) 'The Beckford Report: a critical appraisal', *British Journal of Social Work*, 16 (5), 511–30.

Pearson, G., Treseder, J. and Yelloly, M. (eds) (1988) *Social Work and the Legacy of Freud. Psychoanalysis and its Uses* (London: Macmillan).

Pedder, J. (1986) 'Reflection on the theory and practice of supervision', *Psychoanalytic Psychotherapy*, 2 (1), 1–12.

Penn, P. (1982) 'Circular questioning', *Family Process*, 21 (3), 267–80.

Penn, P. (1985) 'Feed–forward: future questions, future maps', *Family Process*, 24 (3), 299–310.

Pilalis, J. and Anderton, J. (1986) 'Feminism and family therapy – a possible meeting point', *Journal of Family Therapy*, 8 (2), 99–114.

Pincus, A. and Minahan, A. (1973) *Social Work Practice: Model and Method* (Itasca Illinois: Peacock).

Pottle, S. (1984) 'Developing a network–orientated service for elderly people and their carers', in Treacher and Carpenter (1984).

Preston-Shoot, M. (1985) 'An evaluation of a policy of family involvement in one FSU from the families' perspective', *FSU Quarterly*, 36, 52–64.

Preston-Shoot, M. (1988) 'Is your social services job a danger to your health?' *Social Work Today*, 20 (4), 27.

Preston-Shoot, M. (1989) 'Time for positive action on dementia', *Social Work Today*, 20 (29), 14–15.

Preston-Shoot, M. and Williams, J. (1987) 'A model for evaluating the effectiveness of practice', *Practice*, 1 (4), 393–405.

Prodgers, A. (1979) 'Defences against stress in intake work', *Social Work Today*, 11 (2), 12–14.

Reay, R. (1986) 'Bridging the gap: a model for integrating theory and practice', *British Journal of Social Work*, 16 (1), 49–64.

Reder, P. (1986) 'Multiagency family systems', *Journal of Family Therapy*, 8 (2), 139–52.

Reder, P. (1988) '"Because:" a suggested contribution to systemic and strategic therapy', *Journal of Family Therapy*, 10 (1), 75–81.

Reder, P. and Kraemer, S. (1980) 'Dynamic aspects of professional collaboration in child guidance referral', *Journal of Adolescence*, 3, 165–73.

Rojek, C. (1986) 'The "subject" in social work', *British Journal of Social Work*, 16 (1), 65–77.

Rosenfeld, H. (1987) *Impasse and Interpretation* (London: Tavistock).

Ruddock, M. (1988) 'A child in mind, a lost opportunity', *Social Work Today*, 19 (20), 14–15.

Rycroft, C. (1968) *A Critical Dictionary of Psychoanalysis* (London: Nelson).

Rycroft, C. (1975) 'Psychoanalysis and the literary imagination', in C. Rycroft, (1985) *Psychoanalysis and Beyond* (London: Chatto and Windus).

Sandler, J. (1976) 'Counter–transference and role–responsiveness', *International Review of Psychoanalysis*, 3, 43–7.

Sandler, J., Dare, C. and Holder, A. (1973) *The Patient and the Analyst. The Basis of the Psychoanalytic Process* (London: Maresfield Reprints).

Sayers, J. (1988) 'Feminism, social work and psychoanalysis', in Pearson *et al.* (1988).

Seagraves, R. and Smith, R. (1976) 'Concurrent psychotherapy and behaviour therapy', *Archives of General Psychiatry*, 33, 756–63.

Segal, H. (1973) *Introduction to the Work of Melanie Klein*, 2nd edn (London: Hogarth Press).

Segal, H. (1977) 'Countertransference', *International Journal of Psychoanalytic Psychotherapy*, 6, 31–7. Reprinted in H. Segal (1986) *The Works of Hanna Segal* (London: Free Association Books).

Sein, E., Fundudis, T. and Kolvin, I. (1987) 'A behavioural and systems approach to family therapy: a position paper', *Journal of Family Therapy*, 9 (4) ,339–53.

Selvini Palazzoli, M. (1985) 'The emergence of a comprehensive systems approach. Supervisor and team problems in a district psychiatric centre', *Journal of Family Therapy*, 7 (2), 135–56.

Selvini Palazzoli, M., Boscolo, L., Cecchin, G. and Prata, G. (1978) *Paradox and Counterparadox* (New York: Jason Aronson).

Selvini Palazzoli, M., Boscolo, L., Cecchin, G. and Prata, G. (1980a) 'Hypothesising – circularity – neutrality: three guidelines for the conductor of the session', *Family Process*, 19 (1), 3–12.

Selvini Palazzoli, M., Boscolo, L., Cecchin, G. and Prata, G. (1980b) 'The problem of the referring person', *Journal of Marital and Family Therapy*, 6, 3–9.

Sheldon, B. (1978a) 'Social influence: social work's missing link', in M. Olsen (ed) *The Unitary Model: Its Implications for Social Work Theory and Practice* (Birmingham: Birmingham University/British Association of Social Workers).

Sheldon, B. (1978b) 'Theory and practice in social work: a re–examination of a tenuous relationship', *British Journal of Social Work*, 8 (1), 1–22.

Sheldon, B. (1986) 'Social work effectiveness experiments: review and implications', *British Journal of Social Work*, 16 (2), 223–42.

Skidmore, D. (1988) 'Attachment theory and the work of the probation officer', *Practice*, 2 (1), 31–46.

Skynner, A. (1976) *One Flesh, Separate Persons* (London: Constable).

Skynner, A. (1979) 'Reflections on the family therapist as family scapegoat', *Journal of Family Therapy*, 1 (1), 7–22.

Skynner, A. (1981) 'An open systems, group-analytic approach to family therapy', in A. Gurman and D. Knisbern (eds), *Handbook Of Family Therapy* (New York: Brunner/Mazel).

Skynner, A. (1982) 'Frameworks for viewing the family as a system', in A. Bentovim, G. Gorell-Barnes and A. Cooklin (eds) *Family Therapy: Complementary Frameworks of Theory and Practice*, Vol. 1 (London: Academic Press).

Slipp, S. (1984) *Object Relations: A Dynamic Bridge Between Individual and Family Treatment* (New York: Jason Aronson).

Smale, G. (1983) 'Can we afford not to develop social work practice', *British Journal of Social Work*, 13 (3), 251–64.

Smith, D. and Kingston, P. (1980) 'Live supervision without a one-way screen', *Journal of Family Therapy*, 2 (4), 379–87.

Smith, G. and Harris, R. (1972) 'Ideologies of need and the organisation of social work departments', *British Journal of Social Work*, 2 (1), 27–45.

Smith, P. (1984) 'Social service teams and their managers', *British Journal of Social Work*, 14 (6), 601–13.

Specht, H. and Vickery, A. (eds) (1977) *Integrating Social Work Methods* (London: George Allen and Unwin).

Spillius, E. (ed)(1988) *Melanie Klein Today, Vol. 1: Mainly Theory* (London: Routledge & Kegan Paul).

Stein, J. and Gambrill, E. (1977) 'Facilitating decision making in foster care', *Social Service Review*, 51, 502–11.

Steiner, J. (1976) 'Some aspects of interviewing technique and their relationship with the transference', *British Journal of Medical Psychology*, 49, 65–72.

Stevens, R. (1983) *Freud and Psychoanalysis* (Milton Keynes: Open University Press).

Stevenson, O. (1986) 'Guest editorial on the Jasmine Beckford Inquiry', *British Journal of Social Work*, 16 (5), 501–10.

Stevenson, O. (1988) 'Law and social work education: a commentary on "The Law Report"', *Issues in Social Work Education*, 8 (1), 37–45.

Stevenson, O. and Parsloe, P. (1978) *Social Services Teams: The Practitioner's View* (London: HMSO).

Stewart, R., Peters, T., Marsh, S. and Peters, M. (1975) 'An object-relations approach to psychotherapy with marital couples, families and children', *Family Process*, 14, 161–78.

Stierlin, H. (1977) *Psychoanalysis and Family Therapy* (New York: Jason Aronson).

Storr, A. (1989) *Freud* (Oxford University Press).

Street, E. (1981) 'The family therapist and staff–group consultancy', *Journal of Family Therapy*, 3 (2), 187–99.

Sutcliffe, P., Lovell, J. and Walters, M. (1985) 'New directions for family therapy: rubbish removal as a task of choice', *Journal of Family Therapy*, 7 (2), 175–82.

Sutherland, J. (1963) 'Object–relations theory and the conceptual model of psychoanalysis', *British Journal of Medical Psychology*, 36, 109–24.

Sutherland, J. (1980) 'The British object relations theorists: Balint, Winnicott, Fairbairn, Guntrip', *Journal of the American Psychoanalytic Association*, 28, 829–60.

Symington, N. (1983) 'The analyst's act of freedom as agent of therapeutic change', *International Review of Psychoanalysis*, 10, 283–91.

Symington, N. (1985) 'Phantasy effects that which it represents', *International Journal of Psychoanalysis*, 66, 349–57.

Temperley, J. and Himmel, S. (1986) 'Training for psychodynamic social work', *Journal of Social Work Practice*, 2 (3), 4–14.

Thoburn, J. (1986) 'Quality control in child care', *British Journal of Social Work*, 16 (5), 543–56.

Timmins, N. (1989) 'Child abuse makes you blind', *Independent*, 28 February, 15.

Timms, N. and Timms, R. (1977) *Perspectives in Social Work* (London: Routledge & Kegan Paul).

Tomm, K. (1984a) 'One perspective on the Milan systemic approach: part 1: overview of development, theory and practice', *Journal of Marital and Family Therapy*, 10 (2), 113–25.

Tomm, K. (1984b) 'One perspective on the Milan systemic approach: part 2: description of session format, interviewing style and interventions', *Journal of Marital and Family Therapy*, 10 (3), 253–71.

Tomm, K. (1985) 'Circular interviewing: a multifaceted clinical tool', in D. Campbell and R. Draper (eds) *Applications of Systemic Family Therapy: The Milan Approach* (London: Grune and Stratton).

Tomm, K. (1987a) 'Interventive interviewing: part 1: Strategizing as a fourth guideline for the therapist', *Family Process*, 26, 3–13.

Tomm, K. (1987b) 'Interventive interviewing: part 2: Reflexive questioning as a means to enable self–healing', *Family Process*, 26, 167–83.

Tomm, K. (1988) 'Interventive interviewing: part 3: Intending to ask lineal, circular, strategic or reflexive questions?', *Family Process*, 27, 1–15.

Treacher, A. (1986) 'Invisible patients, invisible families – a critical exploration of some technocratic trends in family therapy', *Journal of Family Therapy*, 8 (3), 267–306.

Treacher, A. (1988) 'The Milan method – a preliminary critique', *Journal of Family Therapy*, 10 (1), 1–8.

Treacher, A. and Carpenter, J. (1982) 'Oh no! Not the Smiths again! An exploration of how to identify and overcome "stuckness" in family therapy. Part 1. Stuckness involving the contextual and technical aspects of therapy', *Journal of Family Therapy*, 4 (3), 285–305.

Treacher, A. and Carpenter, J. (eds)(1984) *Using Family Therapy* (Oxford: Basil Blackwell).

Trowell, J. (1986) 'Physical abuse of children: some considerations when seen from the dynamic perspective', *Psychoanalytic Psychotherapy*, 2 (1), 63–73.

Tuckman, B. (1965) 'Developmental sequences in small groups', *Psychological Bulletin*, 63, 384–99.

Ugazio, V. (1985) 'Hypothesis making: the Milan approach revisited', in D. Campbell and R. Draper (eds), *Applications of Systemic Family Therapy: The Milan Approach* (London: Grune and Stratton).

Vickery, A. (1974) 'A systems approach to social work intervention: its uses for work with individuals and families', *British Journal of Social Work*, 4 (4), 389–404.

Von Bertalannfy, L. (1968) *General System Theory* (New York: George Braziller).

Walrond-Skinner, S. (1976) *Family Therapy: The Treatment of Natural Systems* (London: Routledge & Kegan Paul).

Watts, J. (1989) 'Children or parents?' *Observer*, 5 March, 35.

Watzlawick, P., Beavin, J. and Jackson, D. (1967) *Pragmatics of Human Communication* (New York: Norton).

Watzlawick, P., Weakland, J. and Fisch, R. (1974) *Change: Principles of Problem Formation and Problem Resolution* (New York: Norton).

Wendorf, D. and Wendorf, R. (1985) 'A systemic view of family therapy ethics', *Family Process*, 24 (4), 443–60.

Whan, M. (1983) 'Tricks of the trade: questionnable theory and practice in family therapy', *British Journal of Social Work*, 13 (3), 321–37.

Whittington, C. (1977) 'Social workers' orientations: an action perspective', *British Journal of Social Work*, 7 (1), 73–95.

Wieland, C. (1988) 'Femininity as neurosis', *Free Associations*, 13, 48–58.

Wilden, A. (1980) *System and Structure* (London: Tavistock).

Will, D. and Wrate, R. (1985) *Integrated Family Therapy* (London: Tavistock).

Willi, J. (1987) 'Some principles of an ecological model of the person as a consequence of the therapeutic experience with systems', *Family Process*, 26, 429–36.

Williams, J. and Watson, G. (1988) 'Sexual inequality, family life and family therapy' in E. Street and W. Dryden (eds), *Family Therapy In Britain* (Milton Keynes: Open University Press).

Williams, M. (1966) 'Limitations, fantasies and security operations of beginning group psychotherapists', *International Journal of Group Psychotherapy*, 16, 150–62.

Winnicott, D. (1954a) 'Metapsychological and clinical aspects of regression within the psycho-analytical set–up', in D. Winnicott (1958) *Collected Papers: Through Paediatrics to Psychoanalysis* (London: Hogarth).

Winnicott, D. (1954b) 'The depressive position in normal emotional development', in D. Winnicott (1958) *Collected Papers: Through Paediatrics to Psychoanalysis* (London: Hogarth).

Winnicott, D. (1965) *The Maturational Processes and the Facilitating Environment* (London: Hogarth).

Winnicott, D. (1971) *Playing and Reality* (London: Tavistock).

Wootton, B. (1959) *Social Science and Social Pathology* (London: George Allen & Unwin).

Yelloly, M. (1980) *Social Work Theory and Psychoanalysis* (Wokingham: Van Nostrand Reinhold).

Zastrow, C. (1984) 'Understanding and preventing burn–out', *British Journal of Social Work*, 14 (2), 141–55.

Zawada, S. (1981) 'An outline of the history and current status of family therapy', in S. Box *et al.* (1981).

Zinner, J. and Shapiro, R. (1972) 'Projective identification as a mode of perception and behaviour in families of adolescents', *International Journal of Psychoanalysis*, 53, 523–30.

Zinner, J. and Shapiro, R. (1974) 'The family group as a single psychic entity: implications for acting out in adolescence', *International Review of Psychoanalysis*, 1, 179–86.

Index